51 DOCUMENTS:

ZIONIST COLLABORATION
WITH THE NAZIS

51 DOCUMENTS:
ZIONIST COLLABORATION WITH THE NAZIS

EDITED BY LENNI BRENNER

Fort Lee • New Jersey

Barricade Books, Inc.
Barricadebooks.com

The Library of Congress has catalogued the hardcover edition as follows:

Library of Congress Cataloging-in-Publication Data
Brenner, Lenni, 1937–
    51 Documents: Zionist collaboration with the Nazis / Lenni Brenner
        p. cm.
    Includes bibliographical references and index.
    ISBN1-56980-235-1 (casebound)
    1. Zionism--History--20th Century. 2. Germany--Politics and government-
    -1933–1945. 3. Jews--Palestine--Politics and government--20th century.
    4. Holocaust, Jewish (1939–1945) 5. Germany--Ethnic relations. I.Title.

DS149.B844 2002
320.54'095694--dc21

                                                            2002026066

22nd Printing
Manufactured in U.S.A.

CONTENTS

v

Contents

Contents

Contents

INTRODUCTION

This book presents 51 historic documents to indict Zionism for repeated attempts to collaborate with Adolf Hitler. The evidence, not I, will convince you of the truth in the issue.

Most selections formed the basis of my 1983 book, *Zionism in the Age of the Dictators*. An unknown Trotskyist doesn't expect a *London Times* review. Yet they liked it: "Brenner is able to cite numerous cases where Zionists collaborated with anti-Semitic regimes, including Hitler's." Moscow's Stalinist *Izvestia* said likewise, and the book became well known worldwide to specialists in Zionism. However, mainstream book reviewing in my America was then fanatically defensive of Israel.

The *New Republic* raged against me for being the historic source of Jim Allen's 1987 play, *Perdition*. Americans never heard of it, but theater historians will testify that, thanks to Zionist efforts to suppress it, it is one of the most famous plays in British history. I replied. But the magazine's notoriously eccentric publisher wouldn't run it, violating the right of reply upheld even by most Zionist reviewing journals.

A *Village Voice* editor told me they wouldn't review the book. "If you don't like it, set up your own paper." So it went, and the general public in modern Zionism's second home never heard of the tome.

However, the media's silence in regard to my book isn't the cause for modern American ignorance of Zionism's Holocaust role. In 1948, Albert Einstein wrote a letter to *The New York Times*, denouncing Menachem Begin and his Zionist Herut/Freedom Party as "closely akin in its organization, methods, political philosophy and social appeal to the Nazi and Fascist parties."

In 1960, *Life* magazine ran some of Adolf Eichmann's memoir, written in hiding. He described deals with Hungarian Zionist Rezsö Kasztner. In 1961, celeb writer Ben Hecht published *Perfidy*, exposing Kasztner.

In 1963, Hannah Arendt critiqued the Zionist role in her celebrated *Eichmann in Jerusalem*, getting their customary brickbat reviews in return. Lucy Dawidowicz translated a secret German Zionist offer of collaboration with Nazism in her *Holocaust Reader*.

None of these triggered significant public reevaluation of Zionism. Unless dead Yanks are involved, most Americans stay away from reading about foreign history and politics like the devil hates holy water.

Serious intellectual interest in anything "political"—Lincoln, whatever—is far too much to expect of 47 percent of Americans, certain the God of Abraham created the world, much like it is, in the last 10,000 years. (Others believe dinosaurs and humans coexisted because they saw them together in a cartoon.)

Jewish readers are actually two publics. The exploding, worldly, Jews are the ca. 50% and growing, who reject Judaism as an intellectual broomcloset in a hyperscientific age. Since they usually encountered Zionism connected with Judaism, most have no interest in reading about it, as typical ex-Catholics don't read about Catholic politics.

But the imploding religious Jews are commonly worse. There are ca. 15,000-plus Orthodox who see Zionism as a monstrous secular perversion of their religion. However, for most Orthodox, political reading means a glatt or hyper-kosher Zionist propaganda weekly, and a daily run by nitch-market con-artists, "Jew-wooers" in this case, who pander to their readers' illusions.

Many members of the Conservative and Reform sects are troubled by Israel, which doesn't permit their rabbis to perform legal marriages. But they resolve their inner conflict, not by reading about or acting against what they know is bigotry, but by psychic flight from the topic.

Be also apprised that the Arab and Muslim publics are no better. An Iranian Shia Muslim daily pirated my second book, *The Iron Wall*. They decided that my figure, six million Jews killed by Hitler, was too high. Six became one.

The classic proverb stands: Fools outnumber the wise in every country in the world. Yet historians should—and I will—try to reach America's "We the People," for all the stats. But the facts re historic and political illiteracy raise profound questions about the ability of democracy to cope in an age of war, terror and revolution, and they can't be ignored without destructive consequences. They will be dealt with in my last chapter, "Final Thoughts on the Final Solution."

But now Israel is everyday's TV news, and at least the historically educated, Jew and gentile, are grasping that fuller understanding of Zionism, with its 200 A-bombs, is essential to a sophisticated world politics. Today, with the internet, talk radio, public access TV, and a sharp decline of Zionist sentiment among America's Jews, the general public and media, the stark record will assuredly batter through any obstacles to reach serious researchers, well beyond specialists.

In any case, as Shakespeare insists that "brevity is the soul of wit," there is a short intro note to the selections, so you can understand it on your own. You also get a glossary of foreign terms, organizations, etc.

Then, after you've cast your verdict, I allow myself the short closing essay.

Readers seeking detailed amplification of the material herein are referred to my two books, available in major university and public libraries, and presently on the internet:

<www.marxists.de/middleast/brenner/index.htm>
<www.marxists.de/middleast/ironwall/index.htm>

As the documents are from five languages, with those in English written over decades in American and British formats, each piece is edited on its own, without format unity across the collection.

Italians say traduttori, traditori—translators, traitors. But mine did excellent work. I thank Hagai Forschner for his treatment of Yitzhak Gruenbaum's Hebrew "About the Holocaust and about the Reaction." Professor Egon Mayor was more than generous in providing me with a provisional translation, prepared for him, of Rezsö Kasztner's Report on his negotiations with the Nazis. Henry Black was then invaluable in scrutinizing it, and translating other German documents.

However, if there is a translating traitor, it's me. I don't speak German, Hebrew, Italian or Russian. Yet I had the chutzpah—Hebrew for audacity—to "correct" my translators' phrasing, and I take full responsibility for any errors of omission or commission.

Prosecution without a defense is automatically suspect. But here most selections are from Zionist sources, some specifically written to justify their policies. Most pieces are complete letters, articles, memos, speeches. Others are complete book chapters. Other documents had to be carefully excerpted to eliminate irrelevant or repetitious material.

One is new to the scholarly world. In 1981, I taped Joachim Prinz, the leading Zionist rabbi and wannabe collaborator in Nazi Germany. I discussed him briefly in my book. The tape, excerpted extensively here, is being sent to the archives of the American Jewish Congress, which elected him its president, 1958-1966, and the Conference of Presidents of Major Jewish Organizations, which he chaired, 1966-1968.

The documents are laid out in broad subject fields. All movements are locked into their historic matrix. Zionism defined itself re anti-Semitism and racism before Hitler. Therefore six documents from the pre-Nazi period are presented first for context.

As the movement was organizationally split during the Nazi era, a picture of the World Zionist Organization's policies is followed by an examination of the rival Zionist-Revisionists. That, in turn, is followed by the record of "the Stern Gang," a splitoff from Revisionism.

"The child is father to the adult." So every contemporary movement is the product of its past, and there is no way to understand an important ideology without studying its history. Many will be upset. The material here is shocking. But all of it is true.

—Lenni Brenner
2002

PART I
Zionism and anti-Semitism
Before Hitler

THEODOR HERZL
"Conclusion"
The Jewish State
1896

A common belief among pro-Zionist Jews is that Zionists warned Jews of the coming Holocaust. That's folk history.
    Theodor Herzl (1860-1904) founded the World Zionist Organization.--LB

How much has been left unexplained, how many defects, how many harmful superficialities, and how many useless repetitions in this pamphlet, which I have thought over so long and so often revised!

But a fair-minded reader, who has sufficient understanding to grasp the spirit of my words, will not be repelled by these defects. He will rather be roused thereby to cooperate with his intelligence and energy in a work which is not one man's task alone, and to improve it.

Have I not explained obvious things and overlooked important objections? I have tried to meet certain objections; but I know that many more will be made, based on high grounds and low.

To the first class of objections belongs the remark that the Jews are not the only people in the world who are in a condition of distress. Here I would reply that we may as well begin by removing a little of this misery, even if it should at first be no more than our own. It might further be said that we ought not to create new distinctions between people; we ought not to raise fresh barriers, we should rather make the old disappear. But men who think in this way are amiable visionaries; and the idea of a native land will still flourish when the dust of their bones will have vanished tracelessly in the winds. Universal brotherhood is not even a beautiful dream. Antagonism is essential to man's greatest efforts.

3

But the Jews, once settled in their own State, would probably have no more enemies. As for those who remain behind, since prosperity enfeebles and causes them to diminish, they would soon disappear altogether. I think the Jews will always have sufficient enemies, such as every nation has. But once fixed in their own land, it will no longer be possible for them to scatter all over the world. The diaspora cannot be reborn, unless the civilization of the whole earth should collapse; and such a consummation could be feared by none but foolish men. Our present civilization possesses weapons powerful enough for its self-defense.

Innumerable objections will be based on low ground, for there are more low men than noble in this world. I have tried to remove some of these narrow-minded notions; and whoever is willing to fall in behind our white flag with its 7 stars, must assist in this campaign of enlightenment. Perhaps we shall have to fight first of all against many an evil-disposed, narrow-hearted, shortsighted member of our own race.

Again, people will say that I am furnishing the Anti-Semites with weapons. Why so? Because I admit the truth? Because I do not maintain that there are none but excellent men amongst us?

Will not people say that I am showing our enemies the way to injure us? This I absolutely dispute. My proposal could only be carried out with the free consent of a majority of Jews. Action may be taken against individuals or even against groups of the most powerful Jews, but Governments will never take action against all Jews. The equal rights of the Jew before the law cannot be withdrawn where they have once been conceded; for the first attempt at withdrawal would immediately drive all Jews, rich and poor alike, into the ranks of revolutionary parties. The beginning of any official acts of injustice against the Jews invariably brings about some economic crises. Therefore, no weapons can be effectually used against us, because these injure the hands that wield them. Meantime hatred grows apace. The rich do not feel it much, but our poor do. Let us ask our poor, who have been more severely proletarized since the last removal of Anti-Semitism than ever before.

Some of our prosperous men may say that the pressure is not yet severe enough to justify emigration, and that every forcible expulsion shows how unwilling our people are to depart. True, because they do not know where to go; because they only pass from one trouble into another. But we are showing them the way to the Promised Land; and the splendid force of enthusiasm must fight against the terrible force of habit.

Persecutions are no longer so malignant as they were in the Middle Ages? True, but our sensitiveness has increased, so that we feel no diminution in our sufferings; prolonged persecution has overstrained our nerves.

Will people say, again, that our enterprise is hopeless, because even if we obtained the land with supremacy over it, the poor only would go with us? It is precisely the poorest whom we need at first. Only the desperate make good conquerors.

Will someone say: Were it feasible it would have been done long ago? It has never yet been possible; now it is possible. A hundred—or even fifty years ago it would have been nothing more than a dream. Today it became a reality. Our rich, who have a pleasurable acquaintance with all our technical achievements, know full well how much money can do. And thus it will be: just the poor and simple, who do not know what power man already exercises over the forces of Nature, just these will have the firmest faith in the new message. For these have never lost their hope of the Promised Land.

Here it is, fellow Jews! Neither fable nor deception! Every man may test its reality for himself, for every man will carry over with him a portion of the Promised Land—one in his head, another in his arms, another in his acquired possessions.

Now, all this may appear to be an interminably long affair. Even in the most favorable circumstances, many years might elapse before the commencement of the foundation of the State. In the meantime, Jews in a thousand different places would suffer insults, mortifications, abuse, blows, depredation, and death. No; if we only begin to carry out the plans, Anti-Semitism would stop at once and forever. For it is the conclusion of peace.

The news of the formation of our Jewish Company will be carried in a single day to the remotest ends of the earth by the lightning speed of our telegraph wires. And immediate relief will ensue. The intellects which we produce so superabundantly in our middle classes will find an outlet in our first organizations, as our first technicians, officers, professors, officials, lawyers, and doctors; and thus the movement will continue in swift but smooth progression.

Prayers will be offered up for the success of our work in temples and in churches also; for it will bring relief from an old burden, which all have suffered.

But we must first bring enlightenment to men's minds. The idea must make its way into the most distant, miserable holes where our people dwell. They will awaken from gloomy brooding, for into their lives will come a new significance. Every man need think only of himself, and the movement will assume vast proportions.

And what glory awaits those who fight unselfishly for the cause!

Therefore I believe that a wondrous generation of Jews will spring into existence. The Maccabeans will rise again.

Let me repeat once more my opening words: The Jews who wish for a State will have it. We shall live at last as free men on our own soil, and die peacefully in our own homes. The world will be freed by our liberty, enriched by our wealth, magnified by our greatness. And whatever we attempt there to accomplish for our own welfare, will react powerfully and beneficially for the good of humanity.

VLADIMIR JABOTINSKY
"A Letter on Autonomy" (1904)
Israel Among the Nations
Zvi Zohar, Ed., (1966)

Vladimir (Ze'ev) Jabotinsky (1880-1940) later founded the Zionist-Revisionist movement, the central ideological component of the Likud, Ariel Sharon's party.

In 1904 the gifted linguist was a leading figure in Russian Zionism. Autonomism was then a "contender" among the ideologies competing for the support of eastern European Jewry.

In the wake of conquest of "the colored races," Europe's capitalist intelligentsia became infected with "social Darwinism." German soil was for those with German blood, etc. Many Zionists translated this into Jewish soil for Jewish blood. They saw the medieval rabbis' opposition to converting Christians (in response to persecution for it) as fortuitous. The "shell" of religious restrictions preserved the "nut" of Semitic racial purity.—LB

My dear sir, the question that you posed is of such importance that I hope you will permit me to reply to you in print. You formulate your question as follows:

"I, too, doubtlessly admit that a preservation of the specific national traits not only does not stand in contradiction to the ideal of progress but, on the contrary, is desirable, and even essential, for progress; for we understand progress as an aspiration for variegation, for a profusion of tones and nuances and not for monotony. For that reason I believe that every nation is in duty bound to preserve its uniqueness (obviously while at the same time acquiring all the values of general human civilization) while not hindering and belittling the traits and uniqueness of other peoples. I fail, however, to understand why you think the possession of their own specific territory to be a sine qua non for the preservation of national singularity. Just imagine a people which though scattered over the length and breadth of a large territory, like the United States for example, also enjoys the privileges of national autonomy. It looks upon North America as upon its homeland, loves it and serves it faithfully, and regards all its inhabitants who are members of another nation, as brethren—but at the same time enjoys the right of living in accordance with its specific spiritual outlooks, to establish its own national schools of all grades and types, to teach in them in its own language, send its national representatives to Congress in Washington, and to the various town councils, promulgate laws of its own within the spheres defined by the Constitution of the country. For that purpose, it will have at its disposal, apart from the House of Representatives and the general municipalities, also national institutions for autonomous government—a central institution and local institutions; and finally it will maintain special courts of its own to deliver judgment in disputes between members of the nation and, if need should arise, will have also a national army of its own, to form part of the general army of the United States. After all, what can hinder this nation from preserving its specific national character for the everlasting. Surely we know from experience that conquerors desirous of obliterating the nation conquered lay hands first of all on the schools, on the courts, on the institutions of self-government and on the army. It is clear, therefore, that so long as those four institutions remain in the hands of that landless people and it is at liberty to administer and conduct them at will, it is not threatened by the dangers of assimilation."

First of all, permit me one remark. You err in thinking that I say that "it is unavoidable that we, living on foreign soil can acquire such extensive rights on an unprecedented scale." I will not say anything of the kind. I do not see anything in it that is unavoidable—in the course of time of course. In Czechoslovakia, for example and in other regions of the Austro-Hungarian empire various peoples will, in the end, have to agree to that form of state which you propose. There are apparently localities there in which people belonging to various nations live side by side and there is no possibility of making territorial distinctions between one nation and another. But the question arises: Does the autonomism which you propose ensure a preservation of the Jewish national ego? Apparently you believe that the essential condition for the preservation of nationalism is an act of will and that it is sufficient for a people to want to preserve its national ego. Of course, you are not oblivious of the fact that such will must find practical foundations in the life of the people and it must be effected in certain deeds, otherwise it is doomed to slow atrophy and the people will become assimilated with its surroundings without any resistance. But so long as the will for national self-preservation is in existence, and is strong in the heart and the soul of the people, and derives sustenance from that root of its existence, it will not deviate even an iota from its free will and mount the road of assimilation. Not even its dispersion amongst strange nations can prove a danger to it. The question, however, is whether autonomism ensures the preservation of those factors capable of awakening and constantly encouraging in the Jewish people the instinctive desire to preserve its original national ego?

Let us consider this question.

Some years ago I asked myself the question whence stems that feeling of national ego that is so deeply implanted in us? Why is our language so beloved among us (obviously for those of our people who have succeeded in preserving the language)? Why does our national anthem, and even the tune of it without the words, engender such tremendous emotions within us? Wherein lies the source of this spiritual bond of attachment to that specific national character which is so strong and for the preservation of which people are willing to undergo torture and suffering? The answer that first rose to my mind was; its roots lie in the education that everyone one of us receives. The form of life in which we have been brought up has remained dear and closely ingrained in us throughout our lives. On second thoughts, however, I came to realize that this answer is erroneous. In the first place, I observed people whose education had transcended the confines of our national life; people who had never witnessed even the "Seder" ceremony in their childhood, who had never in their lives been in a "Sukkah" on the Feast of Tabernacles, who had never played with a "dreidel" on Chanukah and had not succeeded in retaining their childhood memories even a single beautiful scene of Jewish religious national life. On the other hand, they did remember many repulsive and insulting things; there were some among these people whose parents too had been brought up in this spirit and yet when the time came there was something that awoke in the hearts of these people; they began contemplating their deeds and actions, they began yearning for a national existence and even drew near to same in order to study and to imbibe it. Secondly, aren't we witnesses to frequent manifestations of a whole generation rising against the forms of life which it had been brought up? And if education itself hasn't the power to create within us that spiritual bond with a certain form of life and preserve it within us for the duration, and if such bond is created at times also outside the field of education; say, despite the form of education we receive, it is clear that the source of national feeling to be sought not in a man's education. And what is that? I contemplated this question and arrived at the conclusion that it lies in a man's blood. And I abide by this outlook even at present. That feelingof national ego is deeply ingrained in a man's "blood"; in his racio-physical type, and in that alone. We do not believe that the independent spirit lies in the body; we believe that a man's spiritual outlooks are primarily determined by his physical structure. No education—neither the family or the surroundings, can transform a man on whom nature has bestowed a calm temperament into a stormy and tempestuous character and vice versa. The spiritual structure of a people reflects the physical type in a more pronounced and full-form than the spiritual outlook of the individual. The nation molds its national and spiritual character in that it adapts that character to its physical-racial type, and no other spiritual outlook on the basis of the physical type is possible. From the point of view of customs and manners, form of life changes of course as time goes on, but the national ego is to be traced not in customs and manner. And when we speak of the structure of a spiritual ego, we obviously have in mind something deeper. This something expresses itself at different times in various external manifestations, dependent on the period and on the social surroundings, but this "something" in itself remains unchanged and immutable so long as the physical-racial type is preserved.

For that reason we do not believe in spiritual assimilation. It is unconceivable, from the physical point of view, that a Jew born to a family of pure Jewish blood over several generations can become adapted to the spiritual outlooks of a German or a Frenchman. A Jew brought up among Germans may assume German customs, German words. He may be wholly imbued with that German fluid but the nucleus of his spiritual structure will always remain Jewish, because his blood, his body, his physical-racial type are Jewish. The basic features of his spirit are a reflection of the basic traits of his body. And a man whose body is Jewish cannot possibly mold within himself the soul of a Frenchman. The spiritual assimilation of peoples whose blood is different is impossible of effectuation. It is impossible for a man to become assimilated with people whose blood is different from his own. In order to become truly assimilated he must change his body. He must become one of them in blood. In other words, he must bring into the world through a whole string of mixed marriages, over a period of many scores of years, a great-great-grandson in whose veins only a minute trace of Jewish blood has remained, for only that great-great-grandson will be a true Frenchman or a true German by his spiritual structure. There is no other way. So long as we are Jews in blood, the sons of a Jewish father and mother, we may lie open to oppression, degradation and degeneration but not to the dangers of assimilation in the true sense of the word—assimilation in the sense of a complete disappearance of our spiritual ego. Such danger does not threaten us. There can be no assimilation so long as there is no mixed marriage. But the moment that the number of mixed marriages is on the increase, and account for the majority of marriages, only then will the children be half Jews in blood and so the first breach will be created for the inception of true and complete assimilation which can never be remedied. An increase in the number of mixed marriages is the only sure and infallible means for the destruction of nationality as such. All the nations that have disappeared in the world (apart from those, of course, who were completely massacred or who disappeared as a result of abnormal conditions of existence) were swallowed up in the chasm of mixed marriages.

The thing that you propose does not in actual fact threaten us, neither massacre nor mass extermination. But the implementation of your plan—autonomy in the Golah, on strange land, is likely to lead our people, by natural means and by unavoidable necessity, to a gradual increase in mixed marriages, which will exceed in number all other forms of marriage and hence to the complete disappearance of the Jewish nation as such from the face of the earth.

Present day society is split-up into classes and groups, which look upon one another with jealousy or disregard or simply with hatred. For that reason, the overwhelming number of marriages take place within the same group and class. But surely, we are all aspiring to a period when there will be no reasons for jealousy between nations or hatred between the wandering national groups of humanity, when such national groups will live in good neighborly relations and profess mutual respect and complete agreement.

Just imagine this picture of good neighborly relations in the future when our offspring will be living at peace among a strange people and constitute perhaps only one-twentieth of the general population which, far from oppressing them, will recognize their autonomous rights, look upon them as children of the same motherland, even as they look upon their own children, and when there will be no vestige of animosity towards the Jews. It is then that the Jew will draw near and seek the companionship of the non-Jew with the same ease and freedom as he does that of the Jews. Seeing, however, that the Jews are a minority, they will naturally move among the majority groups of the population. These conditions will lead naturally and freely to an increase in mixed marriages. The children born of such marriages will be no longer full Jews but only half-Jews. Vis á vis the "main" population this will be an insignificant and unnoticeable admixture, but as regards the Jews who are a minority, this will mean the inception of complete assimiliation. The number of such marriages will increase ten fold, for the very reason that the Jews everywhere constitute a small minority numerically. This will lead in actual fact to a complete assimilation of the Jewish race among the non-Jewish majority. Seeing, however, that the specific national spiritual trait can continue to exist only under conditions of the preservation of the physical-racial type, it follows that with the physical assimilation of the Jew among the non-Jewish majority, the Jewish character as a specific cultural-national unit will also disappear. The specific national character is preserved so long as there exists among the people the desire to preserve it. Such aspiration continues to exist so long as its real nucleus continues to exist—in other words, that specific "blood." Without those physical roots, the spiritual flavor is bound to wither, the will to preserve the specific national trait will wane and so the specific Jewish characteristics will slowly dissolve in the strange waters surrounding them. This will mark the end of the battle waged by the Jewish people for national existence, a battle that is unprecedented in the annals of history, a titanic battle that has been waged over so many generations.

I don't know what you will reply to this, but I can foresee with almost complete certainty two reasons that you are going to adduce, and I should like at once to reject them. I can foresee them, because your comrades in thought have more than once used the very same two arguments. In the first place, they said the Jews, at any rate in Russia, densely populate certain towns so that there is no ground to believe that they will all arise and scatter over the length and breadth of Russia when they will be allowed to do so. Large Jewish masses will remain living within the present "pale of residence" and there they will by no means be such a negligible minority which will necessarily lead to an overwhelming increase of mixed marriages. I should like to reply to this argument as follows: Even at present, the Jews constitute only about 14% of the general population in the "pale of residence." If the gates of exit should be opened, this percentage would obviously be considerably reduced through emigration to other regions. True, the Jews constitute a much larger percentage of the urban population, nonetheless they are a minority also there. However, with the industrial development of the country, the stream of large numbers from the villages to the towns will increase, so as to double, or perhaps treble the number of non-Jewish residents in the towns, with the result that the Jews are likely to become a minority even in Berditchev. The most interesting point of all, however, is that the reason adduced by your comrades in thought already constitutes a rejection of the Zionist outlook. Here one already senses an admission of the principle that the preservation of nationality is impossible if that nation constitutes a numerically weak minority in a certain territory. It contains, as it were, a denial of your slogan which regards the necessity of territorial concentration as a mere prejudice, because so long as the nation enjoys autonomy, the fact that it is scattered down does not constitute a danger.

The second argument of your comrades in thought is generally couched as follows: We demand full rights for the self-assertion of every nation, regardless of the territory in which it finds itself. A nation deprived of this right must fight for it, and acquire it. We are the greatest enemies of the suppression, whether forcefully or by artificial means, of national rights. But if this autonomy will lead naturally, and unaccompanied by painful manifestations, to a fusion of our people with the surrounding population, we do not regard that as a disaster. We can oppose it only if such fusion with the strange majority is brought about by oppression and by suffering; but what is wrong with it if "it takes place by mutual agreement and by peaceful means; through freewill marriage, where no one is oppressed or insulted?"

The reply to these words must necessarily be couched in stringent form because herein is revealed the deep chasm between two outlooks. Our own outlook—that of the preservation of the special character of nations is necessary for progress and even if one national unit should disappear from the world this loss in itself is an event to be reckoned with, but it is a loss for humanity as a whole and one must not spare any sacrifices in order to avert such damage. You, however (if you are in agreement with the argument quoted above) apparently find that the preservation of national singularity is of no importance whatever, and that only one thing should be aspired to, that no one should oppress this nation but that of its own free will and painlessly it will take steps leading to the assumption of the foreign mask. You are not responsible for that deed and you are not sorry if it is done. That particular national unit is of no consequence to you, and not held in holiness by you. If it is in existence, well and good; if it disappears, well, it might as well do so. All you hold holy is the principle of freedom and justice. All these are laudable sentiments—this love for justice and freedom and this sense of respect for the things held holy by strangers. Do not, however, call yourselves by the name of "nationalists." Only those can call themselves "nationalists" who desire to preserve national integrity for the everlasting and at all costs. And if you come to realize that through this new path your call will lead to the ancient grave of assimilation, do not keep silent over it. Announce it far and wide. Call yourselves publicly "the painless suicide party"—the party submitting by honorable means and by degrees. By no means, however, call yourselves nationalists lest others, by mistake, follow in your path who, in their heart of hearts, desire for our nation a life of everlastingness and do not want our disappearance.

True, one of the most prominent literary representatives of autonomism once told me in the course of a conversation, "Even if we are subject to the danger of annihilation through a wave of intermarriage, this danger will become a real menace only when the last spark of hatred between Jew and Gentile will be extinguished. Do you really hope that this will ever happen? What optimism on your part! I believe that autonomism will save us from direct oppression because it will educate us both in spirit and in matter and that it will free us from the derision of the peoples. However, I do not delude myself by these false hopes and undoubtedly I can foresee that that consciousness of strange surroundings will continue to remain an everlasting division between our offspring and those of our neighbors. Each of them will treat the other better, but will more fully appreciate members of his own nation than the Jews, so that mixed marriages will even then be exceptions."

Perhaps this is also your opinion? Perhaps you or many of your friends who think like you, are not responsible deep down in your hearts to the establishment of a full and conditionless peace? Possibly you are prepared to acquiesce on a basis of social-political equality plus national integrity and you will not be sorry if the main population of the country will continue to regard your children even then as second rate citizens, as Nordau put it. In other words, let them think of us as they will, as long as they do not oppress us and interfere with our wanting to remain Jews. But even if you should acquiesce in these prospects, your children will never do so and will not be thankful to you for having done so. With the improvement of cultural conditions in which the present generation has been educated and brought-up, it is becoming increasingly sensitive to all moral insults, be they ever so slight. The Negro in the period of slavery paid no attention to insults, because he had become accustomed to something much more painful than that—to the lashes of the whip. To us and to you, even the least vestige of an insult is often as painful as a slap in the face, because we have been brought up under more civilized conditions. The Jews of Spain, in the period of their persecution, would have been indescribably happy to be allowed to live in the same conditions as our brethren in Rumania. Nowadays, however, even an Italian "of the Mosaic faith" who enjoys an ideal equality of rights, and marches in full freedom to the full heights of social and political life in Italy, nonetheless suffers deep down in his soul because he feels clearly enough that, with all the attitude of respect and friendship that is evinced by the true Italian towards him, there is nonetheless something that can never be entirely covered up, some vestige of disregard for the "second rate citizen." I shall remind you of the story (it always rises to my mind whenever I speak of Italian Jews) of the princess who was so pampered that the presence of a single pea under her cushion did not allow her to sleep all night. A generation brought up in a sense of fine nationalism, which had never experienced a feeling of oppression, will never put up with an incomplete attitude of respect on the part of the people among who it lives; on no account will it suffer the constancy of "second rate existence." A solution of the Jewish problem implies the granting of full and complete equality to our nation, on a par with all the nations of the earth. If there should remain even a single vestige of disrespect, then to the extent that the culture of our children will rise, their suffering at that measure of inequality will be increased, and then that "cursed problem" will rise to the fore again.

"And then possibly the Master will once more imprint the mark of strangeness on our foreheads, and a deceived and suffering-laden people will once more go in search of a new homeland."

The Jewish question can be solved—either completely and to the end or it cannot be solved at all. If autonomism does not serve as a full solution, reject it. If autonomism serves as a full solution to the Jewish question, if it really and truly assures us of full spiritual equality with the other sections of the population around, it must in the end lead also to complete assimilation with the peoples around us. A preservation of national integrity is impossible except by a preservation of racial purity, and for that purpose we are in need of a territory of our own where our people will constitute the overwhelming majority. If you should ask me in a sense of revolt and outrage: but surely in that case you want segregation at all costs! I would answer that one must not be afraid of words and not of the word "segregation." The poet, the scholar, the thinker, everyone who must engage in creative work and give expression to his personality must cut himself off and remain alone with himself during the duration of his work; he must shut himself in his own study-room and not see anyone because it is impossible to write poetry or to propound philosophical theories with the noise of conversation going around. No creativeness is possible without segregation. And if the poet or the scholar writes in such segregation things which profit the community as a whole, it follows that their segregation is a civic duty. The nation, too, must create. National-spiritual creativeness is the goal of existence of every nation, otherwise it has no raison d'être. For the fulfillment of this task a creative nation is in need of segregation: it must shut itself in, just as the creative personality of the individual is in need of privacy. And if the nation has not yet become a cadaver it will create new values in its segregation and when it creates such values it will not keep them to itself but will place them on the common international table for the general good, and so its segregation will be looked upon with favor by humanity.

You write in your reply: "Even he among us who agrees with your proofs that autonomism does not ensure the preservation of Jewish national existence as such, even he must nonetheless retort that we have no right to look into such a distant future. To be sorry of the fact that at sometime in the future, say hundreds of years hence, the Jewish nation should disappear painlessly among the non-Jewish masses around it means giving way to sentimentalism at the time when there is such real stress surrounding us, a lack of all civic rights and ignorance. We call ourselves "nationalists" for the following reason. We establish that there is a real strong urge among our people to preserve our nationalism; we recognize the plausibility of such aspiration and for that reason we want to achieve by the shortest possible means, conditions under which the nation will be able to maintain and develop its own culture so long as it desires to do so. If, however, by slow degrees, without suffering and without shocks, this aspiration should disappear in the nation itself, who is entitled to impose upon the nation an independence of which it is no longer desirous? On the contrary come and present your arguments to a laborer who earns a few coppers a day for the maintenance of his family and he will say: "This is far too delicate a question for me: I am faced by two tasks. The one is to raise my wages to such an extent as to allow me a comfortable existence; the other is to be a good Jew because deep down in my soul there is an urge to be a Jew. To worry about what will take place 10 generations hence—whether the Jewish people will continue to exist then or will slowly disappear from the face of the earth—that is beyond me, because I have more pressing needs at the moment, which are of more immediate importance to me than those conjectures of the future." And this laboring man will be 100% right.

Let's clarify this question. Apparently you are of the opinion that it falls to the duty of the poor Jewish laborer to struggle and strive for the fulfillment of his interests, apart from which he must not, and need not care for anything. I fully agree with this. Apart from this, however, you maintain that the interests of the working Jew demand the free and normal fulfillment of all his justified claims, including the fulfillment of his nationalist needs, so long as these exist. The interests, however, do not include the assurance of the everlasting existence of our people, even at the cost of sacrifices. On this point I cannot agree with you.

I think that the point of view of the poor man is the same with me as with you. I believe that the poor laborers constitute the greater majority of mankind. For the time being this is still an ignorant majority, bereft of an understanding for their situation. In the course of time, however, they will gain knowledge and come to realize their situation and so will become very strong and unvanquishable. For that reason, when I speak of the future I draw no line of distinction between the laboring classes and the rest of humanity. Hence, if we realize that some ideal is beneficial and important for mankind, we also admit that the implementation of this idea devolves wholly on laboring humanity, whereas they have shrunk from it, have acted without understanding, like people who are not yet fully conscious of their needs and the interests of their class. After all, what are the interests of humanity if not the class interests of the workers? In this matter, neither I nor you can evince any doubt, nor any of the people professing our social outlook.

For that reason I would appreciate your point of view if it had been expressed by one of our assimilationist friends. They believe that the preservation of our unique national traits is a hindrance to unity, and leads to strife. For that reason they hope that all the nations will sometime in the future merge and form one flock. But how this will happen and what will be the nature of this new mixed race; will it consist only of the white races or will it admit also the Negroes? Exact details have not yet been laid down by our assimilationist friend. I shall not, however, question you as to these details, because you insist on calling yourself not "assimilationists" but by the name of "nationalists." It follows that your point of view is an entirely different one. The merging of all races and nations into the one race of the future, so much so that a citizen of Kamchatka and a resident of Tunis will be welded into people evincing one spiritual-racial characteristic and be of the same physical-racial type, is not an assimilation in which you believe. On the contrary, in the first place you aver that the distribution of mankind into various racial-cultural types will never be blurred; secondly, it does not in any way hinder unity and a life of peace and prosperity; thirdly, such distribution is beneficial and is in keeping with the spirit of progress; it is desirable just as variety in nature is desirable. If you do not think so and if you advise Jews to struggle for national autonomy, in other words to fight for their national integrity, it is clear that you do not regard such separateness as something devoid of value for progress and for humanity.

If that be so, I hope you will forgive me but I fail to understand how it is possible to argue that the concern for the continued existence of one of the most gifted national groups on a sound foundation is not included in the interests of the laboring classes? I ask your forgiveness, but I must say that in this line of thought there is some measure of denigration of the laborer and of his universal task. It is as though one were to declare in his name: since we have no time at present for statues and pictures, just set fire to the museums and art galleries of Dresden and Florence. I don't care a fig about them. This view is not correct, my dear sir. In countries where the proletariat has already achieved a degree of spiritual development they appreciate, to no less a degree than the other strata of society, the treasures of art. Because they understand that the cultured and happy society of the future will be in need of everything of technical development, of philosophy, of music. For that reason, Raphael, Kant, Chopin, all of them form part and parcel of the treasures of a nation and of the social values of humanity and it is only the boor and barbarian who can fail to appreciate them. A class that has realized the value of its task in the world, that has come to understand that they are at one with humanity, cannot by any means declare that they profess no interest in anything apart from plenty and equanimity. All that is of importance to humanity is held dear by them also. If the separate development of national groups is of benefit to the advancement of humanity, then surely a developed and self-conscious proletariat cannot shirk this problem and cannot announce that it has no need of astronomy or of the history of the ancient East. A laborer who has developed and who has arrived at a complete state of consciousness cannot say: "I don't care a fig whether the Jewish nation exists or not, so long as no one persecutes them, so long as their assimilation, if it takes place at all, takes place without suffering and without acts of aggression." Among the various tasks which must be implemented for the good of humanity, the free development of national groups is important and of great value to the same extent as individual freedom and social equality. For the achievement of this end, generations of our people for the last 2,000 years have daily offered innumerable sacrifices, and out of a natural instinct, although they were hungry and bereft of rights. So much the more must the developed and conscious Jewish laborer of the 20th century be prepared for all sacrifices, famine and suffering, if these be required for his national existence and if he has fully understood the value of his task in the world and the importance of his national mission.

Apart from these reasons, however, I do not after all, understand what are the "sacrifices" that you speak about. Zionism of course demands "acts of heroism"; it will also demand no small measure of patience, perseverance and devotion.... But will it demand sacrifices? In speaking of "sacrifices" demanded by Zionism from the Jewish laboring masses, you apparently have in mind the fact that immigration and the establishment of an independent state will bring upon our laboring masses such suffering, which they could avoid if they remained in the places in which they are registered according to their passport, and if they strove for autonomy. This point of view is very strange. I was always under the impression that since time immemorial, immigration served as a means of freeing oneself from suffering rather than bringing upon oneself new suffering.

What are "the sacrifices to the Zionist Satan" about which you spoke? What are the real possessions or hopes which the poor Jews must renounce when they leave the Galician or Rumanian townlets for "the old-new homeland"—"Altneuland"?

I shall never join those people who were prepared to promise the Jewish masses that they would find in their "Altneuland" a paradise waiting in readiness for them. I can foresee a lot of hard work, a lot of failures, mistakes and disappointments. Perhaps I can foresee also cruel clashes with external forces. But I can foresee also "acts of heroism" and "sacrifices" but not these "sacrifices" with which you threaten us. But the experience of history—an experience that is not written in books but inscribed on the pages of Life—the experience of large Jewish communities at present living in peace and prosperity in countries overseas is guarantee of the fact that it would not be to their detriment if these Jewish masses understood these acts of heroism and brought these sacrifices. I shall not deny that if I thought otherwise, if I knew for sure that the assurance of our national independence required many sacrifices from our poor classes, and the postponement for a hundred years of their economic liberation, even then I should not hesitate to call them to make these sacrifices for the sake of Zion, even though it be to their own detriment. Perhaps no one would answer the call. Nonetheless, I would make it because it is preferable in my opinion to put off economic liberation for a century or two rather than die as a nation for eternity. But there is no need for that. Our soil, which is purchased by the means provided by the nation, is national property right from the very beginning. Our Congress, which is created through the general election of men and women, will continue to be created by them even though it no longer be called Congress but "House of Representatives." In bearing all this in mind, and in recalling the experiences of history which have been borne out so gloriously, and, remembering that many large scale migration movements have already proved justified, we demand calmly and resolutely of our laboring classes that they undertake also acts of heroism and bring sacrifices because we know that in that new-old land of settlement, where for the first time they will be able to mold their fate by their own hands—there they will find favorable ground and circumstances for such work and it will depend on them whether they lag behind economic progress in Europe, or they pass ahead of it by giant strides and capture their happiness that lies ahead.

CHAIM WEIZMANN
"To Ahad Ha'am"
December 14–15, 1914
(in) Meyer Weisgal (Ed.),
The Letters and Papers of Chaim
Weizmann, v. VII

Chaim Weizmann (1874-1952) later became Israel's first President. Ahad Ha'am (One of the People) was the pen name of Asher Ginzburg, an early Hebrew writer. Conservative Arthur Balfour (1848-1930) had been Britain's Prime Minister. In 1917, as Foreign Minister, he became the crucial patron of Zionism, announcing the "Balfour Declaration," proclaiming imperialist support for a Jewish national home in then Turkish-ruled Palestine. Cosima Wagner was the widow of Richard Wagner (1813-1883), Germany's anti-Semitic musical titan. She later became a friend of Hitler. Houston Stewart Chamberlain (1855-1927) married Wagner's daughter. Claude Montefiore was a leading anti-Zionist assimilated British Jewish leader.--LB

Dear Asher Isayevich,

In fact I should have written to you yesterday, but I was so tired after my return from London that I decided to do nothing all day. Now I want to tell you that I saw Balfour at midday on Saturday. The interview lasted an hour and a half. Balfour remembered everything we discussed eight years ago, and this made it unnecessary for me to explain once again the nationalist formulation of the Jewish question. I gave him a brief summary of what has been done over these years, told him about the Sprachenkampf, about the Technical College, the University project, the Secondary School, Bezalel. This came to him as a revelation. When I expressed my regret that our work had to be interrupted, he said: You may get your things done much quicker after the war. He then expounded to me his view of the Jewish question, and said that in his opinion the question would remain insoluble until either the Jews here came entirely assimilated, or there was a normal Jewish community in Palestine—and he had in mind Western Jews rather than Eastern. He told me that he had once had a long talk with Cosima Wagner in Bayreuth and that he shared many of her anti-Semitic ideas. I pointed out to him that we too are in agreement with the cultural anti-Semites, in so far as we believe that Germans of the Mosaic faith are an undesirable, demoralizing phenomenon, but that we totally disagree with Wagner and Chamberlain as to the diagnosis and the prognosis; and I also said that, after all, all these Jews have taken part in building Germany, contributing much to her greatness, as other Jews have to the greatness of France and England, at the expense of the whole Jewish people, whose sufferings increase in proportion to "the withdrawal" from that people of the creative elements which are absorbed into the surrounding communities—those same communities later reproaching us for this absorption, and reacting with anti-Semitism. He listened for a long time and was very moved—I assure you, to tears—and he took me by the hand and said I had illuminated for him the road followed by a great suffering nation. He then told me of a conversation with Claude Montefiore who had come to him three months ago to ask B. to intercede on behalf of the Rumanian Jews, and said: What a great difference there is between you and him. For you are not asking for anything—he said—you demand, and people have to listen to you because you are a statesman of a morally strong state. I then drew his attention to that fatal error into which West European statesmen have fallen, looking at East European Jewry as at a Pack of Schnorrers, Western Jews contributing to the propagation of this view. Our bodies are in chains, but we are trying to throw off our chains and save our soul. He asked me whether I wanted anything practical at present. I said no, I merely wished to explain to him how great and deep is the bloodstained tragedy of the Jews. I'd like to call on him again, with his permission, when the roar of the guns had stopped. He saw me out into the street, holding my hand in silence, and bidding me farewell said very warmly: "Mind you come again to see me, I am deeply moved and interested, it is not a dream, it is a great cause and I understand it."

WINSTON CHURCHILL

"Zionism Versus Bolshevism. A Struggle for the Soul of the Jewish People."

Illustrated Sunday Herald,
February 8, 1920

Winston Churchill is perhaps the most over-esteemed figure of 20th century politics. The arch-imperialist was the prime foreign backer of the anti-Semitic 'White Guard' Tsarist counter-revolutionary pogromists during the Russian revolution. Two years after writing this article, he became a passionate supporter of Benito Mussolini. He was cautiously sympathetic to Hitler until he realized that the Nazis were a threat to the British power.—LB

Some people like Jews and some do not; but no thoughtful man can doubt the fact that they are beyond all question the most formidable and the most remarkable race which has ever appeared in the world.

Disraeli, the Jewish Prime Minister of England, and Leader of the Conservative Party, who was always true to his race and proud of his origin, said on a well-known occasion: "The Lord deals with the nations as the nations deal with the Jews." Certainly when we look at the miserable state of Russia, where of all countries in the world the Jews were the most cruelly treated, and contrast it with the fortunes of our own country, which seems to have been so providentially preserved amid the awful perils of these times, we must admit that nothing that has since happened in the history of the world has falsified the truth of Disraeli's confident assertion.

Good and Bad Jews

The conflict between good and evil which proceeds unceasingly in the breast of man nowhere reaches such an intensity as in the Jewish race. The dual nature of mankind is nowhere more strongly or more terribly exemplified. We owe to the Jews in the Christian revelation a system of ethics which, even if it were entirely separated from the supernatural, would be incomparably the most precious possession of mankind, worth in fact the fruits of all other wisdom and learning put together. On that system and by that faith there has been built out of the wreck of the Roman Empire the whole of our existing civilization.

And it may well be that this same astounding race may at the present time be in the actual process of producing another system of morals and philosophy, as malevolent as Christianity was benevolent, which, if not arrested, would shatter irretrievably all that Christianity has rendered possible. It would almost seem as if the gospel of Christ and the gospel of Antichrist were destined to originate among the same people; and that this mystic and mysterious race had been chosen for the supreme manifestations, both of the divine and the diabolical.

"National" Jews

There can be no greater mistake than to attribute to each individual a recognizable share in the qualities which make up the national character. There are all sorts of men—good, bad and, for the most part, indifferent—in every country, and in every race. Nothing is more wrong than to deny to an individual, on account of race or origin, his right to be judged on his personal merits and conduct. In a people of peculiar genius like the Jews, contrasts are more vivid, the extremes are more widely separated, the resulting consequences are more decisive.

At the present fateful period there are three main lines of political conception among the Jews, two of which are helpful and hopeful in a very high degree to humanity, and the third absolutely destructive.

First there are the Jews who, dwelling in every country throughout the world, identify themselves with that country, enter into its national life, and, while adhering faithfully to their own religion, regard themselves as citizens in the fullest sense of the State which has received them. Such a Jew living in England would say, "I am an Englishman practicing the Jewish faith." This is a worthy conception, and useful in the highest degree. We in Great Britain well know that during the great struggle the influence of what may be called the "National Jews" in many lands was cast preponderatingly on the side of the Allies; and in our own Army Jewish soldiers have played a most distinguished part, some rising to the command of armies, others winning the Victoria Cross for valour.

The National Russian Jews, in spite of the disabilities under which they have suffered, have managed to play an honorable and useful part in the national life even of Russia. As bankers and industrialists they have strenuously promoted the development of Russia's economic resources, and they were foremost in the creation of those remarkable organizations, the Russian Cooperative Societies. In politics their support has been given, for the most part, to liberal and progressive movements, and they have been among the staunchest upholders of friendship with France and Great Britain.

International Jews

In violent opposition to all this sphere of Jewish effort rise the schemes of the International Jews. The adherents of this sinister confederacy are mostly men reared up among the unhappy populations of countries where Jews are persecuted on account of their race. Most, if not all, of them have forsaken the faith of their forefathers, and divorced from their minds all spiritual hopes of the next world. This movement among the Jews is not new. From the days of Spartacus-Weishaupt to those of Karl Marx, and down to Trotsky (Russia), Bela Kun (Hungary), Rosa Luxembourg (Germany), and Emma Goldman (United States), this worldwide conspiracy for the overthrow of civilization and for the reconstitution of society on the basis of arrested development, of envious malevolence, and impossible equality, has been steadily growing. It played, as a modern writer, Mrs. Webster, has so ably shown, a definitely recognizable part in the tragedy of the French Revolution. It has been the mainspring of every subversive movement during the 19th century; and now at last this band of extraordinary personalities from the underworld of the great cities of Europe and America have gripped the Russian people by the hair of their heads and have become practically the undisputed masters of that enormous empire.

Terrorist Jews

There is no need to exaggerate the part played in the creation of Bolshevism and in the actual bringing about of the Russian Revolution by these international and for the most part atheistical Jews. It is certainly a very great one; it probably outweighs all others. With the notable exception of Lenin, the majority of the leading figures are Jews. Moreover, the principal inspiration and driving power comes from the Jewish leaders. Thus Tchitcherin, a pure Russian is eclipsed by his nominal subordinate Litvinoff, and the influence of Russians like Bukharin or Lunacharski cannot be compared with the power of Trotsky, or of Zinovieff, the Dictator of the Red Citadel (Petrograd), or of Krassin or Radek—all Jews. In the Soviet institutions the predominance of Jews is even more astonishing. And the prominent, if not indeed the principal, part in the system of terrorism applied by the Extraordinary Commissions for Combating Counter-Revolution has been taken by Jews, and in some notable cases by Jewesses. The same evil prominence was obtained by Jews in the brief period of terror during which Bela Kun ruled in Hungary. The same phenomenon has been presented in Germany (especially in Bavaria), so far as this madness has been allowed to prey upon the temporary prostration of the German people. Although in all these countries there are many non-Jews every whit as bad as the worst of the Jewish revolutionaries, the part played by the latter in proportion to their numbers in the population is astonishing.

"Protector of the Jews"

Needless to say, the most intense passions of revenge have been excited in the breasts of the Russian people. Wherever General Denikin's authority could reach, protection was always accorded to the Jewish population, and strenuous efforts were made by his officers to prevent reprisals and to punish those guilty of them. So much was this the case that the Petlurist propaganda against General Denikin denounced him as the Protector of the Jews. The Misses Healy, nieces of Mr. Tim Healy, in relating their personal experiences in Kieff, have declared that to their knowledge on more than one occasion officers who committed offenses against Jews were reduced to the ranks and sent out of the city to the front. But the hordes of brigands by whom the whole vast expanse of the Russian Empire is becoming infested do not hesitate to gratify their lust for blood and for revenge at the expense of the innocent Jewish population whenever an opportunity occurs. The brigand Makhno, the hordes of Petlura and of Gregorieff, who signalized their every success by the most brutal massacres, everywhere found among the half-stupefied, half-infuriated population an eager response to anti-Semitism in its worst and foulest forms.

The fact that in many cases Jewish interests and Jewish places of worship are excepted by the Bolsheviks from their universal hostility has tended more and more to associate the Jewish race in Russia with the villainies which are now being perpetrated. This is an injustice on millions of helpless people, most of whom are themselves sufferers from the revolutionary regime. It becomes, therefore, specially important to foster and develop any strongly-marked Jewish movement which leads directly away from these fatal associations. And it is here that Zionism has such a deep significance for the whole world at the present time.

A Home for the Jews

Zionism offers the third sphere to the political conceptions of the Jewish race. In violent contrast to international communism, it presents to the Jew a national idea of a commanding character. It has fallen to the British Government, as the result of the conquest of Palestine, to have the opportunity and the responsibility of securing for the Jewish race all over the world a home and a center of national life. The statesmanship and historic sense of Mr. Balfour were prompt to seize this opportunity. Declarations have been made which have irrevocably decided the policy of Great Britain. The fiery energies of Dr. Weissmann, the leader, for practical purposes, of the Zionist project, backed by many of the most prominent British Jews, and supported by the full authority of Lord Allenby, are all directed to achieving the success of this inspiring movement.

Of course, Palestine is far too small to accommodate more than a fraction of the Jewish race, nor do the majority of national Jews wish to go there. But if, as may well happen, there should be created in our lifetime by the banks of the Jordan a Jewish State under the protection of the British Crown, which might comprise three or four millions of Jews, an event would have occurred in the history of the world which would, from every point of view, be beneficial, and would be especially in harmony with the truest interests of the British Empire.

Zionism has already become a factor in the political convulsions of Russia, as a powerful competing influence in Bolshevik circles with the international communistic system. Nothing could be more significant than the fury with which Trotsky has attacked the Zionists generally, and Dr. Weissmann, in particular. The cruel penetration of his mind leaves him in no doubt that his schemes of a worldwide communist State under Jewish domination are directly thwarted and hindered by this new ideal, which directs the energies and the hopes of Jews in every land towards a simpler, a truer, and a far more attainable goal. The struggle which is now beginning between the Zionist and Bolshevik Jews is little less than a struggle for the soul of the Jewish people.

Duty of Loyal Jews

It is particularly important in these circumstances that the National Jews in every country who are loyal to the land of their adoption should come forward on every occasion, as many of them in England have already done, and take a prominent part in every measure for combating the Bolshevik conspiracy. In this way they will be able to vindicate the honor of the Jewish name and make it clear to all the world that the Bolshevik movement is not a Jewish movement, but is repudiated vehemently by the great mass of the Jewish race.

But a negative resistance to Bolshevism in any field is not enough. Positive and practicable alternatives are needed in the moral as well as in the social sphere; and in building up with the utmost possible rapidity a Jewish national center in Palestine which may become not only a refuge to the oppressed from the unhappy lands of Central Europe, but which will also be a symbol of Jewish unity and the temple of Jewish glory, a task is presented on which many blessings rest.

ALBERT EINSTEIN
"Assimilation and Nationalism"
About Zionism: Speeches and Letters
Translated and Edited by Leon Simon

Note: Albert Einstein (1879-1955), was a guest of honor at the establishment of the Jewish Agency, the WZO's executive in Jerusalem under the British. He was also a pacifist, socialist, world federalist, etc. His political innocence is legendary among historians. His pontificating on interracial sex puts even the moronic in oxymoronic to its ultimate test. Let it be a red light warning to all: Except to ask questions, never talk about what you don't know.—LB

[This volume is composed of translations of extracts from speeches and letters delivered and written by Professor Einstein during the last nine or ten years. The speech or letter form has not been preserved, and short passages of purely ephemeral interest have been omitted here and there. The arrangement is roughly, but not strictly, chronological.—L.S. London, September 1930]

ASSIMILATION AND NATIONALISM (1921)

The rebuilding of Palestine is for us Jews not a mere matter of charity or emigration: it is a problem of paramount importance for the Jewish people. Palestine is first and foremost not a refuge for East European Jews, but the incarnation of a reawakening sense of national solidarity. But is it opportune to revive and to strengthen this sense of solidarity? To that question I must reply with an unqualified affirmative, not only because that answer expresses my instinctive feeling, but also, I believe, on rational grounds. Let us glance at the history of the Jews in Germany during the last century or so. A hundred years ago our ancestors, with very few exceptions, still lived in the Ghetto. They were poor, and were separated from the Gentiles by a barrier of religious traditions, secular forms of life and legal restrictions. In their spiritual development they were confined to their own literature and were influenced but faintly by the immense impetus which the Renaissance had given to the intellectual life of Europe. But in one respect these men, humbly placed and scantly regarded as they were, had a distinct advantage over us. Each one of them was bound by every fiber of his being to a community which embraced his whole existence, of which he felt himself a full member, and which made on him no demand that ran counter to his natural mode of thought. Our ancestors of those days were rather cramped both materially and spiritually, but as a social organism they were in an enviable state of psychological equilibrium. Then came emancipation. It opened undreamt-of vistas of progress. Individual Jews rapidly became at home in the higher strata of economic and social life. They eagerly absorbed the brilliant achievements of Western art and science. They threw themselves with ardor into these developments, and themselves made contributions of permanent value. In the process they adopted the ways of life of the non-Jewish world, became increasingly estranged from their own religious and social tradition, acquired non-Jewish habits, customs and modes of thought. It seemed as though they were going to be completely dissolved in the surrounding peoples, so much more numerous than themselves, so superior in their political and cultural organization, and that in a few generations no visible trace of them would remain. The complete disappearance of the Jews in Central and Western Europe seemed inevitable. But things turned out differently. Nations with racial differences appear to have instincts which work against their fusion. The assimilation of the Jews to the European nations among whom they lived, in language, in customs, and to some extent even in the forms of religious organization, could not eradicate the feeling of a lack of kinship between them and those among whom they lived. In the last resort, this instinctive feeling of lack of kinship is referable to the law of the conservation of energy. For this reason it cannot be eradicated by any amount of well-meant pressure. Nationalities do not want to be fused: they want to go each its own way. A state of peace can be brought about only if they mutually tolerate and respect one another. This demands above all things that we Jews become once more conscious of our nationality, and regain the self-respect which is necessary to our national existence. We must learn once more to avow our ancestry and our history; we must once more take upon ourselves, as a nation, cultural tasks of a kind calculated to strengthen our feeling of solidarity. It is not sufficient for us to take part as individuals in the cultural work of mankind: we must also set our hands to some work which can serve the ends of our corporate national existence. In this way and in this way only can the Jewish people regain its health.

It is from this point of view that I look upon the Zionist movement. History has today allotted us the task of contributing actively to the economic and cultural reconstruction of Palestine. Inspired men of genius and vision have laid the foundations of our work, to which many of the best among us are prepared to devote their whole lives. It were well if all of us felt the full significance of the work and contributed each his utmost to its success.

It was in America that I first discovered the Jewish people. I have seen any number of Jews, but the Jewish people I had never met either in Berlin or elsewhere in Germany. This Jewish people, which I found in America, came from Russia, Poland and Eastern Europe generally. These men and women still retain a healthy national feeling; it has not yet been destroyed by the process of atomization and dispersion. I found these people extraordinarily ready for self-sacrifice and practically creative. They have, for instance, managed in a short time to secure the future of the projected University in Jerusalem, at any rate so far as the Medical Faculty is concerned. I also found that it was mostly the middle classes and the ordinary folk, and not those enjoying a high social position or any natural advantages, who had most conspicuously preserved the healthy feeling of belonging together and the willingness to make sacrifices. The impression that I gained there is that if we really succeed in establishing a nucleus of the Jewish people in Palestine, we shall once more have a spiritual center, notwithstanding that the great majority of us are scattered over the world, and the feeling of isolation will disappear. That is the great redeeming effect which I anticipate from the rebuilding of Palestine.

VLADIMIR JABOTINSKY

"The Iron Wall (We and the Arabs)"
Rassvyet, Berlin, November 4, 1923

[Note: The Iron Wall is the ideological underpinning of Zionist-Revisionism, the ideology of the Likud, the party of Binyamin Netanyahu. Col. Blimp colonialism has never had a more articulate champion, and it was the basis of the movement's orientation towards Mussolini in the '30s. It first appeared in English in South Africa's November 26, 1937 Jewish Herald.—LB]

The Iron Wall
Colonisation of Palestine
Agreement with Arabs Impossible at Present
Zionism Must Go Forward
By Vladimir Jabotinsky

It is an excellent rule to begin an article with the most important point. But this time, I find it necessary to begin with an introduction, and, moreover, with a personal introduction.

I am reputed to be an enemy of the Arabs, who wants to have them ejected from Palestine, and so forth. It is not true.

Emotionally, my attitude to the Arabs is the same as to all other nations — polite indifference. Politically, my attitude is determined by two principles. First of all, I consider it utterly impossible to eject the Arabs from Palestine. There will always be *two* nations in Palestine -- which is good enough for me, provided the Jews become the majority. And secondly, I belong to the group that once drew up the Helsingfors Programme, the programme of national rights for all nationalities living in the same State. In drawing up that programme, we had in mind not only the Jews, but all nations everywhere, and its basis is equality of rights.

I am prepared to take an oath binding ourselves and our descendants that we shall never do anything contrary to the principle of equal rights, and that we shall never try to eject anyone. This seems to me a fairly peaceful credo.

But it is quite another question whether it is always possible to realise a peaceful aim by peaceful means. For the answer to this question does not depend on our attitude to the Arabs; but entirely on the attitude of the Arabs to us and to Zionism.

Now, after this introduction, we may proceed to the subject.

Voluntary Agreement Not Possible

There can be no voluntary agreement between ourselves and the Palestine Arabs. Not now, nor in the prospective future. I say this with such conviction, not because I want to hurt the moderate Zionists. I do not believe that they will be hurt. Except for those who were born blind, they realised long ago that it is utterly impossible to obtain the voluntary consent of the Palestine Arabs for converting "Palestine" from an Arab country into a country with a Jewish majority.

My readers have a general idea of the history of colonisation in other countries. I suggest that they consider all the precedents with which they are acquainted, and see whether there is one solitary instance of any colonisation being carried on with the consent of the native population.
There is no such precedent.

The native populations, civilised or uncivilised, have always stubbornly resisted the colonists, irrespective of whether they were civilised or savage.

And it made no difference whatever whether the colonists behaved decently or not. The companions of Cortez and Pizzaro or (as some people will remind us) our own ancestors under Joshua Ben Nun, behaved like brigands; but the Pilgrim Fathers, the first real pioneers of North America, were people of the highest morality, who did not want to do harm to anyone, least of all to the Red Indians; and they honestly believed that there was room enough in the prairies both for the Paleface and the Redskin. Yet the native population fought with the same ferocity against the good colonists as against the bad.

Every native population, civilised or not, regards its land as its national home, of which it is the sole master, and it wants to retain that mastery always; it will refuse to admit not only new masters but, even new partners or collaborators.

Arabs Not Fools

This is equally true of the Arabs. Our peace-mongers are trying to persuade us that the Arabs are either fools, whom we can deceive by masking our real aims, or that they are corrupt and can be bribed to abandon to us their claim to priority in Palestine, in return for cultural and economic advantages. I repudiate this conception of the Palestinian Arabs. Culturally they are five hundred years behind us; they have neither our endurance nor our determination; but they are just as good psychologists as we are, and their minds have been sharpened like ours by centuries of fine-spun logomachy. We may tell them whatever we like about the innocence of our aims, watering them down and sweetening them with honeyed words to make them palatable, but they know what we want, as well as we know what they do not want. They feel at least the same instinctive jealous love of Palestine, as the old Aztecs felt for ancient Mexico, and the Sioux for their rolling Prairies.

To imagine, as our Arabophiles do, that they will voluntarily consent to the realization of Zionism, in return for the moral and material conveniences which the Jewish colonist brings with him, is a childish notion, which has at bottom a kind of contempt for the Arab people; it means that they despise the Arab race, which they regard as a corrupt mob that can be bought and sold, and are willing to give up their fatherland for a good railway system.

All Natives Resist Colonists

There is no justification for such a belief. It may be that some individual Arabs take bribes. But that does not mean that the Arab people of Palestine as a whole will sell that fervent patriotism that they guard so jealously, and which even the Papuans will never sell. Every native population in the world resists colonists as long as it has the slightest hope of being able to rid itself of the danger of being colonised.

That is what the Arabs in Palestine are doing, and what they will persist in doing as long as there remains a solitary spark of hope that they will be able to prevent the transformation of "Palestine" into the "Land of Israel."

Arab Comprehension

Some of us have induced ourselves to believe that all the trouble is due to misunderstanding — the Arabs have not understood us, and that is the only reason why they resist us; if we can only make it clear to them how moderate our intentions really are, they will immediately extend to us their hand in friendship.

This belief is utterly unfounded and it has been exploded again and again. I shall recall only one instance of many. A few years ago, when the late Mr. Sokolow was on one of his periodic visits to Palestine, he addressed a meeting on this very question of the "misunderstanding." He demonstrated lucidly and convincingly that the Arabs are terribly mistaken if they think that we have any desire to deprive them of their possessions or to drive them out of the country, or that we want to oppress them. We do not even ask for a Jewish Government to hold the Mandate of the League of Nations.

One of the Arab papers, "El Carmel," replied at the time, in an editorial article, the purport of which was this:

> The Zionists are making a fuss about nothing. There is no misunderstanding. All that Mr. Sokolow says about the Zionist intentions is true, but the Arabs know that without him. Of course, the Zionists cannot now be thinking of driving the Arabs out of the country, or oppressing them, nor do they contemplate a Jewish Government. Quite obviously, they are now concerned with one thing only—that the Arabs should not hinder their immigration. The Zionists assure us that even immigration will be regulated strictly according to the economic needs of Palestine. The Arabs have never doubted that: it is a truism, for otherwise there can be no immigration.

No "Misunderstanding"

This Arab editor was actually willing to agree that Palestine has a very large potential absorptive capacity, meaning that there is room for a great many Jews in the country without displacing a single Arab. There is only one thing the Zionists want, and it is that one thing that the Arabs do not want, for that is the way by which the Jews would gradually become the majority, and then a Jewish Government would follow automatically; and the future of the Arab minority would depend on the goodwill of the Jews; and a minority status is not a good thing, as the Jews themselves are never tired of pointing out. So there is no "misunderstanding." The Zionists want only one thing, Jewish immigration; and this Jewish immigration is what the Arabs do not want.

This statement of the position by the Arab editor is so logical, so obvious, so indisputable, that everyone ought to know it by heart, and it should be made the basis of all our future discussions on the Arab question. It does not matter at all which phraseology we employ in explaining our colonising aims, Herzl's or Sir Herbert Samuel's.

Colonisation carries its own explanation, the only possible explanation, unalterable and as clear as daylight to every ordinary Jew and every ordinary Arab.

Colonisation can have only one aim, and Palestine Arabs cannot accept this aim. It lies in the very nature of things, and in this particular regard nature cannot be changed.

The Iron Wall

We cannot offer any adequate compensation to the Palestinian Arabs in return for Palestine. And therefore, there is no likelihood of any voluntary agreement being reached. So that all those who regard such an agreement as a condition sine qua non for Zionism may as well say "non" and withdraw from Zionism.

Zionist colonisation must either stop, or else proceed regardless of the native population. Which means that it can proceed and develop only under the protection of a power that is independent of the native population— behind an iron wall, which the native population cannot breach.

That is our Arab policy; not what we should be, but what it actually is, whether we admit it or not. What need, otherwise, of the Balfour Declaration? Or of the Mandate? Their value to us is that an outside Power has undertaken to create in the country such conditions of administration and security that if the native population should desire to hinder our work, they will find it impossible.

And we are all of us, without any exception, demanding day after day that this outside Power should carry out this task vigorously and with determination.

In this matter there is no difference between our "militarists" and our "vegetarians." Except that the first prefer that the iron wall should consist of Jewish soldiers, and the others are content that they should be British. We all demand that there should be an iron wall. Yet we keep spoiling our own case, by talking about "agreement," which means telling the Mandatory Government that the important thing is not the iron wall, but discussions. *Empty rhetoric of this kind is dangerous.* And that is why it is not only a pleasure but a duty to discredit it and to demonstrate that it is both fantastic and dishonest.

Zionism Moral and Just

Two brief remarks:

In the first place, if anyone objects that this point of view is immoral, I answer: It is not true; either Zionism is moral and just, or it is immoral and unjust. But that is a question that we should have settled before we became Zionists. Actually we have settled that question, and in the affirmative. *We hold that Zionism is moral and just. And since it is moral and just, justice must be done, no matter whether Joseph or Simon or Ivan or Achmet agree with it or not.*

There is no other morality.

Eventual Agreement

In the second place, this does not mean that there cannot be any agreement with the Palestine Arabs. What is impossible is a voluntary agreement.

As long as the Arabs feel that there is the least hope of getting rid of us, they will refuse to give up this hope in return for either kind words or for bread and butter, because they are not a rabble, but a living people. And when a living people yields in matters of such a vital character it is only when there is no longer any hope of getting rid of us, because they can make no breach in the iron wall. Not till then will they drop their extremist leaders whose watchword is "Never!" And the leadership will pass to the moderate groups, who will approach us with a proposal that we should both agree to mutual concessions. Then we may expect them to discuss honestly practical questions, such as a guarantee against Arab displacement, or equal rights for Arab citizens, or Arab national integrity.

And when that happens, I am convinced that we Jews will be found ready to give them satisfactory guarantees, so that both peoples can live together in peace, like good neighbours.

But the only way to obtain such an agreement, is the iron wall, which is to say a strong power in Palestine that is not amenable to any Arab pressure. In other words, the only way to reach an agreement in the future is to abandon all ideas of seeking an agreement at present.

PART II
The World Zionist Organization
and Nazism Before the Holocaust

HARRY SACHER

"Review of Dr. Gustav Krojanker, *'Zum Problem Des Neuen Deutschen Nationalismus'* "

Jewish Review
London, September 1932

Note: This is an early sign of what was to come when the Nazis took power on January 30, 1933.—LB

Dr. Krojanker's theme is actual and important, his handling of it rather perverse. There is a considerable parade of philosophical principle, which on strict analysis seems to lead to nowhere or nothing in particular. His argument runs that, for Zionism, Liberalism is the enemy; it is also the enemy for Nazism; ergo, Zionism should have much sympathy and understanding for Nazism, of which anti-Semitism is probably a fleeting accident.

Put thus barely, the case does not seem to have a very close correspondence with the realities, and looks dangerously like one of those abstract "rational" constructions which Dr. Krojanker condemns in a fashion wearing thinner than he suspects. As might be guessed, Dr. Krojanker brings the two actual enemies together by defining Liberalism in terms that Liberals in this country at least would reject, and Nazism in terms which even a Nazi might think excessively charitable. About the whole exposition there is a definite flavor of the tactical.

Dr. Krojanker is convinced that liberalism is dying and damned, and that Nazism belongs to the new order. It is important, therefore, to detach Zionism from the collapsing world and fit it into the coming. It may be clever, but it is hardly wise to be premature in reading the Burial Service or precipitate in celebrating the bar mitzvah. His bar mitzvah of Nazism sounds, indeed, very like a baptism, for he wants to add to it the most characteristic qualities of Liberalism. Dr. Krojanker finishes up like a wrestler who finds himself, after much twisting and turning, facing opposite to the direction in which he began.

"Palestine Drive to Continue"
Israel's Messenger
Shanghai, May 1, 1933

> *Note: Zionist colonization costs money. In good times it primarily came from profits of sympathetic Jewish businessmen. The 1929 Depression hit them like everyone else, and the Jewish Agency/WZO had to look elsewhere for the wherewithal to keep afloat in an all-to-material world.—LB*

New York, March 17

By a unanimous decision of leaders in the Palestine movement in America, it was voted at an emergency executive meeting held Tuesday night of members of the Greater New York American Palestine Campaign Committee to continue "without hesitation without loss of enthusiasm and without cessation of effort" with the American Palestine Campaign, the fund-raising effort which enables the Jewish Agency for Palestine to maintain colonization, education, immigration and sanitation activities in the Jewish homeland. The emergency meeting summoned by Louis Lipsky national chairman of the American Palestine Campaign, and Morris Rothenberg, president of the Zionist Organization of America, was in response to an alarming cablegram that had been received from the executive of the Jewish Agency in Jerusalem, which indicated that a financial collapse is imminent for the Jewish Agency in Palestine, and warning that Jewish relations with the government and economic stability of Jews in Palestine would be disastrously affected. Two factors were said to be responsible for the decision to go ahead with Palestine fund-raising: "An unabated confidence in the strength of America," which was expressed in a formal resolution; and the events of the last few days in Germany, which were spoken of by Abraham Goldberg at the meeting as "the turning point in the history of modern Jewry."

"The Zionist Federation of Germany Addresses the New German State"

In Zwei Welten
Tel Aviv, 1962
English translation in Lucy Dawidowicz [Ed.]
A Holocaust Reader, pp. 150–5

Note: This document, the credo of the German Zionist Federation during the '30s, was unknown to the Jewish public until it was published, in German, in Israel in 1963.—LB

June 21, 1933

I

The situation of the Jews in Germany has, through the events and through the legislation of the most recent time, undergone a development which makes a fundamental clarification of the problem desirable and necessary. We consider it an obligation of the Jews to assist in the untangling of the problem. May we therefore be permitted to present our views, which, in our opinion, make possible a solution in keeping with the principles of the new German State of National Awakening and which at the same time might signify for Jews a new ordering of the conditions of their existence.

These views are based on an interpretation of the historical development of the position of the Jews in Germany, which, by way of introduction, may be briefly outlined here.

II—Historical Summary

The emancipation of the Jews, begun at the end of the 18th, beginning of the 19th century, was based on the idea that the Jewish question could be solved by having the nation-state absorb the Jews living in its midst. This view, deriving from the ideas of the French Revolution, discerned only the individual, the single human being freely suspended in space, without regarding the ties of blood and history or spiritual distinctiveness.

42

Accordingly, the liberal state demanded of the Jews assimilation into the non-Jewish environment. Baptism and mixed marriage were encouraged in political and economic life. Thus it happened that innumerable persons of Jewish origin had the chance to occupy important positions and to come forward as representatives of German culture and German life, without having their belonging to Jewry become visible.

Thus arose a state of affairs which in political discussion today is termed "debasement of Germandom" or "Jewification."

The Jews at first did not even recognize this difficulty, because they believed in an individualistic and legalistic solution of the Jewish question. Zionism (since 1897) was the first to disclose to the Jews the nature of the Jewish question. Zionist insight also enabled Jews to understand anti-Semitism, which they had fought until then only apologetically. The unsolved Jewish question was recognized as the basic cause of anti-Semitism; hence, a constructive solution of the Jewish question had to be found. To this end the benevolent support of the non-Jewish world was sought.

Zionism

Zionism has no illusions about the difficulty of the Jewish condition, which consists above all in an abnormal occupational pattern and in the fault of an intellectual and moral posture not rooted in one's own tradition. Zionism recognized decades ago that as a result of the assimilationist trend, symptoms of deterioration were bound to appear, which it seeks to overcome by carrying out its challenge to transform Jewish life completely.

It is our opinion that an answer to the Jewish question truly satisfying to the national state can be brought about only with the collaboration of the Jewish movement that aims at a social, cultural and moral renewal of Jewry—indeed, that such a national renewal must first create the decisive social and spiritual premises for all solutions.

Zionism believes that a rebirth of national life, such as is occurring in German life through adhesion to Christian and national values, must also take place in the Jewish national group. For the Jew, too, origin, religion, community of fate and group consciousness must be of decisive significance in the shaping of his life. This means that the egotistic individualism which arose in the liberal era must be overcome by public spiritedness and by willingness to accept responsibility.

III—Proposals

Our conception of the nature of Jewry and of our true position among the

European peoples allows us to frame proposals on the regulation of the situation of the Jews in the new German state which are not considerations based on accidental constellations of interests, but which pave the way for a real solution of the Jewish question that will satisfy the German state. In this we are not concerned with the interests of individual Jews who have lost their economic and social positions as a result of Germany's profound transformation. What we are concerned with is the creation of an opportunity for the existence for the whole group, while preserving our honor, which is our most precious possession. On the foundation of the new state, which has established the principle of race, we wish so to fit our community into the total structure so that for us, too, in the sphere assigned to us, fruitful activity for the Fatherland is possible.

We believe it is precisely the new Germany that can, through bold resoluteness in the handling of the Jewish question, take a decisive step toward overcoming a problem which, in truth, will have to be dealt with by most European peoples—including those whose foreign policy statements today deny the existence of any such problem in their own midst.

Relationship to the German People

Our acknowledgement of Jewish nationality provides for a clear and sincere relationship to the German people and its national and racial realities. Precisely because we do not wish to falsify these fundamentals, because we, too, are against mixed marriage and are for maintaining the purity of the Jewish group and reject any trespasses of the cultural domain, we—having been brought up in the German language and German culture—can show an interest in the works and values of German culture with admiration and internal sympathy. Only fidelity to their own kind and their own culture gives Jews the inner strength that prevents insult to the respect for the national sentiments and the imponderables of German nationality; and rootedness in one's own spirituality protects the Jew from becoming the rootless critic of the national foundations of German essence. The national distancing which the state desires would thus be brought about easily as the result of an organic development.

Thus, a self-conscious Jewry here described, in whose name we speak, can find a place in the structure of the German state, because it is inwardly unembarrassed, free from the resentment which assimilated Jews must feel at the determination that they belong to Jewry, to the Jewish race and past. We believe in the possibility of an honest relationship of loyalty between a group-conscious Jewry and the German state.

IV—Emigration

This presentation would be incomplete, were we not to add some remarks on the important problem of Jewish emigration. The situation of the Jews among the nations and their recurrent elimination from professional categories and economic means of livelihood, as well as desire for a normalization of living conditions, force many Jews to emigrate.

Zionism wishes to shape Jewish emigration to Palestine in such a way that a reduction of pressure on the Jewish position in Germany will result.

Zionism has not been satisfied merely to set forth a theoretical conception of the Jewish question, but at the practical level has initiated a normalization of Jewish life through the founding of a new national settlement of Jews in Palestine, their ancient homeland. There about 230,000 Jews have already to date been settled in a normal stratified community. The basis of Jewish settlement is agriculture. All kinds of labor—in agriculture, manual trades, and industry—are performed by Jewish workers, who are inspired by a new, idealistic work ethic. The Palestine movement has always been encouraged by the German Government; it is a fact that the significance of Palestine for German Jewry is constantly growing.

For its practical aims, Zionism hopes to be able to win the collaboration even of a government fundamentally hostile to Jews, because in dealing with the Jewish question not sentimentalities are involved but a real problem whose solution interests all peoples, and at the present moment especially the German people.

The realization of Zionism could only be hurt by resentment of Jews abroad against the German development. Boycott propaganda—such as is currently being carried on against Germany in many ways—is in essence un-Zionist, because Zionism wants not to do battle but to convince and to build.

V—Foreign Policy Consequences

We believe that the proposed regulation of the Jewish question suggested here would entail important advantages for the German people, which would be felt also beyond German borders. The idea of nationhood, so important for the German people scattered through the whole world (Germandom abroad), would undergo a decisive deepening and strengthening by a statesmanlike action on the part of the new Germany.

Millions of Jews live as national minorities in various countries. During the negotiations about the protection of minorities, at the end of the war, formulas and arguments prepared by Jewish national movements were widely accepted by all states; they led to provisions on the basis of which German minorities, like others, assert their rights today. If consideration is given to the strong community of interests among national minorities, which as repeatedly found expression and which certainly would figure in quite another way if the position of the Jews in Germany is to be regulated through recognition of their special character, the political situation of a portion of the German people all over the world can arrive at an emphatic advancement. This advancement would consist not only of ideological reinforcement of the validity of the principles of nationality proclaimed by the Reich Chancellor in his address of May 17, but could also take the form of direct cooperation among minorities in different countries.

We are not blind to the fact that a Jewish question exists and will continue to exist. From the abnormal situation of the Jews severe disadvantages result for them, but also scarcely tolerable conditions for other peoples. Our observations, presented herewith, rest on the conviction that, in solving the Jewish problem according to its own lights, the German Government will have full understanding for a candid and clear Jewish posture that harmonizes with the interests of the state.

"Agreement for Transferring Property from Germany to Palestine: Details of the Three Million Mark Agreement"

The Zionist Record
South Africa, September 20, 1933

The World Zionist Organization's collaborationist policy came to full fruit in its Ha Avara or Transfer agreement with the Nazis.

The conditions of the pact changed over the '30s, always in favor of the Hitlerites.—LB

Berlin, August 31st

The Ministry of Economic Affairs has today published the full text of the decree providing for the transfer of Jewish property from Germany to Palestine.

The decree, which is numbered 54, and is dated August 28th, states that an agreement was concluded "with the Jewish bodies concerned," for "promoting Jewish emigration to Palestine by releasing the necessary sums without putting excessive strain upon the foreign currency funds of the Reichsbank, and at the same time for increasing German exports to Palestine."

The Reichsbank is for this purpose opening two special accounts for the Bank of Temple Society, it states, in favor of the Anglo-Palestine Bank.

Special account No. 1, which is limited to three million marks, may be used for paying in investment sums of more than fifteen thousand marks for buying German goods, and the amount paid in will be credited to the emigrants in Palestine pounds by the Anglo-Palestine Bank.

Special account No. 2 is designed for payments by German Jews who wish to invest in Palestine now, but are not intending to emigrate there until later.

Anyone is allowed to pay in up to fifty thousand marks, also for the purpose of buying German goods, the amount being payable in Palestine.

It is explicitly emphasized that these accounts cannot be used for other purposes than for investments in Palestine. A special Trustee Corporation has been founded for advising prospective emigrants.

TEXT OF THE AGREEMENT

Berlin, September 1st

The full text of the decree issued by the Federal Minister of Economic Affairs setting out the terms of the agreement said to have been concluded "with interested Jewish quarters" to make possible the transfer abroad of property belonging to German Jews, mainly to Palestine, is published here by the Boersen Courier and reads as follows:

(1) Transfer of property to Palestine.

(a) Transfer of amounts exceeding 15,000 marks necessary for establishing a means of existence.

In order to promote the emigration of German Jews to Palestine by allocating the requisite sums, without unduly straining the exchange reserves of the Reichsbank, and at the same time to increase German exports to Palestine, an arrangement has been concluded with the participating Jewish bodies on the following lines:

Emigrants who have obtained the sanctions of the Emigration Advisory Office that they require sums in excess of the minimum amount of £1,000 necessary for the admission to Palestine to enable them to establish themselves in Palestine may within the limits of this sanction obtain permits to pay an amount in excess of this sum of 15,000 marks into a Special Account No. 1 to be opened by the Reichshauptbank in the Bank of Temple Society, Ltd., in favor of the Jewish Trust Corporation to be established in Palestine (and pending the establishment of this Trust Corporation, in favor of the Anglo-Palestine Bank, Ltd.).

This Special Account No. 1 for which, together with a second Special Account No. 2 a total amount of three million marks is envisaged, will be administered by the Temple Bank as a trust account for the Jewish Trust Corporation referred to. The account will be used for the purpose of paying for exports of German goods to Palestine.

The emigrants will receive in Palestine pounds the equivalent value of their payments from the Trust Corporation according to the quantity of German goods disposed of in Palestine.

A Palestine Trust Corporation for Advising German Jews, Ltd., with its seat in Berlin, at Friedrichstr. 218, has been established for the purpose of advising German Jews who wish to utilize this form of capital transfer to Palestine. In issuing permits, attention should be directed to this office.

(b) Payments of up to 50,000 marks per person for immediate invest-ment for emigration at a later date.

A Special Account No. 2 has been opened for the Bank of Temple Society, Ltd., at the Reichshauptbank. On the request of German subjects of Jewish nationality (deutschen Staatsangehoerigen juedischen Volkstums) who do not wish to emigrate now, but desire to create now a homestead in Palestine, the exchange office can issue to them permits for paying amounts up to a maximum of 50,000 marks per person into this account (equally in favor of a Jewish German Trust Corporation to be established in Palestine, and pending its establishment in favor of the Anglo-Palestine Bank, Ltd.).

Special Account No. 2 will in the same way as Special Account No. 1 be utilized to pay for deliveries for German goods in Palestine, with the differ-ence that this account will be dealt with only after Special Account No. 1 has been liquidated. Emigrants, too, can receive permits to pay into Special Account No. 2 sums in excess of the sums recognized by the Emigration Advisory Office, but equally up to a maximum of 50,000 marks per person.

If any person who has not yet surrendered his inland residence, acquires by means of payment into Special Account No. 2 credit deposits with the Trust Corporation in Palestine in Palestine pounds, in return for sales of goods, this credit is to be claimed through the Reichsbank. The Reichsbank is prepared, however, to leave over this credit for the person to whom it is due for a period of six months, and to extend this term at the request of the Palestine Emigration Office in Berlin.

If such an inlander wishes to utilize his credit for the purchase of land in Palestine or other purposes there, he should ask for the necessary permission through the appropriate exchange and economic body, submitting a confir-mation of the serious intention of the applicant from the German Consul-General in Jerusalem.

Consent for the utilization of the credits cannot be given for other pur-poses than for use in Palestine.

"B'nai B'rith and the German-Jewish Tragedy"
B'nai B'rith Magazine
May 1933

If anyone asked New York Times *readers to name one Zionist organization, they would most likely give the Anti-Defamation League, whose letters and ads appear regularly. But it wasn't Zionist in the '30s. It represented the Jewish upper-class, which didn't come over to Zionism until its acceptance by Washington, after the Holocaust.*

The '30s ADL was then just a desk in the office of the B'nai B'rith, a fraternal order established by 19th Century German immigrants. The order spoke for it. Altho the present ADL claims to be the shock troops of the fight against anti-Semitism, readers will see why it rarely mentions what it did against Hitler, and the surge of American Jew-hatred, in the wake of his 1933 triumph.—LB

Criticism is heard: B'nai B'rith did not join the public protests against the German-Jewish tragedy! The power of B'nai B'rith was not exploited sufficiently in the public press! What an opportunity B'nai B'rith had to keep its fame on the front pages in this crisis!

Such things have been said.

The members of this organization have cause to be proud of their affiliation with a Jewish body that obscured its own prestige in order to serve its German brethren the better. Not the glory of B'nai B'rith but the safety of German Jews was paramount at the moment, and quietly B'nai B'rith moved to the defense of these brethren through the strong hand of the State Department.

What was the position of American Jewry in the tragic hour? It was as if a robber had entered one's house and seized one's child and held it for a shield... "You shoot at me and you kill your child!"

What does a man do in such a pass? Shoot? He puts aside his pistol. He considers other means of meeting the crisis.

With the Hitler government threatening reprisals against Jews, should B'nai B'rith have rushed forward with loud protests? In the eyes of the unthinking this might have enhanced the prestige of B'nai B'rith... "How courageous is B'nai B'rith!" they might have said.

B'nai B'rith put aside the opportunity for valor (5,000 miles from the scene of danger!) and with what power is in its hand and in cooperation with other Jewish agencies, set in motion the diplomatic efforts that are already historic. Aye, B'nai B'rith might have thrown itself alone into the breach so that it could be said of it, "Singlehanded this organization battles for the rights of Jewry." But B'nai B'rith greatly desires unity in Israel and it marched with other organizations and still so marches.

If there has not been complete unity in Israel in this crisis, it is no fault of B'nai B'rith.

Weeks before the German-Jewish tragedy became the pain of all Jewry, B'nai B'rith, conscious of forebodings, took steps, met with the leaders of other organizations, considered what was best to do, having always in mind that nothing ought to be done that would endanger rather than mitigate the unhappy situation of the German Jews.

This policy directs and will continue to direct every move of B'nai B'rith acting in cooperation with the American Jewish Committee. We have no quarrel with other organizations that went their own way to make public protest. We believe, however, that time will show that the policy of B'nai B'rith is founded on better wisdom. We regret that in the momentous hour American Jewry is not united.

Even those who were at first hot for public protest have come to see that discretion is the better part of valor in an hour when lives are in the balance. They have announced that "In deference to the wishes of the State Department" they "refrain from making (further) comment on the tragic situation of the Jews in Germany."

For B'nai B'rith there was, besides, a poignant special cause to restrain it from action that might seem rash in the moment. It has fraternal ties with many Jews in Germany where the finest of Jewry is included in the membership of B'nai B'rith. Hostile public words or actions by B'nai B'rith in

America might have reflected dangerously on the B'nai B'rith of Germany of whom it might have been said by their enemies, "They have instigated their fellow members in America against us."

The conscience of B'nai B'rith could never have acquitted itself had any ill-considered action by the Order in America caused injury to our brethren in Germany.

And what of the future? It may be answered that B'nai B'rith in cooperation with the American Jewish Committee is alert; that things are being carefully done; that perfect unity of speech and action exists between the B'nai B'rith and the American Jewish Committee.

If the Jews desire the unity of all Israel in America in the presence of this tragedy they can have it by demanding it of the organizations that represent them. As for B'nai B'rith, it feels that its action in this crisis will make a worthy chapter of its history.

MOSHE BEILINSON
"The New Jewish Statesmanship"
Labor Palestine
February 1934

*Labor Zionist Moshe Beilinson had previously represented
Italian Zionism in pledging loyalty in the '20s to Mussolini's new
Fascist regime. Now the editor of the daily* Davar *could soar to
new heights, defending the pact with the head devil.—LB*

I

For decades after the Jewish people had come into political and social contact with the outside world, after the Ghetto walls had been overthrown, our
main weapon for the defense of our life and our rights was the protest.
Whenever the injustice done to us became unbearable, we appeared before
the nations and the great men of the world—whether the latter were ruling
potentates, financial magnates, or popularly elected representatives, or
whether they were savants and molders of public opinion—and complained
of our lot, and called upon them, in the name of their sacred principles or
vital interests, to do justice to us, or to prevail upon others to put an end to
the injustice. Nor was there any essential difference, but one merely of form
(which is a product of time and place), whether our protest or demand were
intended for financiers and ministers of State or the socialist masses, or
whether our protest and demand took the form of a secret memorandum, of
backstairs diplomacy (shtadlanuth), or of an angry speech or article. The
underlying principle was ever the same: The poor and persecuted people,
who is powerless to shape its own life and to defend its existence and its
rights, begs, asks, or demands help from other people.

For decades we were placed in this position without being able even to
inquire whether this was a useful or honorable course. It was not a matter of

choice, but of necessity. We were used to this way, and in the end it naturally became a tradition.

As for the practical results, let us admit that they were meager indeed.
Here is a striking example: All our efforts in the course of decades did not
succeed in destroying the reign of persecution not only in the vast empire of
the Tsars, but even in the relatively tiny Roumania. Nor was the post-war
attempt—in the selfsame Roumania, in Soviet Russia as regards its attitude
toward Zionism and Hebraic culture, in Hungary, and in many localities in
Poland—exactly encouraging. The result was virtually nil. And yet we moved
heaven and earth. Who can count the number of speeches, articles, memoranda, sessions, mass meetings, all devoted to the Jewish question; who can
enumerate the statesmen and public men, authors, scientists, and humani-
tarians whom we enlisted for the cause, and who can estimate how much
energy, how much strength and money we sank into the work?

Some may say, this war of protest, lasting for decades, cannot be mea-
sured by practical standards. The very war is its own reward: it is of great educational value to the Jewish people itself. For a people that protests is certainly holding itself erect. Nor must we minimize the organizational importance of this war, which unites as in one army the "human dust" that is scattered throughout the diaspora.

One may be pardoned for doubting that "holding oneself erect" means
to be forever turning to others with pleas, demands, protests; and this doubt
manifests itself even at the very moment that the speaker or writer, be he Jew
or Gentile, is showering brimstone itself upon the heads of the nations for
the wrong done to Israel, to the "eternal people," to the "people of the Bible,"
to the "people that gave humanity," etc. One may well wonder if the silence
of the "Ghetto Jew," whom recent generations have learned to despise so
much, did not express more self-respect, more contempt for the evil doer
than all the memoranda, speeches, and articles demanding justice for the
Jews with which we have flooded a wicked world.

Furthermore, from the educational and organizational point of view
there was no little harm in this course in that, under its influence, we became
accustomed to ask others for aid and succor. We got used to rely on others.
We formed the habit of depending on their protection. And once more, there
was only an apparent difference between intercession with the ruling poten-
tate or financial mogul and appeals to the principles of right and to the sentiment of solidarity of the socialist masses. Some of us relied on the self-inter-
est of our neighbors; some, on the enlightenment of our neighbors, and

some, again, on the principle of absolute equality, transcending all class and race divisions, which was destined to win over our neighbors; the common denominator was reliance on others. From the educational standpoint, too, there was a serious flaw, for, at bottom, the Jewish passivity, the inability of the people to take hold of its own life and to shape it according to its will, endured, while the war of protest covered this internal impotence with a deceptive mask of false activity, with a mask of gatherings, mass meetings, demonstrations, and the like. The Jew saw he possessed a weapon for protecting his life and the rights of its brethren, a weapon which consisted wholly in making demands on others; he was inclined to believe that he was faced with one task only: to set in motion the machinery for making demands, to deliver a speech, to sign a petition, to call on some cabinet member or public man, to attend a meeting or demonstration; and having performed this task, he felt he had done his part.

And if we do not wish to deceive ourselves, we must perforce admit that the organizational results are also meager, for the scattered members of our people in the diaspora have remained scattered and strangers to one another; and the external binding force of the "common protest" is devoid even of a trace of that cohesion which the despised Ghetto knew. The psychological attitude of the Western Jew toward the persecuted Jews of Eastern Europe is proof of that.

In recent years, ever since we departed—under the pressure of circumstances of time and place which are beyond our control and of which we have no right to boast—from the course of backstairs diplomacy and adopted the course of popular demonstrations, the protest has become, as it were, an organic part of Jewish nationalism; and the nationalist Jew who does not participate with all his energy in the work of protesting, his nationalism and patriotism at once become suspect, and he finds himself today in a very courageous minority.

The truth of the matter is that this course, in all its aspects, backstairs diplomacy and protesting alike, is nothing but an organic law of Jewish assimilationism, whose essence consists in relying on others, in shrinking from an independent Jewish policy, in the aspiration and endeavor to change the Jewish people from the object to the subject of history. The face of this endeavor, which is hidden at times, does not shed its revolutionary character. The Jewish people has ceased to stand under the protecting wing of other peoples; it is going back to its own country, there to spin its own life. From this territorial point of view there follows inevitably an ideological and psychological corollary: the Jewish people has ceased to rely on the understanding of others, their education, progressivism, and kindness; it takes its fate into its own hands.

It was solely due to lack of historical and psychological comprehension that even Zionism, at any rate official Zionism as distinguished from practical development work in Palestine and oppositional Zionism, associated itself with this policy of protest and also judged the height of nationalism by the loudness of the protesting voice. Perhaps this was caused by the weakness of Zionism in its practical work in Palestine, for the protest, even in the form of a stormy demonstration, has always been the weapon of the weak, and willy-nilly we, too, had to resort to it as long as the practical endeavor in Palestine was small and meager and did not figure as an important factor in the life of the Jewish people. But the moment Palestine ceased to be an abstract matter and became for us a perceptible and concrete reality and, therefore, an essential factor in the solution of the Jewish question, it was inevitable that a charge should also ensue in Jewish statesmanship.

II

This change commenced at the 18th Zionist Congress in regard to the German question. On the face of it, what could we have expected from this Congress, according to the traditional way? A delegation of Germans ascends the platform at the Congress and severely arraigns the unjust and cruel regime in the Germany of Hitler, and one by one the delegates to the Congress take the floor and swear not to abandon their brothers in Germany, and call upon the whole civilized world, upon all men of conscience and righteousness, to come to the aid of the persecuted Jews of Germany. But that was not what happened at this Congress. Why? Was it because Nordau was no longer among the living, and there was none to make the whole world ring with a cry of lament over the calamity? Or was it because our hearts had become unfeeling? But not in decades had we seen the people, in all its habitations, trends, and layers, so shocked as it was at the sight of the sufferings of the present exiles from Germany. Perhaps it will be said that the fear of Hitler was upon the Congress delegates. But this was not the first time that we had to stand before a powerful and arrogant man, and we had known how to protest even in the presence of the Russian Czar, the Roumanian noble, and the French anti-Dreyfusard general; and sentiments of pity for the Jews of Russia, Roumania, and France had not prevented us from realizing what was necessary in war, as we then understood it.

It must be that the Eighteenth Zionist Congress, for the first time since the removal of the Ghetto barriers, took stock of the defensive policy which had become traditional.

For, upon the outbreak of the German calamity, we did everything in strict conformity to the tradition in all its particulars. We wrote articles, delivered speeches, called meetings, went to the good men and great among the Gentile nations, lamented bitterly, and invoked their aid and protection, while we for our part proclaimed a boycott against German goods, at times also against the German language, books, and motion pictures. And all this was done according to the "Jewish tradition": without a concentration of forces and without unity of command, as a sort of guerrilla war on the part of the Jewish people against the Hitler regime, in which we did not even bother to formulate our "peace terms," and did not know on what conditions we would be willing to suspend hostilities.

After several months of this activity, the Zionist Congress had a right to ask, What have we accomplished? Answer: so far, nothing at all. The lot of the German Jews has not changed for the better. On the contrary, it is daily growing worse. To be sure, there has been no repetition of the terrible scenes of April 1; but the intention of humiliating all the Jews of Germany and of eradicating them from the economic and cultural life of the country—this intention is stronger today than ever before. And should it be said, the war has been in progress too short a time for us to appraise its value; let us continue it until victory is attained, we may ask in turn, and what, pray, will this victory be? And should the answer simply be this: the restoration of full rights to the German Jews; it is for this that we have declared war, and it is on this condition that we will make peace, and this will be the victory—may we not be pardoned for asking. Indeed?

Let us overlook the practical question of whether the achievement of this victory is within the bounds of possibility in the near future, even if we were to suppose—a supposition which is unfounded—that a radical change will before long take place in the German government. As a matter of fact, there is room for much doubt if even a democratic, Socialist, or Communist revolution would be able to bring tangible alleviation to the Jews of Germany, or to eradicate the seeds of hatred and poison which have been planted by the Nazi movement and Nazi regime in the heart of the German people. Furthermore, even another revolution would be unable and unwilling to attack the vast Aryan army which has managed to capture the position and livelihoods of "exiled Judah." However, even if we suppose a return to the status existing before the Hitler revolution to be within the realm of political possibility, even then the Jewish democrat, liberal, socialist, assimilationist may perhaps be satisfied with his reinstatement in equal rights, but a Zionist cannot rest content with this, since he has a special conception, since this is not the ideal of Zionism nor the alter for its sacrifices. For this equality, and even more, prevailed for 14 years. Only now, with the anti-Jewish measures, expulsions, and removals from places of employment, are we beginning to realize great and powrful were he positions which the Jews captured in the Germany of the Weimar Constitution. But did we Zionists say then that this had solved the problem of German Jewry, and that this was the ideal of world Jewry? Did we not warn the Jews of Germany against their complete faith that "they had their own Jerusalem, and its name was Berlin"?

The conception of Jewish history which is peculiar to Zionism is a cruel one and does not permit us to envisage victory in a return to the status quo, namely that German Jews shall again be professors at German universities, Jewish merchants shall again hold honored places in German commerce, and Jewish writers and artists, etc. No, this return to the status quo, the hope for which is so steadily diminishing, cannot be regarded as victory. And now, with the German disaster, we cannot, even if we would, content ourselves with anything less than victory, which has only one meaning: the solution of the Jewish question. In the face of the events in Germany, we must not look toward any goal that stops short of this; and all this guerrilla war we have waged during the last few months, who can tell whether it is capable of leading us to this goal?

The Eighteenth Congress was alive to the imperfections and shortcomings of the "traditional policy" in our defensive war. It recognized that every Jewish community is exposed not only to the danger of degradation and the deprivation of its right, but also to another peril: the peril of self-deception, of dissipating its strength in a futile war for an imaginary victory; and even to a greater menace still: the mencace of being severed from the body of the Jewish people as Russian Jewry has been, and of being cut off from the hope of the Jewish people, from the shores of its Homeland. The Eighteenth Zionist Congress realized that there are values which the Jewish people, and above all Zionism, is bound to fight for, but for well known reasons Zionism must make one value its central concern: the official seal upon the Jew's passport, the seal which enables him to cross the border line between the diaspora and Eretz Israel.

It would be ridiculous to think, or to pretend to think, that the attitude of the Eighteenth Congress towards the German Jewish problem was due to any consideration for the position of the Zionist leaders of Germany or for the fate of their paper, which was suppressed during the sessions of the Congress. To be sure, even such considerations would not be sinful, but it is not here that the cause of the battle fought at the Congress is to be found, nor in the courage of some, nor in the spinelessness of others. The Congress did not "betray"; it triumphed. It was not "afraid"; on the contrary, it had the courage to initiate a new Jewish statesmanship, a Zionist statesmanship, one whose object and fulfilment is the concentration of the Jewish people in Palestine. Verily, the Eighteenth Congress had the courage to destroy the assimilationist tradition whose chief characteristic is a reliance on others and appeals to others, and sought to follow the way of self-reliance and self-help.

Whence this strength? Why did not other generations possess it and employed ineffectual weapons? Palestine - not the abstract, spiritual, and ideological, but the Palestine that is a concrete factor in the solution of the Jewish question - it was this Palestine, by its growth and development, which inspired the Congress with this courage, the courage to renounce the weapon of the weak, the courage to inaugurate a statesmanship befitting a people that is conscious of its own strength. For generations we fought by means of protests. Now we have another weapon in our hand, a strong, trusty, and sure weapon: the visa for Palestine.

III

There is no statesmanship without its perils, and the new Jewish statesmanship is no exception.

We have abandoned a well-trodden and conventional way, which because it was satisfactory—even small and poor satisfaction may be classed as satisfaction—became a real tradition, not only with Stephen S. Wise, who is swayed by histrionics, and not only with Jabotinsky, who is seeking to escape, by means of the campaign in behalf of the German Jews, the doom which is hanging over him, and to hide the kinship, psychological and ideological, of his movement with the nefarious movement which now prevails in Germany. The "traditional way" of Jewish statesmanship is dear to the mass of our people, and the transition to a different statesmanship cannot be achieved without pain, without self-mastery.

For many sides the complaint is heard, World Jewry is now embattled against Hitler, while you, Zionists, you, Palestinian Jews, are seeking to reach an agreement with Hitler and destroying the unity of the Jewish front. Nay, more, the Socialist and Labor International, the flower of the world's intelligentsia, men of integrity and peace, all lovers of freedom, whom you regard as your allies, are making war upon Hitler, while you are deserting the battlefield.

The complaint bears witness either to an irrational attitude toward the Zionist policy of the Jewish people, or to an inability and perhaps also reluctance to understand the peculiar position of the Jews in the war with the Hitler regime.

To begin with, it is necessary to distinguish between one's opinion of a certain social, ideological, and political force and one's official relations with it. One cannot suspect France of having a friendly attitude toward the Hitler regime—the press, public opinion, and many statesmen in France make no secret of their hostile attitude toward the "new Germany"—but no one would expect the French parliament to declare war at once, this very day, against Germany, and no one would ask the President of France to expel the German ambassador from Paris. The French people, who are well schooled politically, knows how to distinguish between the 2; and he who insists on absolute consistency on the part of the Jewish people does not hold it in particular regard but disdains it, since he does not admit that the Jews are competent to pursue the proper diplomatic policy, that they have something at stake, and that it therefore behooves them, as it does other people, to act prudently.

Another illustration: the foreign policy of Soviet Russia. At the very moment that Mussolini and Kemal Pasha are handing over Italian and Turkish Communists to the public hangman, representatives of the Russian Communist government are sitting in conference with them and trying to conclude agreements and sign treaties with them. To be sure, France does not treat her Communists with special severity; yet those embraces of Daladier or Herriot and Litvinoff and Gorky are a strange sight indeed from the standpoint of psychological and ideological "consistency." Nevertheless it would be ridiculous and childish to protest against this policy. There would only be room for complaint if the spokesmen of Soviet Russia announced that they were inaugurating a "new revolutionary international policy." But since they have given up such lying phrases, and their realistic diplomacy no longer adorns itself with such deceitful trappings, it must be acknowledged that Communist Russia and capitalist and imperialistic France have a right to come to an understanding. (And this would be clearer and more self-evident still if "Izvestia" did not suddenly discover that France was the cradle of "the great Revolution," and if Herriot did not try to concoct a "general human and ethical" basis for the new covenant, and if he did not, in honor of this basis, wax enthusiastic at the sight of starving Russia.) For both Russia and France primarily want—and have a right—to live and not to be the victims of Hitler's predatory designs. And the very same Socialist International which is reported to be "unable to understand" the course of the Zionist Congress toward Germany, greatly rejoices—and rightly—at the rapprochement between Communist Russia and capitalist-imperialist France. Why should that be forbidden to us which is permitted to Litvinoff and Herriot? Can it be that behind the "normal demand" which they are making of us there lurks a certain contempt for us because we too are turning to realpolitik, because we too are following their ways and are unwilling any longer to be at the service of humanity?

Above all, our position differs radically from that of the other forces warring upon Hitler. We have hostages in Germany. Nor are they of the same category as the hostages of socialism, democracy, and communism. The latter are in their own country. Their lives and fortunes depend upon their triumph in their country. For the sake of the triumph of socialism in Germany, it is proper and worthwhile to sacrifice the socialists who live in Germany. We too would not spare our hostages if we believed their fate to be bound up with that of Germany. Perhaps we too would say then, this is our common war and hence we must share in the common sacrifices for the common liberation. However, this is not our goal. From the territorial point of view, our liberation is quite distinct from that of the others. We desire to remove our hostages from the confines of Germany. If we seek an analogy for our situation, we shall find it in those nationals of a belligerent country who are held prisoner in the enemy's country, and the right and effort to secure whose release and exchange for others not even the most ardent champion of war to the bitter end will renounce. And whoever does not acknowledge the right of the Jewish people to deliver its hostages from the Hitlerite captivity, and to deliver them by methods dictated by the objective conditions, shows that he does not take seriously Zionism, as the Jewish political policy, and Palestine, as the Jewish homeland.

Nevertheless, the main difficulty of the new Jewish statesmanship does not lie in theoretical discussions with outside factors, but in the elementary emotions within our camp, a camp used to statesmanship in the "traditional manner" of so many generations. The spokesman of the new statesmanship must be prepared not only to face the charge of "treason" and "cowardice," but to encounter a genuine display of Jewish feeling which has not yet overcome the conventional way and notions that are so hard to resist, even at the moment when one is already reconciled to the need of overcoming them.

These ideological and psychological difficulties remind us a great deal of the complaints which were hurled at Zionism in the beginning. How well we remember the accusation that we were "betraying" the "monotheistic mission of our people among the nations"; how well we remember the charge that we were "running away" from the battlefield of humanity, which, of course, was not in an "Asiatic nook," but on the broad plains of Russia and the United States; how well we remember the reproach that we were indifferent to the fate of the Jewish masses, whose "future" was in the diaspora and not in Palestine. And how long is it since we ceased to be regarded by international socialism as a strange movement, nationalistic and even chauvinistic, petit-bourgeois? In point of fact, we are not wholly cleared of these accusations even now, in these days of Zionist realization in the "Asiatic nook." And the new difficulties will likewise disappear when the outside world, and especially the Jewish world, comes to understand and believe that the Jewish people has decided in all seriousness, having no other choice, that it will alter its life radically, that it will not depend any more on others, that it will resolutely spin its own life in its own land. With this firm resolution and its realization, the Jewish people has ceased to be an exception even in this respect, and is now "like unto all the nations," that is, a people which has something at stake and something to safeguard, a people whose defense is not conducted with the single weapon of protest, of bitter outcry, of plea and demand dinned into the ears of others.

The old statesmanship, which became a tradition with us, was known to us in all its particulars—so much so that it was practically stereotyped. So and so visited the editorial office of a newspaper, such a one called on a cabinet member, and so and so went to Geneva. "International law, minority rights," slogans, mass meetings, street demonstrations, petitions, and the boycott as means. Everything was clear. Now we have a new goal and no longer content ourselves with "arousing world opinion." Our ideal is not the obtaining of rights, citizenship rights or minority rights, for the Jews of Germany, but the obtaining of a Palestine visa for them, in addition to all that is necessary for such a visa so that it, too, may not become a mere scrap of paper. And how is this work to be done? How are we to attain the new goal, insofar as our relations with the Hitler government are concerned? Here it is necessary to search, to inquire, to investigate everything, to try and to try again, for the road is not well trodden and safe. A great deal of deliberation and discipline is necessary in order that we may free ourselves from the antiquated form of warfare and that the new course may not be construed as license for irresponsibility to work its will.

Many and sundry will now try to heap abuse upon the Eighteenth Congress for its attempt to really initiate a new Jewish statesmanship; but if we possess the strength to follow the way of this Congress, the Jewish people are sure to perceive what the "men of protest" have achieved and what we have accomplished, and eventually the Eighteenth Congress will be recorded in the annals of Zionism as a daring and pathfinding congress. But this, as said, depends on one condition: that we possess the strength to follow in the footsteps of the Congress.

The great danger menacing the new Zionist statesmanship—as indeed all statesmanship, even the most correct—is that it may remain a mere declaration unaccompanied by action. The meaning of the new policy is: the transfer of the Jews of Germany to Palestine. It is only for the sake of this that all those painful renunciations were made; it is only for the sake of this that the delegates to the Eighteenth Congress repressed their natural feelings. And unless this goal is reached, our renunciations will prove vain, and the violence we did to our feelings will be like pangs without birth. If our objective is not attained, we shall find ourselves in the embarrassing position of having prematurely thrown away the "weapon of protest," a weapon covered with rust, to be sure, but nevertheless a weapon of a sort, before we had forged a more effective and more appropriate weapon.

Herein lies the danger. However, the responsibility for this does not fall upon the Jewish statesmanship of which Palestine is the cornerstone. Eventually we shall attain this statesmanship, as the life of the Jews in the diaspora, a life without hope and without security, makes it imperative.

CHAIM NACHMAN BIALIK

"The Present Hour"

The Young Zionist
London, May 1934
[From a speech to a press conference
on the Hebrew University]

Chaim Nachman Bialik (1873-1934) was Zionism's star poet.
He thought of the Jews as a pocket-sized master race; if they
wouldn't hang out in gentile fleshpots, and tilled their own
vineyard.—LB

The Wandering Jew

When the political life of the Jewish nation was destroyed, Israel went out
into the wide world and adapted its possessions for a life of wanderings and
vicissitudes. The Jewish people was forced to reduce its "baggage" to the lowest possible minimum—to something which would be easy to take on a journey and which would at the same time be quite indispensable. The nation
exercised restriction and economy upon its possessions. First of all it had to
rid itself of all items which were not absolutely necessary for a people wandering on the highways of the world. Samuel Luzzato once said, "Israel
embarking upon its journey left behind most of its beautiful and exhilarating
poetry and many of its arts.... It preserved only the dry laws and regulations
which ordered its daily life." One might say that only abstract Judaism was
preserved. I once compared this process to an army going out to battle which
does not take fresh bread and fruit as provisions, but dry forms of bread and
dry preserved fruits. Similarly the Jewish people took only its legal codes
which gave a united cultural aspect to all Jewry—which created a portable
state with an ordered way of life and a mutual form of culture, and thereby
safeguarded the nation's existence. Uprooting its culture from its previous
surroundings, from the soil and conditions of Palestine, the nation converted its concrete possessions into abstract, spiritual possessions, better suited to

the needs of its new life of eternal vagrancy. Israel lived a life of brains and spirit and book-learning; negotiation and Pilpul, sharp wits and cleverness—these were her only weapons. Such weapons do not take up much room. They are enshrined within the brain, whence hidden from view they pass from place to place throughout the length and breadth of the world. With this spiritual baggage the Jews were not prevented from penetrating into all nations and all cultures. Possessions of substance and weight are not fitted to be easily transported, whereas thoughts and ideas traverse all barriers and all limits, and penetrate into all hidden nooks and crannies. By such means the Jewish people penetrated into the world, and absorbed its power into all civilizations for its own benefit and for the benefit of mankind as a whole.

Jewish Influence on Modern Thought

We are now living in a very different period—in a period of return. But there is a great similarity between these two occasions. It cannot be doubted that those remnants of idolatry which existed in Christianity were the source and origin of the internal falsehood which was latent within it. On the one hand we find the avowal of principles of complete righteousness commanding one to give one's coat to the man who has stripped off the shirt, to turn the right cheek when the left cheek is struck—and on the other hand deeds of murder and enmity, unceasing warfare and a thoroughly rotten cultural outlook—the sort of outlook which finds a trenchant expression in the latest book of Spengler who holds that the abstract Jewish culture was the thing which crippled the higher type of humanity, spoilt man's teeth and nails—that is, the attributes of the beast in man—and caused the diminution of man's stature as the higher form of life, as the lion of living things. And he urges that, assisted by a new and perfect technical science, Man should once more assume the higher image of an animal with subtle instincts, sharp weapons, teeth and nails. Indeed it is quite true that Judaism, by penetrating into all the nations actually did undermine the remnants of that sort of idolatry. The process of undermining was conducted with the considerable help of Jews—help in a thousand aspects, a thousand forms and a thousand ways, through all the world's languages, by means of assimilation and enlightenment and cosmopolitanism; and also by the belief in the "Jewish Mission" from the early days of emancipation up to the present time. But perhaps the strongest forces in this process were our "apostate" or "assimilated" Jews of all types who entered into the very body of Christianity and stirred its very bowels, and went on slowly undermining the remnants of paganism as a result of their Jewish volition and their Jewish blood. I too, like Hitler, believe in the power of the blood idea. These were the men—although often the names of great non-Jews are called in their stead—who smoothed the roads for the great movements of Freedom all over the world: The Renaissance, Liberalism, Democracy, Socialism and Communism. The entire road, a steep and checkered road—always ascending towards freedom and progress, was marked out principally by all sorts of unnoticed or anonymous Jews. There were apostate Jews who mingled with Gentiles and produced many a great questioner; there was the influence of Jews who merely stood behind the scenes of enterprises in the cause of freedom and liberation; there were professors and teachers of Jewish stock ever since the Middle Ages who produced thousands of pupils to take the lead in liberating movements. Even the Protestant movement had leaders who had been educated by Jewish teachers. And these influences have existed in every age right up to the movements of our own time in which many Jews have participated, openly or secretly. Anti-Semites sometimes have clear discernment. Jewish influence has indeed been very powerful in this connection; we ought not to deny it. Marx was not only a Jew by origin but his way of thinking was Jewish, his sharpness of intellect was Jewish, and one of his grandfathers had been a renowned and sharp-witted Rabbi. Lasalle was also a Jew.

Judaism Equals Liberty
At last the nations have probed the great secret that Judaism, with as much vigor now as ever before, is bubbling and effervescing like a poison, undermining the remnants of idolatry and paganism. Against this the pagan instinct has risen up and is now attempting to fight the final battle against Judaism, the battle of Gog and Magog. There can be no doubt that this battlefront which is being built principally against movements of freedom and modern progress, against democracy and socialism, and against the extension of Man's privileges, in short, against all modern manifestations of freedom—this front is bound to become an international front against various sections of Jewry. I venture to think that Socialism in its best and most perfect form is a fruit of the Jewish spirit—of the prophetical outlook. The Hebrew prophets were the first socialists, preaching Freedom, Equality, and the acknowledgment of human value. "There is one Father for us all; one God hath created us." So were all the words of the prophets one great call for equality. But in our own time we approach these problems with different weapons and with different instruments of thought. And now again war is being declared against us, not in our own country but in the wide world outside, wherever we are found in dispersion; and our enemies wish to smoke us

out from all the holes and clefts in which we were hidden. They wish to exterminate us as bacilli, to drag us forth from all our nests with a view to final and complete destruction.

The Zionist Solution

But history or some instinct of anticipation or some prophetical spirit which has never ceased in Israel, has produced a remedy before the disease. Some 40 or 50 years ago there were men who anticipated the storm which was to break over our heads. Read the words of Pinsker; you will find in them the greatest vision which has been uttered amongst us in the ancient prophetic spirit in our own generation. The very name "Auto-Emancipation" is pregnant of meaning. Pinsker contemplated the future clearly and was not smitten with blindness like our Jewish brethren in Germany who lived in their last stronghold with perfect confidence of eternal existence in their adopted land. They believed that the privileges of emancipation were never liable to be taken away from them. And although Zionists made this historic prognosis 50 years ago, I am afraid that even today German Jews and other sections of Jewry who are in a similar position to them, will not learn the true lesson of these events. Naturally something has been stirred up within them. The disaster was so sudden? But for us there was no surprise; we knew it beforehand. And Jewry decided that if the world banishes us from every center of influence, if they uproot our brains and our influence from the world of our dispersion, we have no choice but to turn back along the road from whence we came, to return to our own country, to concentrate ourselves therein, once more to join our brains to our soil and to enshrine them in solid vessels, fixed and ordered in one place. Thus could we preserve what we have, give it power of growth and development, and add to it as well. Here in this place we must again give practical expression to all our experiences in the course of our history. Here from this place we must realize and proclaim to humanity a new decalogue, based indeed on the old one, but with the difference that it shall be binding not only between man and man, but also between nation and nation. This must be the new addendum to our old foundation. Again in this place we must generate our little sphere of life to serve as a model for a greater life, conceived in the image of true greatness....

The New Idolatry

At the present time also there is an idolatrous Christianity, this time with new idols. The Laws of Race, the modern style of politics, nationalism in the wild form of savage beasts—what are these if not new idols? But this time as well, the world will be compelled to accept certain parts of Judaism in its new form—in the form of a social influence. You can be sure that Hitler and Hitlerism in every part of the world will be forced, as were the worshippers of idols in antiquity, to yield to certain parts of our social religion. But this "present" will be bestowed upon them with the accompaniment of a fierce hatred of the Judaism which forced upon them the principles of its creed. And this hatred will be even more bitter and cruel than in former times, because it is fortified by science, fundamentalism, technique and power of organization. At a time such as this there is only one road open before us: To concentrate our lives, to save the last remnant, to rescue the fugitives from the upheaval, to enable them once more to attach Jewish experience, Jewish brains, Jewish instinct and Jewish feeling to actual, concrete possessions, so as to provide an example not only in words or in proclamation of ideas, but in practical ways of life. This University must accept this great function. It must be the first and preeminent example of the idea of consolidation and concentration in its own sphere; and thereby it must serve as a guide to the whole nation. It must be conscious of the great responsibility resting on it in this hour. It must select and gather in beneath its roof those men who are fitted for the mission of today, men who are prepared to do their work in quiet devotion and faith and tenacity, despite those who long to see us swept away and annihilated from off the face of the earth. We have to continue our task obstinately, so as to absorb and preserve that which is finest throughout the whole world and to make an added contribution of our own.

RAPHAEL POWELL
"Should Jews Join Anti-Fascist Societies?"
The Young Zionist
London, August 1934

Nazism in power inspired imitators everywhere. Thousands joined Sir Oswald Mosely's British Union of Fascists. Even more Jews and leftists battled them in the streets. But British Zionists, mindful of the WZO's good relations with Mussolini, tried to ignore the local crisis. Jews and workers paid no mind to their folly and, on October 4, 1936, 100,000 people defeated the Fascists and 5,000 police in the famous "Battle of Cable Street." London Jews were freed from the Blackshirt menace.—LB

I have been asked whether Jews should join anti-Fascist societies, and I know the answer which would be given by a large number of my friends whose views incline, somewhat more ponderously than my own, to the sinister side of politics.

"Why not?" they reply, and in the majority of cases that provocative question is supported by some such arguments as these:

(1) That the Jew has suffered for hundreds of years from the intolerance of the governments of the world, and that therefore it would indeed be a hardship if his own coreligionists should impose any restriction on his power to think and act as he pleases.

(2) That the Jew, since he cannot withstand anti-Semitism by force, must ally himself with any body of opinion which is opposed to a party which includes anti-Semitism as the pièce de résistance of its policy—even though his ally be the devil himself.

(3) That the Jew, seeking some outlet for his political sense, has been compelled to join the ranks of the Socialists or Communists because only among these has he been received with welcoming arms.

(4) That freedom of thought is much beloved by the Jew, and that therefore he must resist any power which threatens to interfere with that privilege.

These are some of the main augments, and we must take care that, in examining them, our glasses are neither so roseate in hue that we fail to discern their defects nor so dark that we do not appreciate their merits.

In the first place, we must remind ourselves that the question is "should" and not "may" Jews join anti-Fascist societies. No one would deny that a Jew has the power, and few would deprive him of the right to do whatsoever he pleases as long as no restriction is imposed upon him by law. But a difficulty always arises when we try to reconcile individual liberty with public policy. Then are conceived those awkward questions—Is it expedient? Will others suffer? Even if they suffer, can we sacrifice their well-being for the benefit of the whole body of Jews?

Secondly, let us admit that in the majority of cases Jews gravitate naturally, either through force of circumstances or by reason of personal inclination, towards socialistic shades of political thought. The question might still remain—should they display this tendency to the world by the overt act of joining a political party?

It is indeed hard to deny to any man his right to express in action the sentiment that he feels in his heart. Psychologists would say that such repression is dangerous.

At the same time we must realize that when a Jew joins an anti-Fascist society, he brings to that body something more than the mere political views which he may share with his non-Jewish comrades, something stronger than the mere desire to oppose dictatorial methods of government, something more compelling even than a common revulsion against inhuman treatment of fellowmen; for he brings within him that mangled Jewish soul which is the legacy of several thousands of years of persecution. That is why a Jew, whether he is really conscious of the fact or not, is more zealous and more active in the support of those whom he joins, more bitter in his opposition to those who are the common enemy.

But in the mind of that enemy is begotten that eternal fallacious generalization: Since the leaders are Jews, therefore all Jews are surely tarred with the same brush. So all Jews are Socialists or Communists or anti-Fascists—or indeed any other "-ists" with whom Jews may from time to time ally themselves.

Suppose that under a Fascist regime reprisals are used against anti-Fascists, all Jews must suffer. Suppose that such measures are taken only against socialists or Communists, all anti-Fascists are involved, because, of course, all anti-Fascists must be Socialists or Communists. Absurd generalizations if you like—but generalizations which history proves to have been made only too frequently.

So the question looms up once more—Should we?

On the one hand, there may be many who will say that the mischief, if mischief it is, has already been done, so that we may as well be hung for a sheep as for a lamb.

On the other hand, there are others who aver that we owe it to ourselves to encourage the instinct for self-preservation, and that therefore we must seek protective alliances. If the Fascists will not have us – and why should we curry favor with our enemies?—then we must join the opponents of Fascism.

In either case, in my opinion, we would be adopting a counsel of despair. The one answer results from something akin to bravado; the other reveals a lack of independence. Both answers confess weakness.

Meanwhile, there are three ideals which cry aloud for the support of all Jews, and there is a serious danger that they may die for lack of that support. These ideas are: (1) The unity of the Jewish people. (2) The need for a stronger Jewish pride. (3) The building up of Eretz Yisrael. And we are wasting our time wondering whether we should join anti-Fascist societies!

BORIS SMOLAR
"Between the Lines"
The Daily Bulletin
March 8, 1935

Many Zionists opposed the ZVfD/WZO collaborationists. Boris Smolar, chief European correspondent for the Jewish Telegraphic Agency, the Zionist news service, spoke for them.—LB

Zionist Overtures to Nazism

Die Juedische Rundschau, official organ of the Zionist Organization in Germany, has more than once been criticized for its overtures to the Nazi government. It has been pointed out more than once that this organ, while expressing the views of the Zionists in Germany, acts in contradiction with the interests of the general Jewish population in the Reich and with the attitude of world Jewry towards the Nazi regime.

The overture, which this official organ of the Zionists in Germany has just made, demanding from the Nazi government economic equality only, at a time when world Jewry demands the restoration of full rights for German Jews, will again give ground for a new criticism of the German Zionist Organization, which is responsible for the views expressed in the Juedische Rundschau.

Approving a Ghetto

Similarly, criticism may be expected also of the suggestion by the Juedische Rundschau that the Jews of Germany have cultural autonomy under control of the Nazi government. By reducing the Jewish demands to cultural autonomy only, instead of demanding full rights for German Jewry, the Zionist paper actually agrees to limiting the Jews of Germany to a ghetto life.

It is needless to say that the Jews of the world, fighting for the rights of the Jews in Germany, will never agree to the compromise which the Zionist organ in Berlin suggests. The slogan of world Jewry is that there can be no peace with Germany until the Jews are restored to their full and equal rights. Tolerating Jews in commerce is not enough. Limiting Jews to a cultural ghetto life is certainly something which is not in accordance with Jewish demands.

Sanctioning the Nazi Policy

One can understand that a Jewish newspaper which appears in Germany may not be in a position fully to support the demands of world Jewry with regard to the full restoration of Jewish rights. This, however, does not justify any official Jewish organ to come out and to practically agree to the anti-Jewish limitations which exist in Germany. The last is exactly what the Juedische Rundschau has done.

By demanding only economic rights and cultural autonomy under Nazi control, the *Juedische Rundschau* actually sanctions the present Nazi policy of limiting the Jews to commerce and to their innercultural life. It does not demand anything more than the Jews of Germany "enjoy" anyway at present.

A Dangerous Compromise

The Zionist organ in Berlin has long been criticized for its overtures to the Nazi regime. It has been suspected that these overtures are made merely in order to prevent any persecution of Zionism in Germany. Whether this suspicion is correct or not is actually not of importance. The important thing is that the Nazi government takes the Zionist overtures quite seriously, especially since the barter agreements were concluded between Palestine and Germany.

The American Jewish Congress and other Jewish organizations interested in fighting for the full restoration of Jewish rights in Germany should therefore be interested in letting the Nazi government feel that the opinion of the *Juedische Rundschau* is far from coinciding with the sentiments of the Jews of the world.

The Jews of the world will never agree to see the German Jews limited to trading and to internal cultural ghetto life. The Jews of the world demand equality for German Jews in all spheres of life.

Any compromise suggested only weakens the fight which the Jews all over the world are conducting against the Nazi Reich in the hope of forcing the Nazi leaders to abandon the "Aryan paragraph" and to restore the Jews to their full rights.

DR. GUSTAV KROJANKER

The Transfer: A Vital Question of the Zionist Movement

English Edition, Tel Aviv, 1936

Gustav Krojanker, an editor at the oldest European Zionist publisher, emigrated to Palestine in 1932, and continued to advocate full collaboration with Nazism for the Hitachduth Olei Germania, the German Immigrant Association.—LB

I. Two Forms of Jewish Reaction

When, during the past two hundred and fifty years, the Jewry of any land was harried and persecuted—and of the innumerable records of oppression one recalls the Damascus blood libel, the Dreyfus affair, and the incessant tyrannies of Czarist Russia and Roumania—there was an immediate reaction. A wave of indignation swept the Jewish world: protest meetings were held, and the loathsome incident of the day was condemned in the name of humanity. Distinguished Jews stepped into the breach and exerted their influence for justice and against the country in which repression had occurred. Funds were raised and relief committees established.

Yet History ignores these outcries in her cruel, indifferent fashion. Jewry's response to the attacks upon it during those difficult days was that of an exiled people, incapable of any other means of answer. When beaten, it cried out; when ground down, the hurts of those beneath ruthless heel were assuaged; tortured to the very point of death, Jewry tried to retaliate at least with a pinprick. It must be admitted that there were ready ears to hear the appeal; to assuage hurts was a noble mission; and even the prick of a pin was preferable to ineffective silence. But all that may be summed up as Diaspora politics: rebelliousness, which could improve naught, offwarded an event but rarely and never affected the fundamental Jewish problem.

One of the cases which stirred up the whole of Jewry was the Dreyfus affair. It led to Herzl's formulation of the Zionist idea, which inferred a complete contradiction of the ineffective Jewish action. It substituted creativeness for outcry, and the desire for a new, productive life for temporary aid; in place of a resentful mien, it developed a statesmanlike policy, stimulated not by sympathies or antipathies but by national interest. This was a remarkable innovation in Jewish circles, which reacted much as other people react when faced with something surprisingly new: to fight it or ignore it entirely. Forty years have elapsed since that time, Herzl's ideas have won thousands of supporters, and the non-Zionist world has at least become accustomed to the existence of those ideas. The fact of a Jewish Palestine has greatly assisted this achievement: since it is convenient for mankind to acquiesce with facts than disturbingly new conceptions. Moreover, it was easier to accept the fait accompli of Palestine and overlook the fundamentals of the undertaking.

The old Diasporetic psychology, an inheritage of hundreds of years, could not be abandoned overnight; and the new structure reared in Eretz Israel came sooner than the spiritual preparation of those destined to live within it. People are dwelling in that structure or getting ready to take up their abode in an edifice at whose foundation rests a great national policy, and yet their minds are still confused with Exilic thoughts. They have not yet grasped the fact that not a stone could have been laid in Palestine had it not been for the substitution of the ineffectual policy of outcry and indignation by one of upbuilding governed by entirely different laws.

II. Palestine and the German Catastrophe

Had matters evolved in a different way, and the Zionist elements of the Jewish people been of sufficient political maturity to undertake the handling of a real policy of statecraft, then there would today have been two diametrically opposed conceptions on the problem of German Jewry, the pivot of the Jewish question at present, much as Zionism years ago posed a revolutionary concept to the old Diaspora tactics. Moreover, Zionism, which claims to itself the right of spiritually guiding the people, would never have considered it enough to bestow whatever it could by virtue of its practical position in Palestine, but would have utilized this unique opportunity to accomplish a great political undertaking and thus afford a new, active and vital demonstration of the conception of statecraft which lies at the basis of its activity.

What did really happen? The great body of German Jewry, of a high cultural and material standard, was suddenly deprived of the whole foundations of its existence, and forced into exile—something which had not occurred since the time of Spain. Their number was so small as to enable the majority to be absorbed within Palestine in the course of a decade. Until now this small country has taken in almost thirty thousand German Jews, far more than any other country in the world. Not only has it absorbed them, at a time when other countries passed on the refugees one to another and only a small proportion were able to strike new roots, but given them a homeland and a future. Palestine itself has benefited greatly. With the stream of talented people, there was an influx of Jewish capital of a volume unprecedented hitherto. The increase at the same time of labor immigrants from other countries was achieved in great measure by the German newcomers who brought with them the means for existence and expansion for all classes of the people.

Let us now consider that the number of people and the extent of capital which has entered Palestine from Germany until now is only a very small part of the contemplated immigration during the coming few years—to build and develop the land for the benefit of other sections of Jewry. The decisive factor in the objective position of German Jewry vis-à-vis other Jewish elements is that an element of a high cultural order with large funds is coming to Palestine. The rich and the poor are subject to the same oppression: of the wealthy Jews in Poland and Roumania, not to mention other Western lands, only a few inspired by the Zionist ideal are going to Palestine; while from Germany, most everyone given the chance of doing so would join the immigrants. From this point of view it is clear that Zionism has been confronted with an immense task and that it would be failing in its mission if it merely waited those who would find their way to Palestine without its insistence.

III. The Special Aspect of the German Jewish Emigration Problem
German Jews should be enabled to go to Palestine. Whoever contends that they are in any event given the possibility, more or less, of emigrating there like all other sections of the Jewish people, cannot appreciate the special character of the German problem. This special characteristic does not lie in the German currency laws, as might be imagined from a superficial survey, but in the unique fact that a whole body of Jewry is ready simultaneously to migrate, and under certain conditions is equipped for it. No such problem has arisen until now.

Emigration from other countries primarily affected people without means who needed labor certificates, and in addition a small percentage of so-called capitalists who encountered no particular difficulties in leaving their countries of domicile. But in Germany it is necessary at one fell swoop to liquidate considerable capital. The complex question is therefore posed of how to realize this capital—a question that has not in the past faced any other country.

From the principle viewpoint, naturally, it depends upon the wealth of the country which is expelling its Jews and upon the percentage which the Jews own to that national wealth. Theoretically it may be argued that this or the other country can permit its Jewish inhabitants to leave with all their property in the form of cash. Such is not the case in practice. It is just those countries, where the problem arises at all in this form—economic crisis and acute anti-Semitism usually go hand in hand—which cannot afford owing to their economic position to surrender, even with the best of will, a part of their national resource. Certainly Germany is not able to do so, for even before Hitler assumed power, the currency transfer restrictions were most stringent. Germany cannot permit the transfer of Jewish capital in any other form except merchandise, just as ultimately there is no kind of transfer save of goods (one recalls the German reparations system where the statesmen failed to foresee that their countries could be paid only in kind). In short, the question of German currency restrictions is not a specific German problem; it is liable to arise in greater or lesser form in practically every country where a large Jewish body is about to migrate. From an objective point of view, there is really little difference whether the process is voluntary or compulsory; and consequently the Zionists are in error who regard the special practical problem of transfer facing German Jewry as peculiar to the latter and with which Zionism itself cannot be concerned. It is the contrary which is true. The problem of liquidating Jewish capital was a decisive factor in Herzl's first conception (in his "Judenstaat") of the Zionist ideal. He knew nothing, as long ago as that, of currency laws but he was aware that a general process of liquidation had to be established as the central issue, and especially through a Zionist institution. And that was only a small part of Herzl's broader conception. His survey of the situation was devoid of any futile grudge-bearing; he perceived two political factors—an organization of the Jewish people on the one side, and the countries concerned on the other. They were to be partners in a pact: the countries which were to be relieved of their Jewish problem by the departure of the Jews, and the latter, to whom the nations were guaranteeing a homeland, ready to carry out from the practical viewpoint whatever they could in order to achieve this process. The question of transferring capital is thus also a Zionist task.

To be sure, that task has never been actual. Only a few individuals were affected and they had no need of treaties or particular organizations.

Consequently what Herzl wrote on the matter forty years ago was forgotten. Now suddenly an entire Jewry came along, or, better still, is ready to come. Whether voluntarily or by compulsion, it is the first time in history that such an objective situation is created, conforming to Herzl's original conception.

IV. Has Zionism Reacted Properly?

How has Zionism reacted to the situation? That is the real test.

Was the reaction of the Zionist Movement spontaneous, or did it follow on when the Jewish world at large reacted in its Diasporetic fashion? What happened among world Jewry when the Jews of Germany were overtaken by the greatest catastrophe in contemporary history? It was aroused to a storm of protest and indignation; relief funds were started, and a policy of retaliation was decided upon in the form of a boycott. The Diaspora reacted as it was wont to do, as was in the nature of things, and there is nothing really that can be said against this form of response. I repeat that outcry is eventually heard; it is necessary to relieve pain; and to deal a pinprick in retaliation is better than quiescent toleration. But it should be clearly understood that all this has nothing in common with Zionism.

For Zionism the German Jewish catastrophe was not a surprise nor something unexpected. It was an eventuality which at least was within the bounds of possibility, liable to occur at some time or another even in Germany. Zionism had delivered its clarion call in anticipation of a similar situation many years ago, when the Jewish people were still tranquilly somnolent, from the platform at Basle. While as for the assuagement of hurts, it is probable that while others contributed money, the Zionists gave something far more valuable—the life and vigor of innumerable pioneers who in their nationalist idealism prepared the land and thus enabled thirty thousand persons to come and live freely in almost a simultaneous body. It was in the third factor, the great political concept which Herzl had outlined and in which Zionism showed the distinction between a real Jewish policy and one of Diaspora reasoning, that Zionism faltered and hesitated, failing to serve its true purpose. That was because it followed on where the Diaspora led, because it lacked the revolutionary power to overthrow the ghetto psychology—which also exists in Palestine—by its forceful inspiration. Zionism cannot persist or hope to flourish unless it develops to the highest degree its own essential ideology though this be unpopular. The pure Zionist idea was not conceived in any placatory spirit; it was intended gradually to bring about a convincing realization of its force by penetrating the ghetto outlook.

What actually happened after the German disaster, then, was that the

Diaspora came forward with its remedy of a boycott. The Zionist Movement remained silent. True, Palestine absorbed immigrants and thus offered a most important, practical response; but the Zionist idea, whose inception had made the present-day absorption possible, turned its head. Not a word was said; and the Movement failed to rise to the opportunity, for the first time since the Balfour Declaration, of again acting in the spirit of Herzl.

Zionism could well have left the Diaspora to its boycott tactics; in principle it had no concern with such tactics. It might perhaps have considered the practical implications of a boycott—doing harm to the Hitler regime and thus indirectly achieving an improvement in the position of German Jewry— either optimistically or with skepticism, as the case might be; but none of this had any relation to the upbuilding of Palestine. The romanticism of the Diaspora policy, weighed by its likes and dislikes, might have improved or eased the situation in its nonessentials; but it could not affect the fundamental Jewish question which only Zionism has grasped. It was entirely divorced from that sphere. There is the same difference between the Diaspora and Zionist policies as lies between the day-by-day tactics of the Trade Unions and the ultimate Socialist purpose. Trade Unions serve the concrete interests of the workers within the framework of the existing order, while the great parties which lead them aspire at the eventual abolition of the social order. In our own case, it is obviously the bounden duty of Zionism to pursue the ultimate purpose of Palestine, even though sympathetically regarding the day-by-day tactics of the Diaspora.

Instead of obeying the boycott dictates of the Diaspora, the Zionist Movement should from the outset have adopted a Zionist standpoint, or, in other words, it should have endeavored to become the representative of one party to a pact.

When Russia reached an agreement with France, and even sent instructions to the French Communists not to oppose rearmament in their country, no intelligent person believed for a moment that Stalin had suddenly altered his attitude towards the Imperialist Capitalism of France. Obviously, it was just because of the Soviet philosophy that a provisional treaty was made necessary in the contemporary circumstances. The Zionist Movement should have endeavored, in emulation of Stalin's example, either directly or, if this were not possible, then through the medium of foreign institutions, to influence the German Government to enter into a statesmanlike treaty, accepting the situation and trying to derive the utmost advantage from it in the Zionist sense. Such a political treaty would of its very nature have had to be principally an economic one. Germany would have been compelled to grant the largest possible concessions for the transfer of capital, and the Zionist Movement would have had to assist to its utmost the transfer as well as of regulating it for the benefit of an extensive emigration.

Actually official Zionism proposed no such course of action. What happened arose mechanically from the facts of the situation. On the one hand, Palestine Jewry accepted the boycott plan with enthusiasm, and on the other hand, a few people in Germany and Palestine set up the "Haavara" (Transfer) system, a sort of agreement with the German Government for the removal of Jewish capital from that country to Palestine. What the situation urgently required was a diplomatic treaty, and even private or semiprivate individuals and groups could have secured one; what transpired was that Boycott and "Haavara" developed side by side almost peacefully, and were accepted in the same spirit by the official institutions which knew perfectly well whither the state of affairs was leading. As an outcome, they placed no obstacles against "Haavara," and even utilized its services; but, on the other hand, they took no action to explain the matter satisfactorily to public opinion or to adopt a firm attitude towards the street agitators.

Thus it was that the proper Zionist pronouncement essential in the circumstances was not made far and wide. The private Zionist initiative in establishing "Haavara" was howled down by the mob which obeyed its primitive instincts and was stimulated by agitators who took advantage of the situation for their party interests, although some of the criticism may have been genuinely motivated. Possibly the authoritative institutions awaited the decision of Congress to which the discussion of this difficult but important problem had been referred. At all events, confusion and lack of leadership marked a crucial epoch in history.

V. Value of "Haavara" for the German Jews in Palestine

In such wise did the matter begin and so it continued. But the question became far more serious than at its inception, until now it is by far the most significant factor in the life of German Jewry.

When "Haavara" was established, German Jews had two other means of proceeding to Palestine with their capital. Firstly, the German Government still allowed, until the middle of 1934, every emigrant with LP. 1,000 to transfer that amount in currency, and "Haavara" could have limited its activity to salvaging the amounts exceeding LP. 1,000 (up to 50,000 Reichsmarks). Secondly, it was still possible then, outside "Haavara," to transfer capital in the form of "blocked marks" (Sperrmark), which although involving heavy losses was acceptable to people of large fortunes. But since then, the situation has altered completely. The German Government, whose currency position became serious, now refuses to allow emigrants to take in cash the LP. 1,000 they need for "capitalist" visas, but sends them to "Haavara." At the moment there are more than 2,000 families who can bring a total of LP. 2,000,000 to Palestine dependent upon "Haavara." These applicants are constantly growing in number, and would be greater if the potential clients had any hope of receiving the money in Palestine in the near future, particularly now that the method of transferring "Sperrmark," involves a loss of 65 percent. In other words, German Jewry is pent up in a barred citadel from which there is only one narrow egress—"Haavara." It is only along this narrow path that men and money can stream into Palestine. And along this path, too, there is the unique possibility for the immigration of many "certificate" holders without means, as no employment is available without capital investments.

It is true that Zionism preached to German Jewry for many years and encountered deaf ears. But this feature was not, after all, so very much different from the attitude of Jewish communities in other countries. The tempo of immigration increased wherever the pressure was the strongest, and vice versa. At the moment the pressure is strong in Germany and has caused a volte-face among the whole of its Jewry, arousing a ready ear in every Jew. Only those who came to Palestine because of their ideology and at self-sacrifice are entitled to throw a stone at this changed psychology. Those who fled under the pressure of circumstances or those who consider themselves unworthy of a "righteous" attitude, cannot insist upon an explanation of the altered outlook among German Jewry, though, they may pose another important question: How can the newly-won Zionism hope to have any influence over the German Jews, when, at a time when they are in sore need of its support, it proffers them the Diasporetic answer in place of the Zionist message; if it tells them regretfully, "We must sacrifice you, we must sacrifice those potentialities which we can obtain through your medium?"

And why really must we sacrifice German Jewry in the name of a resounding heroic abnegation? We are told that it is because of the supreme purpose, for the sake of Israel, whose honor demands retaliation against Hitlerist Germany, and through it with all those world forces which are striving to deprive Jews of their rights. Yet insofar as national honor is concerned, it appears to me that we are Zionists just because we believe there is only the practical salvation, as honorable to the Jewish people, and that is the establishment of a creative nation in Palestine. All other means, which are nothing but palliatives, are insignificant in relation to this postulate, and the Zionists must, indeed they have the right to participate in them only insofar as specific Zionist functions are not endangered. That must be the rule concerning Hitlerist Germany and Hitlerist factors throughout the world. Zionism seeks something more than equality for individual Jewish communities in various countries; it seeks the equality of Israel among the nations of the world. And it believes that, in the long run, the rights of individuals in the Diaspora can only be guaranteed by such international equality.

Such is the Zionist ideal, and it has found open hearts and ears today in German Jewry. We must draw the practical conclusions. It is another question entirely of how great a strength we possess or whether we can overcome the conditions opposing us. But we dare not concede anything from the outset; we dare not accept with one hand something we have just given with the other.

VI. "Haavara" and Boycott

There are, in addition to this standpoint of principle, practical instances which demonstrate that the ideological negation has actually been greatly weakened.

What is the process achieved through "Haavara"? Jewish property—houses, factories, shops—takes the form of possessions which cannot readily be packed up and brought to Palestine. It is essential to realize them in cash, and in turn to convert the cash into movables, e.g., merchandise. A Jew owning a house may exchange its value for the purchase of machinery so as to establish a factory in Palestine. That is the only method of transferring property and, as explained above, the sole possibility at a time when transfer of assets is proceeding on a larger scale. But the individual cannot always choose this method. The house may belong to a widow who needs no machinery, or the owner may be unable to predetermine a safe economic pursuit in Palestine, and so forth. That is where "Haavara" steps in. It is the intermediary which takes Jewish funds paid over in Germany and purchases for cash the merchandise anybody needs in Palestine. The proceeds are then paid over to the recipients who went to Palestine and they invest the money in Palestinian enterprise. In effect, "Haavara" arranges for the conversion of Jewish houses, factories, and shops in Germany into new Jewish property in Palestine: not necessarily in the form of houses, factories, and shops once more, but as Jewish land, Jewish settlements, Jewish labor.

Anyone refusing to take "Haavara" merchandise is simply rejecting merchandise for which the Yishuv has no need to pay, and which, indeed, comes to Palestine with the immigrants. And, on the contrary, anyone ordering goods from any other country purchases something for which the Yishuv does have to pay, e.g., for which Palestinian money must go abroad.

The promoters of the anti-German boycott probably did not think of this process when they announced their campaign. The confusion arose because of a misunderstanding of the two entirely different processes comprised in the term "export." It is, indeed, difficult to explain to the ordinary man, who reacts to his feelings, that there is an enormous difference between one type of German merchandise to another. No one would object if the German Jews brought their cash with them to Palestine, insofar as that was possible. Money would be acceptable from Germany; but goods, for which after all money is but a token, are refused just because it is not known that Palestine does not have to pay for them, that they constitute additional Jewish capital for Palestine.

The rapid development of the country in the past few years has fully demonstrated the value of this influx. German men and women fulfilled an important function in this development, not only directly in the large amounts of capital imported but indirectly as well in stimulating the influx of capital for investment from other countries. The value of this factor cannot be sufficiently emphasized. It is a well-known axiom that capital attracts more capital, and vice versa. If ever the point is reached at which the stream of capital, which led to the development of the past few years, slows up or dwindles—and there is some danger of this happening—the consequent natural slump will produce a psychological setback: money will leave the country because of diminishing affluence, just as it came here because of growing affluence.

Thus before attempts were made artificially to restrict "Haavara's" activity in its natural market in Palestine, intelligent Zionists should have forestalled them by first giving thought to extending the scope of a system so limited in this small country. Such efforts emerge naturally from the circumstances even without impulsion. The newspapers published a number of reports of several proposals, some of them quite serious, made by leading Jews. The situation, it was pointed out, was providing an incentive to sponsoring fresh opportunities for extending "Haavara." They had one in common: that Palestine might more or less be excluded. Thus, single individuals would be saved—in order to form a new Diaspora and to introduce the Jewish problem into a new land. Palestine, homeland of the Jews, in which the transferred capital was converted into national resources making it possible to embark upon productive upbuilding, will indeed remain excluded unless we do not interfere in time. We shall still have labor immigrants without means, who undoubtedly will be welcomed with open arms especially if they are idealists and capable, but their absorption will be impossible without the corollary capital to create labor opportunities.

To include oneself within the transfer process, to open new possibilities, to guide that transfer to Palestine, are political tasks of first-class magnitude. It is the political task of Zionism today. It is necessary to explain the dire measure of forcing people at all costs to leave a country and at the same time depriving them of the means making that departure feasible. The world, faced with the international problem of a Jewish migration, would undoubtedly appreciate the position. So would Germany, too, if it were shown how to elaborate a solution of the pressure it is exerting upon its Jews. It might even be ready to conclude agreements—if we can only and are prepared to extend the "Haavara" system to other countries. If this is not done by ourselves, it may be done without us, and we shall not only lose the human material and the money but also bring about an economic crisis. Palestine's economic absorption today necessitates not only the same flow of capital as in the past two years, but a much larger one in view of the country's increased capacity for absorption.

Even the boycott leaders will ultimately understand what is necessary to explain to the world and to Germany. They will learn how to differentiate between types of exports; between goods for which payment is necessary and goods which are really another form of Jewish capital; between a constant export trade and a onetime transfer of capital, preserving for the Jews what they might otherwise lose. Under these circumstances there would be no sacrifice of honor in securing an agreement between Germany and Jewish institutions whereby opportunities would be created for transferring capital and a large-scale immigration enabling a practicable and speedy liquidation of the Jewish problem in Germany. Moreover, Zionism can approach Germany as a claimant, since contrary to other countries Palestine is proposing a mass migration in which there are numbers of people without means, and establish a healthy proportion between capital and human material.

Palestine is acting in the spirit of these demands and aspirations through "Haavara" at present only for itself. It is still not achieving this fully, because the Yishuv has not in its attitude to "Haavara" given the full strength which the latter needs. "Haavara" as a diplomatic-political medium, as it should have been conceived in the Zionist spirit, ought to be a kind of commercial-diplomatic monopoly in the negotiations with Germany and really regulate the market, which seems quite impossible now in connection with any other country in the world. As is well-known, Palestine has no protection against "dumping" by any other country, and local products are practically neglected. But as far as Germany is concerned such is certainly not the case. The permits for purchase of goods through "Haavara" are distributed with the assistance of the Palestine Manufacturers Association. Had "Haavara" dealings with a far-sighted community giving the system full authority to operate, then it could have been an ideal method for the control of commerce. Now that "Haavara" lacks the support of the Yishuv, it cannot regulate its advantages freely but must compromise with merchants who, while staunchly upholding a boycott, are ready to forego their views at the price of high rebates.

"Haavara," as required by the political idealism of the Zionist Movement, might have become an ideal instrument for a statesmanlike political economy; "Haavara," as it is—opposed by the Diaspora spirit and fighting its way step-by-step—is actually nothing more than an undeveloped instrument of Zionist activity. Nor would the dissolution of "Haavara" exclude German goods from the market, but thrust them pell-mell into an uncontrolled market indifferent to the claims of Tozereteh Ha'aretz (local products). Such dumping would take its toll on Palestine currency.

VII. Motives of the Political Agitation Against the Transfer

Let us compare the described state of affairs with what irresponsible political partisanship and agitation have made of it. It is of course impossible to ask of the man in the street to understand alone the significance of circumstances far beyond his comprehension. He sees German goods and cannot understand what it means; he reads of occurrences in Germany and his feelings are in turmoil. That is an ordinary process and certain interested elements are able to use it for their party politics.

Naturally the Revisionist Party has, in its own customary manner, made use of this excellent opportunity. It now dubs itself the "New Zionist Organization," and even though there is some doubt as to how far it is really a "Zionist Organization" there can be no denying that it has brought something new into Zionist life. That innovation is a denial of any form of political leadership in Jewry which Zionism claimed for itself. Instead of leading, this organization pursues the primitive instincts which sway the mob from time to time and panders to them so as to be able to trample upon the ruins of the official organization. The innovation introduced is that any means to this end are legitimate. Even though the man in the street may not understand, the leaders are all too knowing. And they, who speak so highly and mightily of statecraft and profound policy, are fully aware in their own minds that not since the Balfour Declaration has there been a similar epoch in history as the present demanding a great political effort so really essential in handling the problem of German Jewry.

The Revisionists had for the nonce a real opportunity of carrying out something about which they had always bragged: to replace a small, practical penetration of Palestine by one of a much broader scope on sound political lines. They would have every justification to recall Herzl's memory, which they call up so often, in this case. Had their program been other than a mere canvassing of votes, had it really some substance, they could have launched a different kind of attack upon the official Organization, in full consonance with the spirit of their program: by pointing out that "Haavara" was allowed to operate without the full weight of official support, without being afforded the political strength, so essential externally and internally, and for failing to change the small stream known as "Haavara" into a great, rushing torrent. They should have contended, in the full spirit of their program, that the Zionist Organization was undertaking something only half-heartedly, that it was obeying a Diaspora policy which had no relation to the Zionist political viewpoint, and in this way losing a priceless creative opportunity, or, as the Revisionists would say, an heroic activity. But as there was nothing popular in such a course of action and it needed leadership instead of instinct, these born heirs of Herzl preferred to adopt the Galuth psychology as their own and to utilize it in Palestine, where the Yishuv had not yet freed itself of the thrall, in order to conduct organized agitation under the guise of "real Zionism."

Moreover, their battle was not so much directed against "Haavara" itself as the Zionist Congress which had agreed to the system with the full consent of two of the leading spokesmen for the boycott movement in America who had become convinced of "Haavara's" justification. The battle, too, was waged against the Executive which, after the Congress, accepted official responsibility for "Haavara." Anyone who still hesitates as to the ultimate advantage of this campaign must ask himself why it was organized on so large a scale against "Haavara" at just this moment and with such violence. Was it because the position in Germany had grown worse? Because "Haavara" had become the only possible means of salvage? Because it was necessary to add an onslaught from Palestine to that by Germany? No. It was because at this moment, after the Congress, it was possible to strike at the official Organization through "Haavara." Truth to say, Revisionism has no other purpose than to try to undermine the official Organization and its institutions wherever possible. This time they found an excellent medium, the instincts of the Diaspora which still rule so strongly among the masses. And real Zionists are in duty bound to show them that nevertheless they were wrong.

VIII. Prospects

Matters have been enlightened to some extent. Congress approved the principle of the "Haavara" system and imposed the responsibility for it upon the Executive. The latter issued a public statement supporting the principle of "Haavara" with its authority. We have consequently emerged from the obscurities of compromise politics which had prevailed but were not admitted as such. A clear light was shed upon the Zionist ideology in Ben Gurion's official statements.

Yet all this is but a beginning. Instead of serving even as a minor instrument within the political framework of a farsighted Zionist policy, "Haavara" in its present form has come into the forefront of discussion not because of its intrinsic worth but by reason of interparty strife. We hope that it has been made clear that this nevertheless will be an external factor leading to the real merits of the discussion, in which there will be no consideration of "Haavara" as it stands, but of the question of whether or not Zionism appreciates the problem confronting it in German Jewry for the first time in its history in the present acute form, and exactly as Herzl foresaw forty years ago. Now, with the lapse of forty years, the Zionist movement must be told of the true state of affairs so that it may comprehend its function in dealing with the situation in the spirit and on the scale conceived by Herzl.

In another twenty years there will probably be no German Jewry worthy of mention. But the fate of the people comprising the body of German Jewry today lies to a great extent in our own hands. We can leave them in Germany, and in ten years at the very latest they will be a community culturally and economically degenerated, of as little value to the structure of world Jewry as the Jews of Russia today. Such will be the consequences of a war waged for the sake of Jewish honor. We can help in the emigration of a great part of them and gather them into the fold of the resurgent Jewish people in Palestine where the future glows brightly. We can use their talents and their capital for the upbuilding of Palestine; and the past two years have shown how important this is. The choice lies within our grasp: Destruction in

Germany, and hard abnegation for Palestine; that is what they call "honor"— or redemption from Germany and a flourishing Jewish homeland—the "national treachery" of which we are being accused.

"Debating the Issues of the Transfer: Is the Agreement Between the Zionists and Germany Justified?"
Call of Youth
January 1936

Berl Locker, headed the Palestinian Poale Zion (Workers of Zion), the Labor Zionist organization. Baruch Vladeck, his opponent, was an editor of Forward, *then the leading Yiddish daily in America and the voice of the older generation of the still huge Jewish working class.—LB*

[The issues involved in the Transfer Agreement have aroused stormy debates in Jewish labor circles where the economic boycott against Nazi Germany is taken seriously. Admittedly, the outstanding proponents of the two sides of the issue are B. C. Vladeck, chairman of the Jewish Labor Committee, and Berl Locker, head of the Poale Zion organization in Palestine. We are glad to present their opinions below.—Editor]

YES! Says Berl Locker
Opponents of Zionism have seized upon the Transfer Agreement, making capital of it in their efforts to discredit the Zionist movement. Their baseless and confused attacks on the Transfer have been, from the beginning, aimed as an attack upon the Jewish worker in Palestine.

A short history of the beginnings of the Transfer movement is perhaps in place so as to clarify misunderstandings. Soon after the ascension to power of the Hitler regime, with its insensate persecution of Jews, there began a wave of emigration of Jews from Germany. Hundreds, and then thousands, of German Jews fled the country; before the conclusion of the Transfer Agreement, Jews leaving the country were allowed to take only up to £1000 in cash. The remainder was taken in merchandise.

So it was not the Zionist movement which originated the transfer movement. Palestine was presented with a fait accompli—German goods were being brought into Palestine by fugitives. Palestine was also presented with the dilemma: shall we boycott these German goods which are coming into Palestine? Can we put pickets in front of such establishments and carry on the Anti-Nazi boycott? No, for this would be not a boycott of German goods, but a boycott against German Jews. To deprive the persecuted German Jews of this last harbor of refuge, this only opportunity to rescue themselves and something of their fortunes from the slough of Nazidom, would be national suicide.

B. C. Vladeck tells these unfortunate Jews not to flee, but to remain in Germany and struggle against Hitler. We cannot, however, be this arbitrary and unreal about the situation. German Jews are leaving Germany. They are emigrating and they wish to save some part of their wealth, instead of leaving it to the German government. And if Jews migrate to Palestine without any private resources, what will they be able to do? Many of the emigrants are middle-aged men and women, for whom the transition to manual labor would be extremely difficult. Even if they could work, there must be industry to absorb them. Unfortunately, the national funds of Palestine (Keren Kyemes and Keren Hayesod) are inadequate and would not suffice to productivize these emigrants with no resources.

It is Vladeck's assertion that withdrawal of Jewish capital from Germany in the form of goods is not so shameful in individual cases; that it is the stamp of approval which the Zionist movement has put upon it which is making the Jews the laughing stock of the world. Let us suppose that we were to allow the emigration movement to proceed unsupervised. What would be the result? German goods would be dumped on the Palestinian market resulting in personal loss, chaos in the Palestinian market, and the disorganization of Palestinian economic life.

At the time that the Transfer Agreement was arranged, Jews leaving Germany were, without restriction, allowed to take out £1000 in cash. When the Havorah (Transfer Agency) was organized, it concerned itself only with transactions involving the surplus above the £1000 which individuals were freely permitted to withdraw. Since then, free withdrawals have been restricted and only 12-15 such withdrawals a month are permitted.

The usual procedure is as follows: the candidate (for emigration) obtains government permission and deposits his money with the Havorah. The Havorah, in turn, deposits these moneys in one of two accounts which it maintains with the German Reichsbank. Account I functions for those Jews who are already in Palestine, or who plan to emigrate there immediately. Account II is for others who are not themselves prepared to emigrate. The account is (temporarily at least—Editor) closed. The maximum that any Jew is permitted to withdraw from the country is 50,000 marks or $20,000 at the German rate of exchange.

The Havorah has thus established a credit with the Reichsbank. It then obtains orders for the German merchandise in Palestine and arranges to pay for these orders with its Reichsbank credit, thus obtaining cash in Palestine and satisfying the merchandise clause of the agreement. The Transfer Agreement prevents the country from being flooded with German merchandise, since goods come in only as there is need for them. It is the only method whereby a German Jew can withdraw more than £1000 of his fortune. Besides, it provides (through Account I) moneys which are invested in the national funds of Palestine.

Before I conclude, I should like to answer one objection of Vladeck's. Vladeck attacks the Transfer Agreement, saying that with the Agreement we are allying ourselves and dealing with the Hitler Government. Has not the Joint Distribution Committee, of whose executive Vladeck is a member, sent $1,000,000 into Germany to help the German Jews? In so doing has it not provided the German government with the valuta which it wants so badly? In attacking the Transfer Agreement for the same reason, Vladeck shows a strange inconsistency.

NO! Retorts B. C. Vladeck

At the recent conference of the "Labor Campaign for Palestine" a resolution was adopted in favor of the boycott of German Goods. Yet at this same conference the Transfer Agreement between the Zionist organizations and Nazi Germany was openly defended—an agreement by which German goods are bought by a Zionist organization in Germany and sold to the Jews in Palestine. You may argue from now till Doomsday, but this is double bookkeeping of the most flagrant sort. That nobody should break the boycott but the Jews of Palestine. And nobody deal with Germany but the Zionist organizations!

The defenders of the Transfer Agreement themselves feel the contradiction of the situation and make attempts to explain it away. One of the explanations is that under this agreement Germany receives no money from other countries, no valuta. That is no excuse. Why does Germany need valuta? Because there isn't enough money in Germany. That is, there is plenty of money, but the government cannot or will not touch private fortunes. What, then, is the function of the Transfer Agreement? It takes the money that Jews own as private capital, and that the government cannot touch, and gives it to the government in return for German goods.

Nor is that all. In order to sell her goods to other countries besides Palestine, the German government is ready to supply up to fifty percent of the cost of these products. It sells special marks with which foreign importers then pay for German goods, and these marks are worth not very much more than one-half the real value of the German mark. But those goods exported from Germany under the Transfer Agreement are paid for, pfennig for pfennig, mark for mark; the German government receives for them twice as much as she would have received if she had exported them to another country.

The second excuse is not really an excuse, but an analogy, and it was propounded, according to the newspaper, by my friend, Baruch Zuckerman. The analogy is as follows: if a child is kidnapped, no one blames the parents when they pay the ransom money, although everyone knows that the kidnapper is an outlaw and a scoundrel. In the same way, in order to save the German Jews, it is permissible to deal with Germany.

This analogy would be a very good one if the premises were the same. But, unfortunately, an altogether different analogy fits the case: a whole family has been kidnapped. The ransom money is paid for one member of the family, thus enabling the kidnapper to torture the rest of the family. If there were only one Jew in Germany or only 1,000 Jews, then Friend Zuckerman's example would be correct. But there are still nearly half a million Jews in Germany, all of whom it is impossible to move in a short time. By giving the Nazis money we strengthen and enable them to persecute the remaining Jews all the more effectively. The moral harm of the Transfer Agreement is so apparent that only the most dull-witted can try to ignore it. The whole organized labor movement and the progressive world are waging a fight against Hitler through the boycott. The Transfer Agreement scabs on that fight.

"But," say the defenders of the Transfer Agreement, "we can't stop to discuss moral effects. We must save the Jews in Germany, and the Transfer is a way out." Let's look into the practical value of the Agreement. We are told that over 30,000 Jews were rescued by the Transfer Agreement. That, to put it bluntly, is a lie. Not 30,000 but between 4 and 5 thousand were settled in Palestine by means of the Transfer, and these were not "saved."

How does the Transfer Agreement work? Israel Karlebech, an eminent Zionist, gave in the Warsaw "Today" of Nov. 1, a clear explanation of the workings of the Agreement. Let us say a German Jew has $1,000 and he wants to take it out with him so that he may settle in Palestine. First of all, he must wait at least a year before he can get permission from the Finance Minister. When he gets the permission the government takes off 20 percent as "flight" tax. He now has $800. Of the $800, the "Havorah" (the Transfer organization) takes approximately 25 percent of the total $1,000, or $250, for various expenses. This leaves $550. Of the $550 he gets 40 percent in notes on the Jewish National Fund, 20 percent in a Palestinian "gesellschaft," 20 percent in a Palestinian cooperative undertaking, and 20 percent in cash. The cash is not turned over to him until two years later and he may not sell any of these holdings. Plainly put, the German Jew is so "saved" that for $1,000 he gets $111 and that only after two years.

It is my contention that the main purpose of the Transfer is not to rescue the Jews from Germany but to strengthen various institutions in Palestine. I have seen figures which show that to date the National Fund has received over three million marks from the Transfer; the workers' union "Nir" over one and a half million marks; the bank "Hapoalim" another half million; and the "Hanuta" two and a half million marks. From the beginning of the Transfer up to the 31st of July, 1935, the "Havorah" exported from Germany products worth about 19 million marks. Of these German Jews with whose money the goods were bought, received only about seven million marks. Over nine million went to strengthen various institutions in Palestine.

There is still another aspect to the question. Because so many German products enter Palestine the market is flooded. New markets are needed. So the German consul in Egypt is approached by the "Havorah" to help sell "Havorah" goods to the Egyptians and is thereby promised especially low prices. The same is done in other countries neighboring to Palestine. Palestine thus becomes the official scab-agent against the boycott in the Near-East.

There have been many protests against the Transfer Agreement—from prominent Zionists themselves. But more amazing than the protests is the silence which has enshrouded it. When the news of the Transfer Agreement first came out, the Zionists denied having anything to do with it. At the 18th Congress in Prague, Berl Locker said: "Not a single Zionist agency has the slightest connection with the Transfer." During that very period the bank "Hapoalim" (of the Histadruth) was raking in money from the Agreement. At the last Zionist Congress the question came up again and there were very heated debates. I have before me the Bulletins of the "Palkor" of the days when the debate was raging. But the only record of it is a few words by Kaponsky and by Meyer Grossman of the Jewish State Party. It was evidently felt that such discussion could not be publicized.

From this I can conclude in only one vein: the Transfer Agreement is a blot on the Jews and on the world and the stain must be wiped away.

PALESTINE
TELEGRAPHIC AGENCY
"German Zionists Seek Recognition"
Palestine Post
January 15, 1936

The Palestine Post *is today the* Jerusalem Post.—*LB*

Berlin. Tuesday—A bold demand that the German Zionist Federation be given recognition by the Government as the only instrument for the exclusive control of German Jewish life was made by the Executive of that body in a proclamation today.

All German Jewish organizations, it was declared, should be dominated by the Zionist spirit.

"Baal Is Not God"

The Congress Bulletin
January 24, 1936

The Congress Bulletin *was the organ of the American Jewish Congress, a leading pro-Zionist organization.—LB*

The demand of the Zionist Federation of Germany that it be given full jurisdiction over the adaptation of German Jewry to the conditions created by the Nuremberg Laws is, in a way, an open defiance of the cultural dictatorship of Georg Kareski which the Nazis have imposed upon the Jews.

The Cabalists of old long ago discovered the dual complexion of ideas. Light and darkness, sacred and profane, God and Satan, all manifest themselves through the same phenomena. Thus it is with nationalism. It can spell salvation, liberation and freedom; it can also spell persecution, enslavement and annihilation.

Hitlerism is Satan's nationalism. The determination to rid the German national body of the Jewish element, however, led Hitlerism to discover its "kinship" with Zionism, the Jewish nationalism of liberation. Therefore Zionism became the only other party legalized in the Reich, and the Zionist flag the only other flag permitted to fly in Naziland.

It was a painful distinction for Zionism to be singled out for favors and privileges by its Satanic counterpart. It became menacing when the chasm dividing the two "step-brothers" of nationalism was lost sight of, and the "kinship" began to produce such an anomaly as Georg Kareski.

Once a leading Zionist, and President of the Berlin Jewish Community, Kareski discovered the "compatibility" between Hitlerism and Zionism and then voluntarily joined the Secret Service of the Reich. He became the Jew who made Hitlerism his Jewish nationalist faith. He openly declared—in

Goebbels' "Angriff"—the Nuremberg Laws to be a "blessing to the Jews." Who but Kareski was to be entrusted with implementing the Nazi-made cultural autonomy for Jews?

This "cultural autonomy" is another example of a Satanic counterpart of an idea. Cultural autonomy signifies the freedom of a group of citizens enjoying full civic equality to develop and sustain their particular historic culture. The Nazi interpretation of cultural autonomy is the imprisonment of an economically, socially and legally disfranchised group within the cultural and physical walls of its historical peculiarities. Excluding Jews from participation in German cultural activities is not sufficient. The Jewish peculiarity must be guarded so that no Aryan sound or thought penetrates the walls of the ghetto. Not only are the Jews limited to their own theaters and concert halls, which no Aryan is permitted to enter, but no Aryan composers may be heard in those concert halls, and no Aryan playwright may be presented on those stages. No medieval Jewish fanatic, in his zeal for separating the Jews from the rest of the world, could have thought of turning national life into such an airtight dungeon.

This is the "autonomy" Georg Kareski accepted from the hands of Dr. Hinkel as a "blessing" for his brethren. Were the Zionist Federation of Germany to submit to this dictatorship, it would indirectly subscribe to the Kareski-Goebbels-Hinkel interpretation of Zionism. It would do so under duress, with the sword of the henchmen over its head, but, nevertheless, do so. The demand for full jurisdiction over Jewish matters, carries the daring implication that no Kareski patronage is acceptable. It is on a par with the stand taken by the Protestant Church against the "coordinating" attempts of the Nazi Bishop Mueller. Since the position of the outlawed Jewish minority can in no way be compared to that of the powerful Protestant Church, the Zionist stand displays that much more courage and determination.

It is immaterial, at the moment, whether or not the German Zionists gain their point. It was imperative, however, to proclaim at any risk, that Baal is not god.

DR. JOACHIM PRINZ
"Zionism Under the Nazi Government"
The New Palestine
September 17, 1937

Dr. Joachim Prinz is one of the most distinguished younger Rabbis of present-day Germany, where he has become the outstanding spokesman of the Jewish community, particularly among the youth. Although his family has lived for many generations in Germany, he has been an active worker for Zionism, even since 1917, and was for many years an Executive Member of the German Zionist Federation. Apart from his fame as an orator and leader, Dr. Prinz has also enriched German Jewish Scholarship, and was the author of the first political book, We Jews, *written by a Jew under the Hitler regime. He has recently settled in the United States of America.—LB*

From the very first day of its establishment, the Zionist movement in Germany has played the role of a prophet of evil. There was never an occasion during the past 15 years when the Zionists of Germany ceased voicing their warnings to German Jews.

I shall never forget the day when Walther Rathenau was killed by two young adventurers who were later decorated and praised for their patriotic deed. It was a Sabbath day. We had gone to the Berlin University to listen to one of Germany's most famous and interesting men, a protestant scholar and ardent fighter for freedom and liberty, Ernst Troeltsch. I shall never forget his pale face, his trembling voice, his eyes full of tears, as he began his lecture with the words: "My friend Walther Rathenau has been shot by one of the young men who pretend to be patriots." His lecture which was supposed to have dealt with questions of philosophy, was transformed into an essay on Rathenau, the Statesman.

In those days, the then German chancellor, Joseph Wirth, a Roman Catholic and President of the Center Party, violently attacked the murderers and those who supported them. Further indictments came from the ranks of the democrats and left-wing parties; but being democrats and friends of liberty they knew only of liberal and very mild methods against a phalanx of soldiers who had resolved to fight for "a new Germany" with all means and without "democratic scruples."

The Jews watched the dangerous interplay with mixed feelings. Most of them were happy to see that enemies of the State, who were at the same time foes of the Jews, were finally being "prosecuted." They were quite sure that nothing more disturbing could happen as long as men like Severing, one of the socialist leaders, and Braun, were the heads of the government. While everybody felt instinctively that Hindenburg's election as the President of the German Reich must be the beginning of the end, most Jews were happy at the election of a man of that dignity and love of justice.

Zionists Warned of Danger
The Zionists in Germany were in a difficult position. Official Jewry was against us. We were a minority, fighting alone against a Jewish world blind even to the already visible facts. From the beginning of the revolution in 1918, the facts were: increasing anti-Semitism, riots in the universities and even on the streets, anti-Semitic pamphlets and newspapers, riots in the smaller towns, and the slow but steady increase of a group of adventurers who were bound together by the so-called "Fronterlebnis" (experience at the front) and headed by a then unknown and later ridiculed man called Adolf Hitler.

We could do nothing but warn. We appealed to the German Jews to face the facts. We cited Theodor Herzl. We tried to make clear that the Jewish question must be solved and that the day would come when the Jews in Germany would have to realize the Jewish question as one of their own problems, a problem of life and death.

In 1930, I had occasion to lecture in the German town of Cassel. My topic was: "The future of the Jews and Nazis." The meeting was overcrowded, but I knew in advance that most of them would be against me. I had committed a crime: I took the Nazis seriously. From the very beginning of that movement, I was convinced that they would succeed. I remember the storm which was created at that meeting when I warned the Jews to repudiate their old view of assimilationism and Germanism. When I reached that point in my address when I described the Nazis as the coming rulers of Germany, the audience began to whistle and shout. One of them cried violently and loudly: "And this man pretends to be a rabbi!"

That was the general Jewish reaction. They did not realize the danger in which they were. They had their own Weltanschauung that meant: to be a good German patriot, to deny even the existence of a Jewish nation and to do everything necessary to prove patriotism. Even when Hitler had already reached power, a great many Jews could not forget the old idols.

Evil Prophecy Came True

But during the days which preceded Hitler, the Zionist movement fought for the acceptance of its own ideals. Against the dream of assimilation we preached the sermon of dissimilation. We asked for Jewish education of the children, increasing interest—moral and financial—in the resettlement of the Jews in Palestine, participation in Jewish world affairs, a changed attitude toward the Ostjuden who came to us in the years after the war and who were regarded—not only by anti-Semitic circles but also by many German Jews—as the cause of all the difficulties. But Zionists preached to deaf ears. Only the youth responded. With times there came an awakening of interest in Palestine, but the majority of the German Jews considered the Zionists to be men of evil who agreed with the Nazis.

The day came when our evil prophecy came true. That day German Jewry suffered the experience of an earthquake. They were overwhelmed by a Jewish and human tragedy which seemed impossible to conceive even in a bad dream. The first of April came. Germans enjoyed that day. They celebrated a new carnival, the "yellow carnival." "Yellow—the color of the Judenfleck" in the middle ages—was the leading color of the day. The long streets in which Jewish shops were found were a single yellow ribbon of insults and outrages.

There was no time then to consider the tragedy and the very touching sentimental and individual problems. Something concrete and practical had to be done. Everybody in Germany knew that only the Zionists could responsibly represent the Jews in dealings with the Nazi Government. We all felt sure that one day the government would arrange a round table conference with the Jews, at which—after the riots and atrocities of the revolution had passed—the new status of German Jewry could be considered. The Government announced very solemnly that there was no country in the world which tried to solve the Jewish problem as seriously as did Germany. Solution of the Jewish question? It was our Zionist dream! We never denied the existence of the Jewish question! Dissimilation? It was our own appeal!

Saving the Remnants

In preparation for that conference, a statement was written which was never published. It was signed by Georg Landauer, who is still in Germany. In a statement notable for its pride and dignity, we asked for a conference to consider the question of the Jewish status. We emphasized that we too were anxious to find a solution of the Jewish problem.

In those early days we believed in the slim possibility of saving the German Jews, but nothing happened. Nothing! We were not even given an answer.

It should be known that during the last four and a half years, not even one Jew was seen or received by any member of the Nazi Government to consider a political question. We dealt only with the officials of the ministries and the police, with the Gestapo, the Jewish department of Goebbel's ministry or with the ministry for economic affairs (on the problems of transfer).

When we realized that the German Government never intended to solve the Jewish problem, and that its only attitude toward Jews was one of humiliation, degradation and the spirit of the *Sturmer*, we turned our thoughts in the direction of saving whatever possible from the enormous bankruptcy of a once wealthy Jewry. That meant constructive tasks.

It was very difficult for the Zionists to operate. It was morally disturbing to seem to be considered as the favored children of the Nazi Government, particularly when it dissolved the anti-Zionist youth groups, and seemed in other ways to prefer the Zionists. The Nazis asked for a "more Zionist behavior."

Zionists Badly Treated

All this was most disagreeable and painful to the Zionists. But the Nazi attitude toward the Zionists was only a facade. In reality, the Zionists were and are miserably treated. Two Zionists were banished from the country without any reason whatever: one of them despite his German citizenship; the other, S. Adler-Rudel, was one of our best experts in social problems. During the years, Zionists have frequently been arrested. Zionist meetings were forbidden or dissolved, sometimes even before the scheduled meeting could be opened (the reason given was that the meeting opened five minutes after the scheduled opening). Zionist officials were and still are frequently called to the Gestapo and examined in not very polite terms. In brief, the seeming pro-Zionist attitude of the German Government is not an expression of, and should not be confused with, cooperation on the part of one side or the other.

But the Zionist task in Germany has consisted, and still consists, of carrying on very specific work: to increase emigration, to establish Jewish schools, to create a so-called Jewish culture (which must be regarded skeptically because of the lack of freedom under which such a culture is produced), to create a new literature for the new Jewish life, to participate in the general daily political tasks of German Jewry, to promote the important and frequently attacked project of Haavarah, etc.

The leadership in these tasks has been provided by a number of institutions. First has been the Judische Rundschau, which proved itself to be the real leader of German Jewry, especially in the early months; the Zionist Organization with all its departments, and the "Reichsvertretung der Juden in Deutschland," the general organization of German Jews.

Kareski's Devilish Role

As the German Jewish community adjusted itself to the new situation, the "Reichsvertretung" and the other Jewish organizations (as, for example, the Jewish community) were reorganized on the basis of the 50-50 principle of the Jewish Agency. The real influence of the Zionist movement constantly increased. That a certain deadlock has now been reached is due to two factors: that most of the Zionist leaders have left Germany, and the existence of a personality who has played a very interesting and devilish role in German Jewry: Georg Kareski. He was once a member of the Zionist Organization, and is now President of the Revisionists in Germany and editor of a bitter newspaper directed against the official of German Jewry and written in the style of the *Angriff.* I hope some day to throw some light on the sad story of the past two years and especially of recent months, in which this man has played a central role.

Suffice it to say that unified Zionist power in Germany has been broken by the dark machinations whose source is well-known to everybody who has had occasion to work in Germany, and who has had to suffer under that influence.

The future of the German Jew is quite clear. No one can doubt that German Jewry must die if the Nazi Government lives, and there can be little doubt that the Nazi Government is very far from dying.

The future of German Jewry is the future of Zionists too. What is being done today in Germany by Jews of various groups is the useless but heroic attempt to make the best of a situation which will forever belong to the tragedy of the Jewish people.

JOACHIM PRINZ AND LENNI BRENNER
Excerpts from an Interview
February 8, 1981

This interview shows that Prinz (1902-1988) definitely thought that Zionism could and should come to an accommodation with Nazism. But he dramatically evolved in the 44 years since he arrived in the U.S. He soon realized that nothing he said in Nazi Germany made sense in the American context, and he jackknifed back into a American liberal version of his pre-Nazi Social Democratic German politics. Eventually, as head of the American Jewish Congress, he marched with Martin Luther King.

I decided that, beyond citing the interview in my book, I would do nothing with it that would embarrass him in his old age. I did the right thing. But now it is obligatory for me to bring the interview to the attention of scholars, for the confirmation it provides re Zionist fantasies about an accommodation with Hitler. But the wannabe collaborator of the '30s was a different man than the gentleman who invited me into his home and honestly answered what he knew would be probing questions.—LB

Brenner:

I came across an article that you wrote, apparently when you came to the United States, for New Palestine.... You say in the article:

"Everybody in Germany knew that only the Zionists could responsibly represent the Jews in dealings with the Nazi Government. We all felt sure that one day the government would arrange a round table conference with the Jews, at which—after the riots and atrocities of the revolution had passed—the new status of German Jewry could be considered. The Government announced very solemnly that there was no country in the world which tried to solve the Jewish problem as seriously as did Germany. Solution of the Jewish question? It was our Zionist dream! We never denied the existence of the Jewish question! Dissimilation? It was our own appeal!... In a statement notable for its pride and dignity, we asked for a conference."

That's the quote. Now, what made you think that the Zionists could deal with the Nazi government?

Prinz:
Well, the Zionists had a theory that we were living in a foreign country. They also accepted the notion of the Jewish people. The German Jews did not accept the notion of the Jewish people. They were not the Jewish people. They were a religious group, different from the Protestants and the Catholics, but nevertheless they were patriotic Germans who happened to be Jewish. But that Jewishness had very little to do with the Jew in Poland or the Jew in Hungary or the Jew in France. They emphasized that they were German Jews and they were Germans first. And that was the opinion of the vast majority of German Jews.

Zionism was a very small movement, attracted very few people, mostly intellectuals. And we all continued to talk about the Jews. The *Rundschau*, last week I spoke to Robert Weltsch, who was the editor of the *Rundschau*, he's now almost 90 years old, and very bright—writes—and I think that in every article he wrote, he wrote about the particular situation of the Jews in the country, and that what we needed really was a country to which we could go without begging, that is a Jewish state, and that the Jews were making a grave mistake of believing that assimilation was possible.

We thought that assimilation was not possible. We were ourselves were very assimilated Jews. I mean, after all, we lived there for many hundreds of years. We were assimilated Jews in terms of acculturation.

Brenner:
Well, what made you think that you could represent the Jews in dealing with the Nazi government?

Prinz:
Oh, we thought, in our discussions with intellectuals in the SS movement, that the time would come when they would say, "Yes, you live in Germany, you are Jewish people, you are different from us, but we will not kill you, we

will permit you to live your own cultural life, and develop your own national capacities and dreams." We thought, at the beginning of the Hitler regime that such a very frank discussion was possible. We found among the SS intellectuals, some people were ready for such a talk. But of course such a talk never took place because the radical element in the Nazi movement won out.

Brenner:

Well, so, in other words, now you said that you thought, you said that your father thought that Nazis were just an episode. But, you say that you thought that, someday, after the riots and the atrocities of the revolution had passed, and a deal would take place. So, didn't you also see the Nazis, in a sense, or the atrocities, as an episode?

Prinz:

No, at the beginning, concentration camps did not exist. Jews were sent to concentration camps in 1938. There were Jews in concentration camps, but so were socialists and other people.

Brenner:

No, but what I'm saying is that what difference really is there between the illusion of your father, that Nazism was just a passing episode, and your feeling that what was going on was just an episode, and that you would be able to...

Prinz:

No, no. I didn't think that what was going on was just an episode, because there was, at that time, no mass murder of the German Jews. That didn't exist. There was such notions that it could take place, but it did in fact take place in 1938, four years after Hitler came to power. It is true that there were Jews who were killed, but the majority of Jews did not leave Germany at that time. Some did. Altogether, I think 200,000 left, maybe a little bit more, but 50 percent of the Jews of Germany were killed.

Brenner:

Now, if someone were to ask you what the Zionist movement did before Hitler came to power to try and stop Hitler? In other words, you said, for example, that the Socialists and Communists fought each other. Did the Zionists tell them to stop fighting? Did the Zionists propose uniting with them?

Prinz:

No, I think that your notion of a Zionist movement as a united movement is wrong. It was not a united...

Brenner:

OK. I accept that, obviously. But did any Zionist come up with a program that was designed to keep Hitler out of power?

Prinz:

I don't think so. I think that the Zionists realized that they were a very small group, that we could discuss with the Germans. We were a people, we were part of the Jewish people, we had no hesitation whatsoever to discuss this matter, we realized that the Jewish problem existed.

Brenner:

What Jewish problem?

Prinz:

The uncertainty of Jewish existence outside of the Jewish state.

Brenner:

Well, do you feel that there is a Jewish problem in New Jersey, for example?

Prinz:

No, no. America is a completely different thing. . . .

Brenner:

...Again, as I say, I'm critical of everybody for their fight, but nevertheless, they fought them.

Prinz:

I think the Socialist movement really failed.

Brenner:

But I have not been able to find any record of the Zionist movement doing anything, prior to Hitler coming to power.

Prinz:

What could they do?

Brenner:

OK. But then they turn around and, as you say, they hope that they could sit down, they who did not fight him, hoped to sit around, afterwards, and negotiate with him.

Prinz:

But for a very, very limited time. Maybe for 2 or 3 months, that we had some hope, we sit together with them, with the Germans, the Germans have decided to have their own government, as Hitler, and they are within their rights to do what they want to do. But we have our own rights. We feel that we lived in Germany, that emancipation is not a reality, and therefore we could sit down with them and discuss the possibility of continuing Jewish life in Germany, under the Hitler regime, with our own cultural values, religious values, and continue to live there. We did not think, at that time, that Hitler would kill the Jews.

Brenner:

Clearly. Obviously. Now you said that there were some people in the SS who were interested in what you people had to say. Did you negotiate personally with...

Prinz:

Yes. For instance, the Germans had decided that no Jewish newspaper could be printed in Gothic letters. There was a newspaper, which incidentally, I was a political editor, which printed the paper in Gothic letters. They were forced to use Latin letters.

The Nazis then went on, on the theory that Jewish life could continue in Germany, within Jewish limits, within Jewish national, cultural and religious limits, and they founded the Kulturbund, which eliminated the Jews from the German theater, Jewish painters could not exhibit, Jewish sculptors could not exhibit, and some of the important conductors became conductors of Jewish orchestras. Jewish actors left the German stage, and we had our own theater. That is, the Germans also thought in terms of continuing Jewish life, separated from the German life, but could continue to cultivate their own heritage.

Brenner:

Would you have accepted that? Did you accept that?

Prinz:

We did accept that. We had, Kulturbund was a flourishing thing. Jews could not go to the theater, I did not go to the German theater, but we had our own theater, we had our own orchestras. Some of the important conductors who later came to America, became conductors of Jewish orchestras because no Jewish violinist, Yehuda Menuchin could not perform in Germany, right?

Brenner:

...OK. I don't know if I'm getting my point across. What I'm trying to say is this: Hitler is coming to power. Should Jews have fought him? Then Hitler comes to power. Should Jews have fought him?

Prinz:

I don't think there was any possibility of us fighting him. I could not fight him, after all, I was a very active political leader. I became a rabbi in 1923. My notion of religion is not theological. I always thought that religion had a say in social matters, in matters of politics, but I don't think that there was a possibility for the Zionist movement—the majority of the German Jews were organized in movements that were very patriotic, for Germany, they of course, didn't think that Hitler would come to power—the Zionists were a movement of only a few thousand in all of Germany, a few thousand. . . .

Brenner:

…The picture that I get is that, as Hitler started to really rise to power, and, as you say, in the period immediately afterwards, that the leaders of the Zionist movement, Blumenfeld, Weltsch, etc., got the notion that, because Zionism didn't believe that the Jews should be in Germany, that they could make a deal with Hitler.

Prinz:

No, no. I think that your notion of making a deal with Hitler is completely wrong. There was no such notion. Don't forget what Weltsch wrote when Hitler came to power, I mean the Judische Rundschau during the Hitler regime—and also don't forget that we had the censorship. You couldn't just write everything. Everything was censored. There were Jewish members of the Gestapo, I think four.

Brenner:

Ok.... In the article that you wrote in 1937, you said, "In a statement notable for its pride and dignity, we asked for a conference".... It says:

"On the foundation of the new state, which has established the total structure so that for us, too, in the sphere assigned to us, fruitful activity for the Fatherland is possible.... Our acknowledgment of Jewish nationality provides for a clear and sincere relationship to the German people and its national and racial realities. Precisely because we do not wish to falsify these fundamentals, because we, too, are against mixed marriage and are for maintaining the purity of the Jewish group."

Now…

Prinz:

Yes, well we never saw Hitler, we never saw Goebbels, we never saw any member of the—we are talking now about a very small group—we were ready, since this was our conviction that we were Jews, we are people Jews, you know, we were national Jews, we were part of the Jewish people in the world. Therefore we thought that we could talk to these Germans, who, after all, acknowledged the reality of national groups. We were the only national group in Germany, we thought that, maybe there's a possibility of establishing ourselves as a national group, with our national culture, and talk to them. But it didn't happen, (but we) thought so.

Brenner:

The memorandum says, "We believe in the possibility of an honest relationship of loyalty between a group-conscious Jewry and the German state."

Prinz:

Right. We thought so. We were mistaken. We thought that, after all, they are nationalists, we are also, Jewish nationalists, and therefore we had something in common. We recognized the fact that the German people had made their decision. It was their decision. They were within their rights because there was a majority of them. Now, we will continue to live in Germany, but we will live as a national group, for the first time recognized, not in terms of emancipation, but as doing away with the national uniqueness of a group, remains, all of them German citizens, of patriotic, we were not patriotic, we were German citizens, but would be recognized—at the same time—the right of the Jews to live as Jews. There was a notion, some of us, thought that let's talk to the intellectuals there, and, you know, I had many discussions with SS intellectuals. I was expelled by Eichmann. I spent my last night in Germany in solitary confinement. So therefore I thought we could talk. Very rarely, SS men began to talk, privately, but the dialogue that we aimed at, never took place.

Brenner:

OK. Now you said, in this memorandum, the ZVfD said that "The realization of Zionism could only be hurt by resentment of Jews abroad against the German development. Boycott propaganda—such as is currently being carried on against Germany in many ways—is in essence un-Zionist, because Zionism wants not to do battle but to convince and to build.... Our observations, presented herewith, rest on the conviction that, in solving the Jewish problem according to its own lights, the German Government will have full understanding for a candid and clear Jewish posture that harmonizes with the interests of the state."

Prinz:

Yes. That was our notion. We were mistaken. It was a romantic notion. We thought now, listen, there's a German government now, based upon a German nationalism. Well, let's sit down together and talk to them. But it never happened.

FRANZ-ALBERT SIX

Report on Secret Commando Matter

David Yisraeli, *The Palestinian Problem
in German Politics 1889–1945*
(Hebrew), Bar-Ilan University,
Appendix (German): pp. 301–4

The Zionists were always more eager to extend their relationship than the Nazis. It was therefore the Haganah, the military arm of the Jewish Agency (de facto the Labor Zionist militia), that obtained permission to negotiate directly with the SS. A Haganah agent, Feivel Polkes arrived in Berlin on February 26, 1937 and was assigned Adolf Eichmann as his negotiating partner. Their conversations were recorded in a report by Eichmann's superior, Franz-Albert Six, found in files captured by the Americans after World War II.

In 1983, I met Yoav Gelber, a scholar at Jerusalem's Yad Vashem Holocaust center. I asked what he knew of Polkes: "The Haganah archives refuses to let me see his file."

On October 3, I went there and asked custodian Chaim Zamir to see the file: "There is no file." "But Yoav Gelber says that you would not let him see the file." "There is no file because it would be too embarrassing."

Presumably, embarrassment would concern 1) Polkes' position in the Haganah hierarchy, 2) his superior, 3) documents by him and others, 4) about him or 5) motivating his negotiations.

The DNB referred to was the Deutsche Nachrichtenbüro, the German News Bureau, simultaneously the Nazi spy apparatus in Palestine. The Wilhelm Gustloff discussed was the leader of the Swiss Nazi Party, assassinated in February 1936 by David Frankfurter, a Jewish student.—LB

Secret Commando Affair Report: Berlin, 17 June 1937
Stamp: Chief Secret Police Personnel
Subject: Polkes, Feivel, Tel Aviv. Born 11 September 1900 in Sokal, Poland
Previous Reference: None

The above-mentioned Jew, Feivel Polkes, who is active as a central figure in the Jewish intelligence service, Haganah, was known here while visiting Berlin between February 26 and March 2, 1937, as referred by DNB correspondent Dr. Reichart.

In connection with the contact made with him at that time, it was found that Polkes is well acquainted with all important matters occurring in the Jewish world. A plan, in coordination with Gestapo (II/B 94), was formulated to enlist Polkes as a steady source of information for the Security Service.

POLKES' BIOGRAPHY

Polkes was born 11/9/1900 in Sokal, Poland (according to his passport, in Tel Aviv or Kloster-Newburg). After finishing his studies in the 8th class of the Jewish Gymnasium in Lemberg, on 26/4/1920, he passed the matriculation examinations on 15/7/20.

He seems to have migrated afterwards to Palestine because, in 1921, he passed the entrance examinations for the Palestinian Zionist self-defense organization.

According to documents in his possession, he worked from 1923 until 23/5/1928 as an accountant in the office of the Sinai Military Railway. He was transferred from there to the "Palestine Railways" when it took over the bureau he worked in.

Now he's active in the Jewish intelligence service "Haganah."

Acccording to his statements, he was in charge of the Palestinian Jews' entire self-defense apparatus during the last Arab uprising.

POLKES' JEWISH-POLITICAL ATTITUDE

In political outlook, Polkes is a national-Zionist. He is against all Jews who are opposed to the erection of a Jewish state in Palestine. As a Haganah man, he fights against Communism and all strivings towards Arab-British friendship.

POLKES INTELLIGENCE JOURNEY IN FEBRUARY/MARCH 1937

In February 1937 he went as a Haganah courier on a trip to Europe and America. He got as far as Paris, never reaching America, being urgently recalled.

This trip gathered information and at the same time, created monetary means for the Jewish Intelligence Service. An examination of his suitcases showed, he was in possession of many addresses of people in Berlin, Vienna, Paris and New York. For example, the Berlin address was: Gerda Wolpert, Tel Aviv, Schiote Israel, House in Berlin: Molkenmarkt 12/13.

For Paris, he possessed, among other things, the address for publisher Fritz Wolff of the "Pariser Tageszeitung," to whom he had an introduction in German, by Karl Loewy (?), presently at Tel Aviv, Ben Ami Street 11.

POLKES' VISIT IN BERLIN

Upon recommendation of the Palestinian DNB-correspondent Dr. Reichert, to whom he sends important news about events in Palestine, he received permission to come to Germany, so that he could be in Berlin from 26/2 until 2/3/37. The costs for the trip and for his Berlin expenses were carried by the Security Service since Polkes had originally intended to travel from Zurich to Paris.

At this time our Security Service made contact with him. In the beginning, he didn't know that he was dealing with a Security Service agent. It was learned that, because of his importance within the Haganah, Polkes knows about all significant matters in the Jewish world. His goal, and the Haganah's, is to create as soon as possible, a Jewish majority in Palestine. Therefore he worked with or against the "Intelligence Service," the "Sûrete Générale," England and Italy.

He stated that he is ready to serve Germany and supply information as long as this does not oppose his political goal. Among other things, he is ready to stand by the interests of German foreign policy in the Middle East. He will try to find the German Reich the oil sources without affecting British spheres of influence, all on the condition that Germany will assist Jewish immigration to Palestine, and on condition that Germany also ease the monetary regulations for these Jewish emigrants.

In connection with other queries, he let it be know that he knew the men and the background of the Gustloff murder. He denied however that the World League was the driving force behind it.

On 2/3/37 he traveled, via Achen, to Paris, and was then urgently called away to Palestine, without making his trip to America.

PROPOSAL

From the above mentioned explanations, it seems that Polkes is ready to provide us with important information for a reasonable reward. His standing promises that important information and material will reach us regarding world Jewry's plans.

The Gustloff murder, the failed assassination attempt against Heinlein, the leader of the Sudeten German Party, and especially the many murder threats and attendant plans of the Alliance Israélite Universelle, Paris, against the Führer, make it absolutely urgent to find contacts to discover the men behind it.

Therefore it is proposed to authorize a connection to Polkes in order to gain him as a steady informant.

For the work of contacting him, we especially suggest SS Group Leader Eichmann of Department II/112, who was in charge of the previous discussion with Polkes in Berlin, and was invited by the latter to visit the Jewish colonies in Palestine as his guest.

Because, according to information from Palestine, Polkes is thought to be vitally needed in the turmoil there, it will be impossible to contact him on neutral grounds. Therefore the only way to enlist Polkes will be by direct contact with him on a trip to Palestine.

For this trip it is possible to get two free tickets from the leader of the Jewish State Zionists and Director of the "Ivria Bank," Kareski. But this might be unwise, as it might reveal that the people visiting Polkes are Gestapo men.

Despite the savings in costs that could be achieved by this, it is advisable that the Security Service itself cover the travel expenses.

If the trip is agreed upon, SS-Hauptscharführer Eichmann will be accompanied by another expert. The couriers will receive press credentials, and the most advisable cards will be those of the "Frankfurter Zeitung" or the "Berliner Tagblatt."

For their personal safety, before the trip, the DNB representative in Palestine, Dr. Reichert, would be notified of their trip via the director of the foreign service of the German News Bureau, Dr. von Ritgen. At the same time, all people in Germany who are suspected of being Haganah men will be put under arrest.

By contacting Polkes, the following matters should become clear.

1) Information about the men behind the Gustloff murder.

2) Information about the work plans and the most important activists of international Jewry.

a) The American boycott organizations.

b) The World League to Fight anti-Semitism

c) Alliance Israélite Universelle, Paris

3) Information about assassination attempts against the Führer (according to unconfirmed reports, there are supposed to be important schemes reported by Gestapo men in Paris. These plans were laid by the Alliance Israélite Universelle, Paris).

4) The Jewish colonization work in Palestine should be thoroughly studied. Recognition of this work therefore appears especially important because, after the proclamation of a Jewish state or a Jewish regime in Palestine, a new political opponent of Germany will rise which will be able to influence Middle Eastern policy. Furthermore, the establishment of a Jewish state might worsen the problem of the Jewish minority residing in Germany.

The study of the interesting question could take place in close contact with the DNB representative in Palestine, Dr. Reichert.

In return, Polkes can be given the following assurances.

1) Pressure can be put on the Reich Representation of the Jews in Germany in such a way that those Jews emigrating from Germany will go exclusively to Palestine and nowhere else. Such a measure lies entirely in the German interest and is already prepared thru measures of the Gestapo. At the same time, Polkes' plans to create a Jewish majority in Palestine would be aided through this measure.

2) Those Jews arrested under suspicion of working for the Haganah would be freed.

3) Additionally, money could be made available to Polkes for his services.

After talking with Assessor Wilmanns of the Reich Economic Ministry, who is an expert on Palestine Transfer affairs, 1,000 Reichmarks for 3/4th of a year would be available thru the Transfer service, so that the Gestapo Security Service would not have any further costs.

Staff leader with a request for Document C.

Report on the Palestine-Egyptian Journey of SS-Hptscharf. Eichmann and SS-O'Scharf. Hagen

John Mendelsohn (Ed.)
The Holocaust, v. 5

On October 2, 1937, the liner Romania arrived in Haifa with two "journalists," aboard, Herbert Hagen and his junior colleague, Eichmann. They met Feivel Polkes, who showed them Haifa from Mount Carmel and took them to visit a kibbutz. But the SS men made a mistake in contacting their local agent. Two days later the British CID expelled them to Egypt. Polkes followed, and further discussions were held in Cairo. In their report on their expedition Hagen and Eichmann gave a careful rendering of Polkes's words at these meetings.—LB

p. 68:
HOW THE TRIP WENT
The trip commissioned by the Group Leader, began on 26.9.37 at 8:50 AM. The trip led across Poland and Rumania. From Constanza, the journey on the steamer "Rumania" continued on 28.9.37. The harbors of Stanbul, Pireus, Beirut and Haifa were touched. We arrived in Haifa on 2.10 at 6 PM, and met on the same day and following days, as we agreed upon in Germany, with the DNB representative in Jerusalem, Dr. Reichert, with whom the contact was arranged with the informer Polkes. An immediate second discussion with Polkes was not possible because he was involved with the unrest before them.

p. 69:
On the 10th and 11th, we had a conversation, as was agreed upon in Haifa, with the informer Polkes, which took place without any difficulties....

pp. 96-100:

That the world's Zionists protested very strongly against this, seems to be not so important for the practical work, that, as Polkes told us, the Jewish nationalists in Palestine would not stand for a delay in the establishment of a Jewish state. He emphasized that until now the English had not yet exhausted credibility. However, if on the part of the English, the tendency would become noticeable to delay the decision because of the recent events, then the Jewish defense organizations would fight open battles against the English! The Zionist state must be established by all means and as soon as possible so that it attracts a stream of Jewish emigrants to Palestine.

When the Jewish state is established according to the current proposals laid down in the Peel paper, and in line with England's partial promises, then the borders may be pushed further outwards according to one's wishes, and eventually, the Negev should be added to the planned Arabic state, in order to win those for the Jewish settlement.

In spite of it, Polkes was convinced that the Jewish state could not be realized next year and perhaps even in the following year. Beyond that, he believed that, after the creation, at least three years were needed in order to secure the state area. Only then one could start with the real work.

His expressions about the Jews coming from Germany were very interesting. He claimed they were unreliable in the Jewish national sense, adverse to work, and trying to emigrate again. In general, those with money went to the U.S.A., in order not to be used for any kind of upbuilding work.

For this reason, they would not be useful for information-carrying work.

Significant for the German emigrant Jews, is the fact that one already heard the mean expression among them, "better back to Germany and a concentration camp then remain in Palestine." Or "it is still better among us in Germany, than in Palestine." Polkes said that, in national Jewish circles for which he worked, he could not tolerate such a position, and therefore those Jews coming from Germany, after taking away their capital, should be put in a communal settlement.

In Jewish nationalist circles people were very pleased with the radical German policy, since the strength of the Jewish population in Palestine would be so far increased thereby that in the foreseeable future the Jews could reckon upon numerical superiority over the Arabs in Palestine.

Considered economically, Palestine looks hopeless. Thus one told us that the main means of payment was checks which nobody cashes, in spite of being completely devalued, continued to be given as payments because complaints about the checks were mostly without success. Sure money would be the German Temple Bank checks. The Temple bank would be the only one who would give you money.

This economic chaos in Palestine will not in the end go back to the fact that the Jews betray each other because, out of a lack of Aryans they can't do business with them, characteristic of the absolutely uselessness of the Jews for the leading of an orderly economy in their own state, that in Jerusalem alone there are 40 Jewish banks which live by betraying their own racial comrades.

III—TALK WITH POLKES

Since, in consideration of the political situation in Palestine, the conversation with the informer Polkes, there, would have been difficulties, this took place thru arrangements of Dr. Reichert on the 10th and 11th of October 1937 in Cairo, in the cafe "Gropi." Since Polkes was already known because of his visit to Berlin, one could immediately continue with the theme.

1) GUSTLOFF CASE

His remark, in connection with his statement in Berlin, that the Reich authorities' theory about the people behind the Gustloff murder was completely wrong, meant that Polkes would now be better informed. He was asked about it by us. In the course of the talk, he tries to talk himself out of it, explaining about how the Alliance Israélite Universelle are a bunch of harmless sheep. He was finally however more definite, and explained that the people behind it should be sought in anarchist circles, persons he did not want to name. He declared however that it would all come about in the Paris Cossack public houses in the Rue Magram, and named hereby also the place of Stelle Adler in Niza, which is a center of joint work of the Deuxième Bureau and Comintern spies.

Polkes, who, thru us, via Dr. Reichert, received £15 per month, promised to thoroughly inform himself of the activities of the Alliance Israélite Universelle, in connection with the Gustloff murder case, and get us some material. He promised to take care of this in 14 days. In the meantime, unrest coming about in Palestine, this could not be achieved, as Polkes, a leading Haganah functionary, has his hand in it.

As a further pressure on him, we mentioned arrested Jewish names in Hamburg, discovered smuggling arms to Palestine. At the name Schalomi, he was startled, and asked us "What are you asking from me to get him free?" We demanded the complete explanation of the Gustloff murder. This he agreed to, however, under the circumstances that Polkes knew we had the mentioned Jew, Schalomi, "his man" (also therefore a Haganah member). Polkes had in the meantime recognized, that thru his awkward beginning behavior, the membership of Schalomi was admitted, and for the rest then, confirming that Haganah agents worked in Germany.

2) CARRYING OUT THE EMIGRATION OF JEWS FROM GERMANY

The Jew Polkes suggested further emigration of Jews from Germany thru a raising of the goods transfer thru "Paltreu" (Palestine Economic Organization of German Jews) and the "Nemico" (Near and Middle East Corporation) allowing 50,000 Jews with £1,000 per head to emigrate. The goods would go to Palestine, Iraq, Turkey and Persia. Since Jews with £1,000 were considered so-called capitalists, could in this case, emigrate to Palestine without the special approval of the English Mandate authorities in charge.

POSITION

We must reject this plan for two reasons:

a) It is not in our interest to send Jewish capital abroad, but in the first line to get the Jewish poor to emigrate on their own. Since the mentioned emigration of 50,000 Jews from the Reich per year would strengthen Jewry in Palestine, leading to a Jewish state, this plan cannot be discussed. It should be prevented.

b) Raising of the goods transfer to the Near and Middle Orient would mean that these countries would be lost as 'foreign-exchange producing countries.' Further, the Ha avara system (Jewish Economic Organization for the Transfer of German-Jewish Emigré Capital), which had been enlarged and extended by the Reich Ministry, would be strengthened.

In spite of it, we left Polkes in the belief that his proposal would interest us, in order to not interfere in the complete explanation of the Gustloff murder....

p. 102:
4) POLITICAL INFORMATION FROM POLKES

Polkes told us that, in a short time, the Soviet Union would publish false documents about Germany and Italy making an agreement whereby Germany would let Italy have a free hand in Spain. For that however, Italy would give Germany a free hand in Poland.

Since the information which Polkes mentioned here would come out of the first source, and would be published in a short time, through the DNB in Cairo to the DNB Berlin, a request was sent to turn them over to the main

Security office, to SS-Sturmbannführer Böhme for his observation. Sturmbannführer Böhme gave them lll 2.

b) The Pan-Islamic World Congress convening in Berlin, according to Polkes, is in direct contact with two pro-Soviet Arab leaders, Emir Shekib Arslan and Emir Adil Arslan.

c) The illegal Communist broadcasting station whose transmission to Germany is particularly strong, is, according to Polkes' statement, assembled on a truck that drives along the German-Luxembourg border when transmission is on the air.

HAYIM GREENBERG
"The Myth of Jewish Parasitism"
Jewish Frontier
March 1942

Labor Zionist Greenberg details the development of Zionist internalized anti-Semitism since Weizmann's statement to Balfour. First of Labor's propaganda ploys, in the '30s and decades after, were bucolic pictures, comic in high-tech Israel today, to Zionists and anti-Zionists alike, of healthy Kibbutznik Jews squeezing milk from healthy Jewish cows, on health-giving Jewish soil. These movement-owned farms were painted to be the antidote to the anti-Semitic/Zionist diagnosis of diaspora Jewry as economically degenerate.—LB

In the anti-Semitic propaganda which has been flooding every country since 1933 a very prominent place is given to the old charge that Jews are parasites in the world's economic structure. As the economic problems in each country become more accentuated and increase in complexity, the average man has more difficulty in finding his bearings in this maze, and easily accepts the truth of the charge. It even influences people who have until lately been comparatively free of anti-Jewish bias.

Jews also have been considerably influenced by the notion that they constitute an unproductive, or even a destructive force, in the world's economy. We speak of Jews as essentially a people of luftmenschen engaged in luftparnosses that is, individuals whose occupations are unsubstantial, who are exploiters, speculators and traffickers in the labors of others.

Signs of this self-condemnation first appear in the literature of our "enlightenment." Jews who felt spiritually emancipated from the civilization of the ghetto even before they were emancipated from its legal disabilities, developed a great admiration for European culture and were in no mean degree affected by its anti-Jewish prejudices. Certainly they shared the European's disdain for the Jew as a trader. During the past hundred years or so wealthy Jews have always been ready to help in the proletarization of Jewry. But their motives were different from those of the Zionists or the nationalists. The latter see in Jewish economic restratification a means to insure a more rounded national existence, or a better possibility for surviving crises, while the former view the transition of many Jews from urban to rural life or from trade to manual labor, mainly as a way of wiping out a blot on the Jewish name.

The views of many Jewish socialists in regard to the economic role of the Jews, have usually been tinged by a certain anti-Semitic bias. This is especially true of Jewish socialists who are not interested in Jewish survival. Not that every Jewish Marxist has actually read Marx's essay on the Jewish question where Judaism is made synonymous with capitalist exploitation, greed and usury. But some of the spirit of that shocking accusation is to be found in the attitude of the average Jewish Socialist.

Non-Jewish socialists, and not necessarily Marxian socialists, have tended to look down on the Jew in the world's economy. The Russian Narodnaya Volya of the late 19th century which glorified the peasant and which was characterized by more humanism than any socialist or reformist movement of modern times, could be expected to be immune from anti-Semitism. Nevertheless, the Narodovoltzi once issued a proclamation to the peasants calling on them "to burn the mansion of the nobility, to rob the estates, and to beat up the Jews." This was not, as some believe, a mere demagogic device to rouse the peasants to revolt by appealing to their prejudices. The authors of this proclamation would not have issued it if they did not, at least vaguely, entertain the idea that the Jew was essentially a "bloodsucker." Socialists and other reformers who stressed the agrarian problem and who saw in the peasant, the chief potential carrier of their ideal, generally tended to see in the Jew the extreme expression of urban life and of the iniquitous exploitation they associate with the city man. This also explains Tolstoy's rather unfriendly attitude towards the Jews, an attitude most eloquently expressed by his repeated failure to speak up on behalf of the persecuted Jews. Tolstoy had the peasant's primitive notions of economic life, the peasant's narrow horizon in determining economic values and the peasant's suspicion of urban sophistication as mere crookedness.

The literary influence of Tolstoy, and the influence of some schools of

Socialist propaganda are largely responsible for the tendency for self-depreci-ation and self-condemnation so common to many Jewish socialists and Jewish intellectuals.

Nor is Zionism free from its share of responsibility. There was a time when it used to be the fashion for Zionist speakers (including the writer) to declare from the platform that "to be a good Zionist one must first be some-what of an anti-Semite." One can sense this attitude in some of Pinsker's writings: there is a great deal of it in Syrkin and in Borochow, the two main theoreticians of the Labor Zionist movement; A. D. Gordon, the author of the idea of the Religion of Labor (Dat Ha-Avoda) wrote, in a spirit of extreme contrition, about the national sins of the Jews which must be atoned for by manual labor; I. H. Brenner, the nearest to Dostoyevsky in Hebrew lit-erature, indulged in a masochistic self-flagellation. To this day Labor Zionist circles are under the influence of the idea that the Return to Zion involves a process of purification from our economic uncleanliness. Whosoever does not engage in so-called "productive" manual labor, is believed to be a sinner against Israel and against mankind.

When addressing the non-Jewish world we become exceedingly apolo-getic and talk of extenuating circumstances to explain our supposedly incriminating economic position. We quote the Bible to prove that as a nation we were born honest toilers of the soil, and that it was the Canaanite, the Phoenician, who used to be the trader of antiquity. We do not dispute the basic fact contained in the accusation against us. We admit, expressly or by implication, that we constitute a useless and unlovely element in the eco-nomic set-up of every country. We merely blame it on our tragic history, on the persecutions and on the disabilities we have suffered.

Our apology is based on ample evidence. There is no doubt that no reli-gious literature (with the possible exception of the ancient Chinese) contains so much glorification of manual labor as do the Bible and the Talmud. Nor can there be any doubt that our history made us a people of traders in a much larger measure than we would have become under normal circumstances. In contrast to the Greeks who looked down upon manual labor as an occupa-tion for slaves, the Talmud takes the view that manual labor is ennobling. Even Plato and Aristotle adopted the dominant Greek attitude, but the Talmud says that if labor was good enough for God when he created the world, it ought to be good enough for anybody. The number of passages one could cite from the Talmud which express the same view is legion, and we have a right to be proud of that attitude. But that does not mean that a man who works hard for his living as an honest storekeeper has reason to be ashamed of his occupation or to feel constantly apologetic. In medieval feudal Europe, manual labor and particularly agriculture were so intimately bound up with the Church that for a Jew in many countries to take to the plough was tantamount to baptism. There are many other reasons for the change in Jewish occupations during the Middle Ages. The recitation of these reasons fills our apologetic literature.

The present economic structure of the Jews may not be ideal, but there is nothing shameful or unethical about it. In the first place, we have more manual workers than it is commonly believed and their numbers have increased in the past few decades. In the second place there is nothing evil or parasitic about useful work which is not manual.

Useful or productive labor does not only mean manual labor or labor engaged in producing things which can be seen and touched and which have physical dimensions. Any work which satisfied human needs or is socially useful is productive work.

Of all great thinkers of modern times Tolstoy probably went furthest in stressing the virtue of simple manual labor. At one time he was under the influence of a homely moralist by the name of Bondarev, who preached the doctrine that only work which helps produce bread is morally good. A peasant who ploughs and seeds corn is a good man, but a farmer who plants oranges or bananas is a darmoyed who eats the bread of idleness, since he wastes his time on producing unnecessary and evil luxuries. At about the same time, Tolstoy was under the spell of another homegrown philosopher, a Swede, who taught that every man must produce the grain for his own food. This Swede reprimanded Tolstoy for drinking tea. Drinking tea, he said, encourages the Chinese peasant to plant the ungodly weed and neglect the cultivation of life-giving rice, thus bringing about famines in China. One day when Tolstoy offered his Swedish friend a glass of milk, he refused, saying, "My mother has been dead a long time, and the cow you have milked is someone else's mother." Tolstoy was tremendously impressed by the argument. Most of us think it ludicrous. But it serves to illustrate the absurd state which may be reached by the consistent application of the idea that only work immediately resulting in concrete goods is socially and economically useful.

Modern Socialism is free from such extravaganzas, since its object is not to limit human needs, but to expand them. The doctrine that man may enjoy only that which he himself produces is alien to a system which looks forward to an abundance requiring an increasing complexity and differentiation of labor. But for many years Socialist theory has stubbornly clung to a dogma that stresses the worth of the producers and the relative worthlessness of the intermediary between the producer and the consumer. A "logical" deduction from such a view would declare the milk wagon driver a parasite, and the cow the only producer in the milk industry.

Bernard Shaw was justified in ridiculing this primitive notion. His illustrations are the country boy who shoos away the birds from the seeded field and who performs by his unsubstantial noises the same function as the village carpenter who builds a gate to keep the cows away from the same field, or the housemaid who has nothing of physical substance to show for her hard labor except the odd broken dish.

No one is a parasite who engages in work which makes life more agreeable, more comfortable, and more abundant for his fellow men. In our modern society, the distribution of goods is indispensable to their enjoyment by the largest possible number. Anyone engaged in distribution—the exporter, the importer, the sailor, the wholesaler, the retailer—is doing useful work. We may hold the view that nationalized commerce is more socially beneficial that private commerce. Yet in principle, there is no moral difference between a merchant operating his own store and an employee of a workers' cooperative or of a Soviet state store. Both earn their livelihood, provided they do their work honestly and conscientiously, and provided they do not resort to cunning to extract remuneration which is not commensurate with their service.

Each one of us owes it to society to do some useful work in order to pay for the things he enjoys as the result of the work of others. But among our creditors, so to speak, are not only the farmer, the tailor and the mason. There are hundreds of people who produce nothing that is tangible, but without whose labor our life would be much harder or would at least lack many of the amenities and the pleasures which we prize. There is the milkman, the grocer, the bus driver, the waiter in the restaurant, the actor, the writer, the radio announcer—even the exterminator of vermin.

Take any typically Jewish occupation which has long been the butt of our moralists and satirists. I for one do not approve of the institution of shadchoness, that is, professional matchmaking. But, after all, this is a matter of taste, and no one forces me to pay for the services of a shadchan if I do not employ him. There are others who do, and what right have I to impose my attitude upon other people? Or take the Jewish clerics—the rabbi, the chazan, the mohel, the shamash, types whom our "enlightened" literature has presented in a most uncomplimentary way —again it is a matter of the point of view. Millions of Jews require the services of these functionaries and are willing to pay for them. Compared to the numerous clerics, monks and nuns of other denominations the Jewish religion has been neither overstaffed nor overpaid. In Poland, before the war, we had several hundred "einiklech," that is, grandsons of famous hasidic rabbis, and we have some of them in this country. These people who trade on their pedigrees constitute to my knowledge the only specific class of unproductive Jews. But then, they are no more so than Siamese twins, or the Dionne quintuplets.

The point I am trying to make is that we have no reason to feel morally apologetic about our economic position. I do not mean to say that all Jews are saints. Nor do I deny the need for a thorough restratification of our economic life. But this restratification ought not to be motivated by a sense of collective guilt. We have to reconstruct our economic life because the present one is fraught with dangers to our well-being, and because a fuller national life requires a more balanced economic set-up. We are not economically wicked. We have not eaten unearned bread all these centuries. And under the conditions of modern society, we have been fulfilling a useful economic function.

I have no reason to be proud of the Jewish saloon keeper in this country, or of his antecedent in Eastern Europe. But I know they have their counterparts among non-Jews. There is nothing edifying about the Jews in the Ukrainian villages under the feudal system who held the keys to the village churches and opened the churches only when the peasants paid the rent. But the keys were placed in the Jews' hands by the greedy and lazy Polish nobility. We are, on the whole, neither better nor worse than others.

The question may well be asked, what of our Labor Zionist ideology? What of our propaganda about ruralization, the dignity of labor, halutziuth? These principles are still sound. A reshaping of Jewish economic life is a historic necessity, and it cannot be accomplished without the popular enthusiasm that Zionism generally and Labor Zionism particularly have aroused for these aims. There is nothing wicked in being a middleman, but it is not sound for a whole people to consist of middlemen. We are building a new nation in Palestine, and we cannot succeed unless we make its economic life varied and many-sided and thereby relatively complete. It requires no effort and no propaganda on our part to create a Jewish merchant class in Palestine. But the emergence of a Jewish agricultural class cannot be a spontaneous process. At this juncture in our history, the creation of a class of Jewish farmers in Palestine is of paramount importance and justifies the expenditure of moral and mental energies that have gone into the effort. Sometimes the enthusiasm of the Palestinian pioneers appears to us at a distance as being too naive and narrow. But taken in its historic perspective this exaggerated glorification of manual labor and its achievements is necessary.

I am not oblivious of the desirability for a restratification of Jewish economic life outside of Palestine, say in the United States of America. I know that our top-heavy economy contains some dangerous possibilities. But mere preaching will not accomplish the desired change. I am not an economist, but I question the feasibility of effecting a complete change in Jewish economic life at the present state of capitalist development in this country. How can we produce large numbers of farmers, coal miners and metal workers? If present conditions make such a feat impossible, there is nothing to be gained by continuous moralizing. If it is possible, it ought to be done. But let us stop apologizing for ourselves.

[The Narodnayha Volya, that is People's Freedom or People's Will, was the fore-runner of the Social-Revolutionary Party which played a leading role in the revolutionary movement until October 1917.]

PART III
Zionist Revisionism, Fascism and Nazism Before the Holocaust

LEOPOLD VON MILDENSTEIN

"A Nazi Voyages to Palestine"

Der Angriff (The Attack)
Berlin, September 27, 1934

A Zionist convinced the Baron, to write a pro-Zionist piece for the Nazi press. He visited Palestine as the six months guest of the WZO and wrote a 12-part series for Der Angriff, *the Nazis' chief party organ. To commemorate his expedition, Propaganda Minister Goebbels had a medal struck: on one side the swastika, on the other the Zionist star.*

The first article testified to the singular truth of the '30s: Everyone, Nazis, Fascists, leftists, other Zionists, saw Zionist-Revisionism as fascist.—LB

On the liner "Moses," a special steamer for Jewish emigrants to Palestine, the Promised Land, a Nazi travels alone, and there observes villages, cities, factories and children's' homes. On his journalistic trip to Jaffa, he gets acquainted with the Jewish immigrants, the difficulties in their travels and the hopes which they have for their new home. On this voyage to Jaffa, most are admitted into the country and keep their passports.

THE PASSPORT CHECK!

A motorboat comes swiftly towards us, the feared passport commissioners. The captain, the 1st officer, the commissary, the doctor, all are ready for the reception. One must be on good terms with the passport commission. First one drinks a glass together, for strength, so that everything may go OK. If the commission denies an immigrant entry, the shipping company must take him back to Trieste. If he still has money, then they can try to get him to pay for the return trip. But if he has nothing, then they must bring him back without payment. That they wish to avoid.

The commission is led by an Englishman, but the real passport inspectors are Palestinian Jews. The great choice begins. Naturally it goes by classes. He who has paid the most, gets in first. Those who have their passports stamped enter the boats with a light heart. To be sure, they are not quiet in the golden freedom. They must first go to the quarantine station, to customs, and then, after three days, return to the quarantine physician. But that is taken very easily, if everything works out fine.

FLYING HERRINGS

We others, who want to go on to Haifa, have time for a rest. In the meantime, the 2nd officer got rid of his freight. That is not so simple. When some herrings are hanging over the boat, one of the containers falls from the winch's wire net into the boat. The cover comes off and the herrings learn to fly. The fast hands of the Arabs catch them quickly and, since they don't want to voluntarily return to the tub, one of the brown men jumps on the container and, under the forceful kicking of his barefeet, the herrings give in. The cover is closed.

When the steward, with his big cowbell, gongs for lunch, the ship starts moving again with a northward course for Haifa, again gliding along the coast. The light brown sand of the steep dunes conceals the fertile coastal land which lies behind. Only occasionally we see a few palm trees. Then comes the wild surf surging onto the steep rocks of the ruins of Atlet. Behind them is Mount Carmel. It is after 4 PM and we are approaching the Haifa mole.

AT THE GATEWAY TO INDIA

There is an entirely different picture than the one in the morning. Mount Carmel falls steeply almost into the harbor. Oaks and pines cover the sloops. At the end, lies a cloister with a light tower, the true sign of Haifa.

To the left of the harbor mole lies the industry of Haifa. A large lighthouse shines over here. Cement works stretch their constantly bellowing gray smokestacks to the blue sky.

The most notable houses of the city have already climbed along the ridge of the mountain. The air must be wonderful. Here below, in spite of the water, it is unbearably hot. The insect swarms seemed to have only been waiting for us. They come in quantities towards us. Their sting carries the Papadadschia, a nasty fever. Their buzzing, much higher in tone then the ordinary mosquito, sounds around us.

Haifa is the only harbor protected by nature on the east coast of the Mediterranean. A strong stone mole goes around the harbor. Mighty cranes stand at the pier. One calls Palestine England's portal to India. Then Haifa is the key to this portal. Here is the only protected harbor on the East Coast. Here will be the greatest airport of the East. Crossroad of the lines from Cape Town and India. Here is the end of the massive pipeline to the Mosul oil fields in Iraq. Here is the terminal of the "all-British railroad," which would connect Haifa with Baghdad and Basra, thus tying together the Mediterranean and the Persian Gulf. And if one should not build this railroad, because today a highway would be more advantageous, so one would have a beginning of this road, which never leaves English protection, and today already basically exists.

The "Martha Washington" is tied to the pier, and the commission comes on board again. I stay on board overnight. My car, which properly has spent the entire trip on board, must be registered. The civil servants aren't there. So, tomorrow, tomorrow!

A JEWISH FASCIST

That is the oriental ointment for all impatient people. When the Arab wants to say something polite to somebody, he says "bukra, insha' allah!" Tomorrow, God willing. If nothing happens tomorrow, God apparently didn't want it. I wait. Besides me, there is also an immigrant Jewish family, that has stayed on board, with the other passengers. Their papers not quite in order. Perhaps tomorrow. In the meantime, passengers for the return trip have come on board. We sit, lonely, in the dining room.

My opposite, a young Palestinian, wears a badge on his lapel. A small seven-armed Menorah. We get into a conversation. He is a Trumpeldor-man. They are followers of a Russian Jewish leader, Trumpeldor, who fell in battle, here in Palestine, shortly after the war, in the fight against the Arabs. He had been a leader of the Jewish Legion. His supporters now represent the Fascist group among the Jews. Radical nationalists, they are adverse to any kind of compromise on questions of Jewish nationalism. Their political party is the "Revisionists." Their leader, Jabotinsky, is the "enfant terrible" of the Zionist Congresses. He cannot forgive the English who, contrary to their promises at the end of the war, disarmed the Jewish Legion in Palestine, instead of having it protect the country. Thus, he is fighting with the English as well as the Arabs. His fighting troopers are uniformed. Khaki pants and chocolate-colored shirts. In addition, they wear shoulder bandoliers. Stars on their shoulders are the signs of their allegiance. On this basis the Jewish self-protection in the country is recruited. And the Jews sometimes need this because the interests of the English are not always the interests of the Jews.

SMUGGLING PEOPLE

I step onto the promenade deck. The steamer is almost empty. Most officers and men are on leave. The steamer, to be sure, only departs tomorrow afternoon. At the gangplank stand Arabic soldiers. The pier is constantly carefully guarded. Even when a steamer arrived, no one could go in the vicinity. Even calling from on board to the pier and the other way was strictly prohibited. He who is on board is in a different world. If some wise guy dares to yell to his acquaintances or family on board, then immediately Arab soldiers rush towards him and swing their batons with threats.

When I again crossed the strictly watched gangplank, then I noticed an Arabic soldier, who winked his eye. As I, full of expectation and astonishment, look at him, he walks ahead of me. Then he turns the next corner of the deck. When I get there, he winks at me, secretively. Finally I become curious and follow him. A second Arab has joined us. He goes around a few corners down a dark stairway. They want to meet with me in the darkness between decks. What is going on? One of them can only speak Arabic. The other speaks bad English. With much eyewinking and gestures, I am asked if I'm allowed off board.

"Why do you want to know that?"

"Well, perhaps there is still a possibility to get into the country." Boats, good friends on shore, darkness. The tender hint of baksheesh cannot be misunderstood.

Therefore I can imagine smuggling people is a good business. If such a poor devil of an immigrant being sent back by the commission faces only the trip back, he must be miserable. The company takes his last money for the return trip. Must he not be open to temptation? Over there, only a few meters away, lies the promised land. There nobody will look for him. With the money left, he will get along. He agrees to the offer and pays. He understands clearly that he risks his life. If the boat is seen, it will be shot at by the harbor watch. But otherwise, he is then free. Who will look for a vanished Jew? I make it clear to my "helpers" that, unfortunately, I could not accept the offer. Fear that I might betray them, suspicion, anger, now show in their eyes. I quiet their fears and retreat slowly back into the light from the lamps.

WE ARE UNLOADED

The morning rises with the harbor astir. My car is now hauled by a crane. With much straining and little help, the Arab porters accomplished the maneuver. Afterwards they want their baksheesh, their tip. And then its a matter of finishing the formalities with the car. I have, so to speak, good luck in Palestine. But I don't know yet if one will ask for custom money. The service centers lie here and there, in the old harbor, partly in the new. Between them there is ten minutes of running and tripping through sand and stones, dust and sand blowing, there and back. That makes me warm, but I have my visa stamps together. The money demanded is small, hardly a pound sterling.

The rest of the gasoline is still there. The luggage must go through customs, then to the car. The harbor longshoremen are organized. A leader watches out. But in spite of that, one is still taken advantage of. If it would go as the carriers want, then two people would rather carry one piece of luggage, instead of the other way around. One group carries the luggage to the customs. One of them pretends to be the overseer and asks for special baksheesh, which he claims. Then he cashes it immediately. He must, of course, go away, suddenly. Soon one notices why. The luggage is hardly at the customs, when they all want their money and disappear. In the meantime, other ones have grabbed the controlled pieces, and I can just about prevent one of the Arabs from putting them into a wagon which, naturally, he operates. In spite of this, naturally, he wants the agreed upon money, plus baksheesh. It comes to a difference of opinion, and the father of the money soon becomes the grandfather of cheapness. He who has never been in the orient cannot appreciate the quarreling and vile manner of this dirty horde. I am glad that I have saved myself and my car, and can disappear thru the harbor gate.

Gas pumps! Gasoline pumps are almost nonexistent. Gasoline, mostly Shell, is sold in 18 kilogram canisters and is directly put into the gas tank. It is much cheaper than in our country, but certainly much dirtier, in spite of the canister. Auto traffic is much less significant than in Europe. One very often sees cars with German licenses. Palestine is completely motorized. The main roads were built after the war by the English. So therefore one can use any kind of car for city and overland traffic. One sees different kinds, but mostly American.

"Stavsky Appeal Allowed: Unanimous Judgement Quashes Conviction: Lack of Corroborative Evidence"
Palestine Post
Jerusalem, July 22, 1934

On the night of June 16, 1933, Haim Arlosoroff, Political Secretary of the Jewish Agency and negotiator of the Ha Avara pact, was murdered. The day before, a Revisionist paper ran an attack on him, declaring that "The Jewish people has always known how to deal with those who have sold the honor of their nation and its Torah, and it will know today also how to react to this shameful deed."

The police had little difficulty catching the Revisionist assassins. The defense resorted to desperate tactics. An Arab, jailed for murder, confessed to killing Arlosoroff, while trying to rape his wife. He recanted, confessed again and recanted, claiming the defendants bribed him to make his confession.—LB

The Court of Criminal Appeal, giving judgment on Friday (as reported in a special edition of *The Palestine Post* on the same day) in respect to the appeal of Abraham Stavsky against his conviction for the murder of Dr. Haim Arlosoroff, set aside the judgement of the Court of Assize and discharged the appellant.

All three members of the Court, the Chief Justice, Justice Baker, and Judge De Freitas, concurred in allowing the appeal and for the same reason: the lack of the corroborative evidence required in criminal cases by Palestine law to support the evidence of a single witness.

The Court rejected the hypothesis, accepted in the dissenting judgment in the Court of Assize, that the crime had a sexual motive. It found that the corroborative evidence led by the prosecution, that of the witness Weiser, the two trackers, and the scratch on accused's hand was not evidence sufficient to corroborate Mrs. Arlosoroff's evidence. The Court saw no reason for criticizing the acceptance of her evidence by the Court of Assize. In England, said the Chief Justice, the conviction would have had to stand.

The full text of the judgement follows:

TEXT OF CHIEF JUSTICE'S JUDGEMENT

This is an appeal from a conviction and sentence to death recorded by the Court of Criminal Assize against Abraham Stavsky.

The accused was charged with two other men, Aba Achimeir and Zvi Rosenblatt. The former was not called upon for his defense, the latter was acquitted.

The Appellant was proved to be a foreigner inasmuch as his passport, issued by the Government of Poland, was put in evidence at the trial. The present Court of Criminal Appeal has, therefore, been constituted in conformity with the last part of Section 3 of the Courts Ordinance 1924 (No. 21 of 1924).

The Judgement of the majority of the Court of Assize, from which there was one dissentient runs as follows:

"The Court by a majority finds that at Tel Aviv on the night of the 16-17 June, 1923, with premeditated intent to kill, the accused Abraham Stavsky did take part in the premeditated killing of Dr. Chaim Arlosoroff, by following him, waiting for him, stopping him and directing the light of an electric torch upon him, and being close by during the commission of the offense: contrary to Article 170 of the Penal Code and Section 3 paragraphs (b) and (c) of the Criminal Law Amendment Ordinance (No. 2) 1927.

As regards the accused Zvi Rosenblatt, the Court does not find the other material evidence required by Section 5 of the Law of Evidence amendment Ordinance 1924 to corroborate his identification by Mrs. Arlosoroff. The accused Rosenblatt is therefore acquitted of the offense of which he stands charged."

It is much to be regretted that the Court of Assize in a case of this complexity and length did not set out more detailed findings of fact than are expressed, or implied, in this judgment, but, at the same time, I cannot agree that as suggested by the Appellant's advocate, the judgment is invalidated for this reason, in view of the proviso to Section 48 (1) of the Trial Upon Information Ordinance 1924.

It is clear from the judgment that the Court in respect of both Stavsky and Rosenblatt believed Mrs. Arlosoroff's evidence of identification, and while in the case of the latter they did not find other material evidence to corroborate this identification, it is equally clear that in the case of the former they did find such evidence.

Mrs. Arlosoroff's evidence of identification has been impugned before us on the ground that before the identification parade she had been shown a photograph of Stavsky.

This photograph was shown to Mrs. Arlosoroff at a time when the only clue with regard to him in the hands of the police was that a clerk in the Immigration office had given information that a person of that name bore a resemblance to the description of the wanted man circulated by the police from the data supplied by Mrs. Arlosoroff.

The police did not know if Stavsky was still in the country and he had not, when Mrs. Arlosoroff was shown that photograph been arrested, although along with other suspects he was being sought.

It is clear from the judgment of the Court of Criminal Appeal in R. v. Haslam (1925) 19 C.A.R. at p. 60 and in R. v. Hinds (1932) 147 L.T.R. at p. 502 that, an arrest not having been effected, there was no irregularity committed in showing Mrs. Arlosoroff the photograph.

The identification parade is further attacked on the ground that owing to the physical distress, naturally enough suffered by Mrs. Arlosoroff, at a parade held within a very short time after the tragedy, Mr. Stafford, a Police Officer, supported Mrs. Arlosoroff with his arm. I am satisfied that it is clear from the evidence that it was only when Mrs. Arlosoroff saw the accused that she was nearly overcome with faintness and had to be supported, and although it is unfortunate it should have been a police officer who gave her support at this juncture, in the circumstances set out I cannot agree that it vitiated the identification.

The presentation of Stavsky in the identification parade unshaven, collarless and coatless, cannot, in my opinion, be objected to, seeing that in the photograph previously shown to Mrs. Arlosoroff he was clean shaven and was wearing a coat, a collar and a tie.

I wish to say here, with all respect to the different view taken in the dissenting judgment in the Court of Assize that the theory that the attack upon the deceased was prompted by improper motives vis-à-vis his wife is, in my opinion, an hypothesis based upon the most flimsy grounds imaginable.

To sum up, I can see no reason whatever for criticizing the conclusion of the Court of Assize in accepting Mrs. Arlosoroff's evidence, and if this case were being heard in England or in most British dependencies, that would be the end of the appeal, and the conviction would have to stand, but the legislature of Palestine has seen fit by Section 5 of the Law of Evidence Amendment Ordinance 1924 to provide that no judgment shall be given in a criminal case on the evidence of a single witness unless such evidence is admitted by the accused person, or is corroborated by some other material evidence, which, in the opinion of the Court is sufficient to establish the truth of it.

The corroborative evidence led by the Prosecution consisted of the evidence of Weiser, the evidence of the two trackers and the evidence as to the scratch on the hand of the accused. It is at this point that is chiefly felt the omission of the Court of Assize to state in their judgment which facts they found established by the evidence of Weiser or the trackers, Irgaig and Abu Ruz, and relied upon as being material evidence which in their opinion was sufficient to establish the truth of the evidence of Mrs. Arlosoroff.

This being so, we have to give independent consideration to each of these items of evidence.

The evidence of the trackers was in many ways unsatisfactory. The undoubted confusion of the tracks which they followed, with tracks showing spur chains that were clearly those of a mounted constable, the accompaniment of certain tracks, as stated by the trackers, with the footprints of a dog, in view of the fact that there is evidence that one police officer was accompanied by his dog, are enough to make it difficult to accept this evidence, especially in view of the circuitous route followed by the debated tracks.

Further, even if the evidence as to tracks on the scene of the crime were unimpeachable, I am satisfied that the footprint parade on the beach was vitiated by the fact the trackers witnessed the identification parade in the station yard at which Mrs. Arlosoroff pointed out Stavsky, that Irgaig there made several of the people in the parade lift their feet for his inspection, that he and Abu Ruz studied such footprints as could be found in the yard and that Abu Ruz, though he says "it was not wrong for me to look at the tracks," immediately afterwards admits "I should have been scolded if an officer had seen me."

Further, Mr. Faraday gave evidence that seeing a tracker, who he believed was Irgaig, bending down to examine the tracks on this occasion in the yard, he told him to go away.

The importance of the scratch on the hand of the accused is minimized by the length of time which elapsed before it was seen by a Medical Officer and is so closely linked up with the suggestion of the prosecution that the route indicated by the trackers involved a passage through a barbed wire fence that, in view of what I have said of the trackers evidence, I need not stop to consider it further.

We come, therefore, to the evidence of Weiser.

The date of the crime was the 16th June. On that night Weiser made a statement to Mr. Spector, the Investigating Officer at Tel Aviv Police Station.

He made a further statement to Mr. Shitreet, the Assistant Superintendent of Police at Tel Aviv on July 3rd.

I am at a loss to know the reason why those two statements, though put in evidence before the Magistrate, were not put in, by the defense or called for by the Court of Assize, especially when I consider the almost innumerable statements of other witnesses that were before the Court, but having learned of their existence from Weiser's evidence before the Assize Court we called for their production under the power conferred upon us by Section 68 (a) of the Trial Upon Information Ordinance 1924.

In the first statement Weiser only spoke of the interloper, at the end of the statement, in reply to a question by the police officer and he then said "I saw a man passing by very near me about two minutes before the occurrence. He was tall, I think he wore a dark blouse, he was bare headed and wore a tie." In this statement he said "I could not see the face of the man who passed by me," and again, "After the shot I did not see any person run away in any direction whatever."

His description of the shooting comes early in the statement "Now I remind myself that soon after the shot I saw the light like that of a small lantern was lit."

In his second statement on July 3rd, Weiser says, "I saw at first the light of a torch light that was lit and immediately put out, soon after that I heard the shot." Later in this statement he says that he saw a man running away up the hill 40 metres off with difficulty, and, of the interloper, he says "I could not recognize him because I did not see his face. I am not certain whether I would be able to recognize his body from the back."

Before the Magistrate, Weiser said that the interloper apparently wore a collar and tie, that three or four minutes after he left he saw the light of a torch and heard a shot. He also says he saw the figure of a person running up the hill of the graveyard.

Finally Weiser told the Court of Assize that at about 10.15 on the night of the crime he was on the sand beside a girl who was asleep, in a spot below the Moslem Cemetery, when a tall, bareheaded man, in a dark suit, collar and tie, came along from the south and stared at him for a minute or two and then went on towards the north, and that about four minutes later he saw the flash of an electric torch and heard a shot and woman's cry, and in a few minutes, after he had overcome his girl companion's reluctance to let him go, he ran up to where the deceased lay wounded.

Much weight was laid by the defence on the fact that the very few minutes deposed to by Weiser as having passed between the interloper's leaving him and the shot, could not possibly be reconciled with Mrs. Arlosoroff's detailed account of the victim and herself being followed and overtaken up the beach as far as the Yarkon, where she and her husband rested for a while, the process being repeated till they returned to the scene of the crime.

I do not attach much importance to this, as the estimate of the passage of time with a man of this type cannot be too rigidly insisted upon.

I wish, however, to emphasize that in the first statement of Weiser there is no suggestion whatever that the stranger stopped, still less that he looked at Weiser, "I saw a man passing by very near me," he says, and later "I could not see the face of the man who passed by me." So far from conveying an implication that the interloper stayed for a perceptible time looking at him, do not the words "pass by," which Weiser used twice, import an uninterrupted walk past him?

But even if this interpretation of the first statement is not accepted, and we believe that the interloper stopped and looked at Weiser what are we to think of Weiser's inability to see the interloper's face, though the latter looked at him for a perceptible time during which Weiser admits that he saw that the interloper was wearing a tie. Again, though in his first statement he said he thought the man was wearing a dark blouse, he later deposed to his wearing a collar, an article of attire which it must be noted was mentioned in the descriptions of the accused circulated by the police on June 17th.

I need not stop to consider the discrepancies in Weiser's statements regarding the question whether the torch was flashed before or after the shot was fired, or whether or not he saw a fugitive or fugitives escaping up the hill near the cemetery.

Mr. Stafford's evidence of the identification parade on July 8th, more than three weeks after the crime at which Weiser picked out Stavsky, runs as follows: "Weiser said of Stavsky, This is the same build and height as the man referred to in my statement."

It is obvious that Stavsky is a tall man of bulky build, but in view of the variations in the evidence of this witness, I cannot hold that an identification, after a lapse of three weeks from one brief sight of a man at nighttime, and, if the first statement is correct, during a fleeting glimpse as he walked by mere similarity of height and build is material evidence sufficient to corroborate

Mrs. Arlosoroff's evidence.

This being so, it is unnecessary for me to deal with the other grounds of appeal, but I wish to add this. Repeated allegations and insinuations were made by the Counsel for the Appellant regarding the conduct of the police in the investigation of this crime; imputations of unfairness and partisanship were freely made, an illicit liaison between the police and the Jewish political party to which the deceased belonged, with a hostile intent towards the accused, who belonged to the opposing party, was alleged.

The Acting Solicitor General, at the close of his address to the Court, wished to deal with this matter, but I told him we do not wish to hear him. My reason was that I did not consider the conduct of the case by the police called for any defence on his part, although it must be admitted that errors and omissions on the part of the police would occur and do occur in a case of this magnitude.

We have heard a good deal in this case of an alleged confession by Abdul Majid, which was afterwards withdrawn, and is said to have been repeated.

The Court of Trial had this witness before it and clearly did not believe him as they did not find in his evidence corroboration of Mrs. Arlosoroff so as to enable them to convict Rosenblatt.

The whole interposition of Abdul Majid in this case leaves in my mind a grave suspicion of a conspiracy to defeat the end of justice by the suborning of Abdul Majid to commit perjury in the interests of the defence.

As I have found that there is not material evidence to corroborate the evidence of the single witness, Mrs. Arlosoroff, it follows that the judgment of the Court of Assize, must be set aside, the conviction quashed, and the Appellant discharged unless detained on any other charge.

—Michael F. F. McDonnell
Chief Justice

JUDGMENT OF MR. JUSTICE BAKER

In a case of this magnitude it is unfortunate that more detailed findings of fact were not recorded. Section 48 of the Trial Upon Information Ordinance, however, provides that no conviction shall be invalid for failure to include in such recorded a finding of a fact; if such fact shall appear to be sufficiently established by the evidence given in the case. Accordingly, it is our duty to see if the fact necessary to support their judgment appears to be sufficiently established by the evidence given in the case.

At the outset I wish to state that I do not for a moment believe that the murder was the result of an attempted sexual attack which counsel for the

Appellant suggests.

The principal evidence in the case against the appellant is that of the evidence of the widow of the deceased who states she saw the appellant and subsequently identified him as being the person who flashed a light on her husband prior to his being shot.

Counsel for Appellant has argued that Mrs. Arlosoroff's original and first description of Appellant was such that it could not possibly tally with the Appellant.

I cannot agree with the contention and I am satisfied that the description she gave does in fact coincide with Appellant's description so far as it is necessary for the purpose of identification.

Subsequently Mrs. Arlosoroff identification parade, and Counsel for Appellant alleges that this was entirely irregular on the following material grounds. First that photos, were shown to Mrs. Arlosoroff including that of Appellant subsequent to orders of arrest having been issued against Appellant, arguing that legal authorities have laid it down that such a procedure is improper and vitiates the identification. I am satisfied after reviewing the authorities, particularly Rex v. Hinds L.T.R. 1932 that the Appellant not having been actually arrested at the time the photos were exhibited, such exhibition was not improper.

The second ground is that the parade was not properly constituted in that none of the persons on parade corresponded with Appellant: and that the officer in charge of the parade was supporting the identifying witness at all material times thereby rendering physical help to her in the identification of the Appellant. I am satisfied from the evidence in the case that the identification parade was properly constituted and properly carried out and that the officer in charge due to Mrs. Arlosoroff's physical distress, supported her, but in no way helped her in the identification of Appellant.

There was evidence before the Trial Court that Mrs. Arlosoroff identified the present Appellant as the man who followed her and her deceased husband and who flashed the lamp on them immediately prior to the murder of Dr. Arlosoroff: and I am satisfied that they were legally entitled to make this finding.

There is no rule in the laws of this country that a Court can act upon the uncorroborated evidence of a single witness other than Road Transport cases, provided the Court is satisfied with such evidence; otherwise this appeal would fail and it would not be necessary to consider the further evidence in the case.

Article 5 of the Law of Evidence Amendment Ordinance 1924 prescribes that the evidence of a single witness must be corroborated by some other material evidence which in the opinion of the Court is sufficient to establish the truth of it.

The Trial Court did not unfortunately specify by what other material evidence the testimony of Sima Arlosoroff was corroborated: but it would appear that the matters relied on by the prosecution were: the evidence of the trackers supported by the scratch found on Appellant's hand; the evidence of one Weiser; the evidence of Abdul Majid.

With regard to the trackers, I am satisfied after reading the mass of evidence thereon that the evidence is so conflicting as to be impossible to find that they identified any of the tracks on the scene of the crime to be those of appellant and not being satisfied that appellant's tracks were found on the scene of the crime, the evidence of the scratch, whatever its merits may be, must fall with the tracks, for it is only evidence in support of the tracker's evidence and cannot be separated.

The reasons for disbelieving the trackers' evidence has been set out in the Chief Justice's judgment: and with these reasons I entirely agree.

With regard to the evidence of Weiser, this witness gave a statement on the night of the murder in which he stated "a man passed very near to me two minutes before the occurrence. He looked at me and proceeded in the direction of the Yarkon: after three minutes I heard the shot, I could not see the face of the man; he wore a blouse, was bareheaded, wore a tie; he was a young fellow of about twenty and several years. After I heard the shot I saw a light like that of a small lantern. I did not see any person run away in any direction whatever." Some 17 days after he gave a further statement, a statement materially varying with the first. In this statement he says "I saw at first a torch light that was lit and immediately put out: soon after that I heard the shot. I asked the fellows to run after them because I saw the figure of a man running up the hill with difficulty. The distance between me and the figure was about forty metres. This figure did not go straight. Sometimes he was bent and made a movement with his hands as a man who intends to go up in a hurry. I could not recognize this man. I did not see his face and I am not certain whether I would be able to recognize his body from the back."

It is noteworthy that in his first statement he saw no one running away.

There is no evidence that Mrs. Arlosoroff mentioned that two persons had participated in the murder; yet 17 days after the occurrence he speaks of following them although he alleges he saw only one person running up the hill: this person, he alleges, he saw on a dark night 40 metres away making movements with his hand going up the side of a hill some hundred metres from the place where the trackers allege they saw tracks going up the hill.

When this witness gave evidence before the Trial Court he stated that the person who passed him stayed for a minute or two and then went on his way to the Yarkon; that he was 1 or 1 1/2 metres away from him: yet he did not see his face.

Some 21 days after the occurrence (after Appellant's description had been broadcast in local papers), he attended an identification parade and there picked out the Appellant, a man whose face he says he never saw and whom he had never attempted to describe before, other than estimating his age, and that he wore a collar and tie, a blouse, and was bareheaded.

These facts, together with the inconsistency of his time with that of Mrs. Arlosoroff, (with regard to the length of time Appellant could have been out of sight of Mrs. Arlosoroff), compel me to doubt whether the man whom he states looked at him and whose face he did not see, he subsequently identified as Appellant. This witness would appear to be one of the many witnesses of this country who must necessarily embellish a true story by such flights of fancy as to render it impossible to give any credence to it or at any rate to determine which part of it is true and which false.

I cannot consider Weiser's evidence as satisfactory or sufficiently reliable to corroborate that of the principal witness in this case.

With regards to the confession of Abdul Majid, I have already expressed an opinion during the hearing of this appeal that the Assize Court could not have attached any importance to it and must have disbelieved the confession, otherwise they could not have found that there was no corroboration to the identification of Zvi Rosenblatt by Mrs. Arlosoroff.

With this finding I am in full accord, and consider that no Court could place any reliance on evidence of this nature, whether preferred for the prosecution or the defence.

I find that the other material evidence required by Section 5 of the Law of Evidence Amendment Ordinance to corroborate the identification by Mrs. Arlosoroff of the Appellant is lacking and that the appeal must be allowed and the judgment of the lower Court quashed.

—F. B. Baker
A/Senior Puisne Judge

JUDGMENT OF JUDGE DE FREITAS

I am in complete agreement with the judgment of the Chief Justice which was arrived at after Baker J. and I had discussed the case from all angles with him.

I have read the judgment of Baker J. with which I agree in principle. I hold that the conviction of the Appellant must be quashed.

There is one point, however, on which I feel I should enlarge: namely the attack by the Defence on the conduct of the case by the prosecution. I am aware that what I am going to say may be misinterpreted as an attempt to whitewash the Police.

Now all intelligent and fair-minded people of this country are well aware of the difficulties of the Police due to a number of factors not the least important being:

(a) the total absence of public opinion;

(b) the part money can play.

When a serious crime is committed in this country a position arises which may be termed Police v. Criminal and Public. Friends of the victims, friends of the accused and busy-body-members of the public harass and tamper with the police in a most reprehensible way.

From the finding of the Court of Criminal Assize it is abundantly clear that in this case the Police were up against a defence which, although with the exception of the confession by Abdul Mejid, was run on stereotyped lines, was nevertheless, very cleverly got up.

I would mention that the confession is not original.

Further, after Mrs. Arlosoroff had identified the Appellant, an atmosphere was generated which increased the difficulties of the Police.

In all the circumstances, while I do not in any way excuse some of the errors of the Police which are apparent in this case, but which can in no way, as it happens, affect this case, I understand that errors which should not be made, may not be avoided entirely in the future until the public gave the police fair play and the support that the police are entitled to demand.

In a word, in my view the public has got a more efficient and more honest police force than it deserves.

—J. M. De Freitas

VLADIMIR JABOTINSKY
"Letter to Colonial Secretary Sir Philip Cunliffe-Lister (7/24/33)"
Shmuel Katz, *Lone Wolf*
v. 2, pp. 1395–8

Jabotinsky at his best was notable for relentless colonialist realism. At his worst, he denied the fact that his followers were assassins and, in time, even that WW II would happen.

He wrote the Colonial Secretary, listing his problems with the court's decision. Cunliffe-Lister tossed it into his round file.—LB

1) The Chief Justice, in announcing the High Court's judgment, said that "if this case had been heard in England the conviction would stand," but, as in Palestine the evidence of one eyewitness was insufficient, and there was no valid corroboration, Stavsky was "discharged." It will be remembered that the Jerusalem District Court, in acquitting Rosenblatt, had used the same argument—absence of corroborative evidence.

2) The Palestine Labor Party thereupon published a manifesto containing the following statement:

"Rosenblatt and Stavsky, who have been freed from any punishment for lack of second eyewitness as required by the Turkish Law still applied in Palestine, have been recognized as murderers also by the High Court. Both the Jerusalem District Court and the High Court have accepted Mrs. Arlosoroff's evidence as true."

3) Police Inspectors Barker and Goffer, according to the Jewish Telegraphic Agency, warned Stavsky and Rosenblatt that "their lives are in danger" and that "the Tel Aviv police cannot be responsible for them."

It appears questionable whether Stavsky and Rosenblatt can sue the Labor Party for libel, as that party can plausibly allege that it only amplified

146

the obvious meaning of the Chief Justice's words; it is still more questionable whether that party can be charged for contempt of court, for when a Chief Justice says that from the point of view of British justice, "the conviction would stand," he may easily be understood to convey that the convicted man is actually guilty though he may have to be discharged because of (Turkish) technicalities.

But Stavsky and Rosenblatt are faced not only with slander against which they can probably find no legal defence; they are faced with danger of violence against which the police declares itself incapable to defend them.

This situation is absurd and should not be tolerated under any civilized government. I refer not only to the police's duty to assume the fullest responsibility for the safety of two inhabitants whom that police explicitly state to be in danger. I especially refer to the statements of the Chief Justice which constitute the very root of this absurd situation. Acceptance of human judgments should also have some reasonable limits, and I am reluctantly compelled to submit that here these limits have obviously been overstepped.

To begin with, the Chief Justice's statement that in England "the conviction would stand" on the ground of Mrs. Arlosoroff's identification is not correct... "In England" such an identification is not admitted at all. In England, the Lord Chief Justice in quashing the sentence of Thomas Dwyer (1924) said: "It is clearly illegitimate, it would be most improper, to inform a witness beforehand, who is to be called as an identifying witness, by the process of making features of the accused familiar to him through a photograph (C.A.C. Vol. 18, Part 8, p. 145). Equally, in quashing the sentence of J. J. Haslam, the Lord Chief Justice [in England] said: "A person who has seen the photograph of an accused person may identify him simply because he has seen a photograph of him. This matter is sufficient to require the Court to quash the conviction." (C.A.C. Vol. 19, Part 3, 1926 p. 59.)

Secondly, I submit that it is most unfair, inhuman, and deadly for the prestige of the judiciary to "discharge" two prisoners with comment which can so easily be construed as stamping them for murderers, and exposing them on high authority to lifelong abhorrence, persecution, and even violence.

You have thought it your duty to abstain from official interference in the case while it was sub judice. It is no longer that; nor is it, properly speaking, a causa judicata, for it is not clear whether the High Court meant to pronounce those men guilty or not guilty.

In consequence, there is already as reported in the English press, a recrudescence of strife in Palestine, unprecedented insofar as its outbursts can now be observed even in places of public worship. Yet it must be feared that this only a beginning; that the strife may assume forms even more dangerous; and that public opinion, Jewish and non-Jewish, all the world over will attribute it, in its present phase, only to the action of the High Court in allowing a judgment, which everybody expected to bring in final appeasement, to be so framed as to encourage and even exasperate dissention.

I can admit no shadow of doubt that such a situation cannot possibly meet with your approval nor toleration.

I respectfully submit that the only means to remove that situation is to have it publicly stated, either by the Palestine High Court itself or by some authority superior to that court, that the unquestionable meaning of both acquittals is that both Rosenblatt and Stavsky have been definitely pronounced not quilty.

"Trace 1933 Murder Weapon to Stern Group Death Squad"

Jewish Journal
August 10, 1973

To this day, Revisionists deny they had anything to do with Arlosoroff's murder. But subsequent evidence confirms their guilt.—LB

Johannesburg (JCNS)—According to a former Palestine Mandatory forensic expert, the murder weapon that killed Haim Arlosoroff, the political head of the Jewish Agency, was a 7.62 Russian Nagant revolver, a type used in "murders connected with the Revisionist Stern group activities."

The man who has made the allegation is Superintendent F. W. Bird, now living in Gaberone, Botswana. (Haim Arlosoroff was taking a stroll with his wife Sima on the Tel Aviv seashore in June, 1933, when two young men approached him. One pulled out a revolver and shot him on the spot. Three men linked with the Revisionist movement were later acquitted of the murder.)

Superintendent Bird has made his claim in a letter to the *Rand Daily Mail*.

He says as a Palestine forensic expert he compared the Arlosoroff bullet exhibits with seized weapons hundreds of times, "all with negative results until the murder of Lord Moyne."

When Lord Moyne (the British Minister Resident in Cairo) was assassinated by members of the Stern group in Cairo in 1944, Superintendent Bird flew to Cairo from Palestine and discovered that Lord Moyne had been shot with a Nagant "and I subsequently proved that it had also been the crime weapon in no fewer than seven previous political murders all connected with Revisionist Stern group activities."

He adds: "I did not give evidence of the Arlosoroff connection at the time of the trial of the two murderers of Lord Moyne as the chain of evidence of the Arlosoroff exhibits had been broken during the eleven year gap." Superintendent Bird said the Nagant revolver which killed Lord Moyne was later presented to King Farouk of Egypt.

VLADIMIR JABOTINSKY

"Jews and Fascism: Some Remarks—and a Warning"

Jewish Daily Bulletin
April 11, 1935

Jabotinsky loved pre-Fascist Italy, where the linguist perfected his Italian, and had no sympathy for Fascism's follow the "head buffalo" leader principle. But he saw Mussolini as a possible substitute Mandatory, to replace London, which was increasingly concerned not to antagonize the Arabs in its vast holdings. He defiantly began to orient towards Rome, confirming the world's unanimous opinion that Revisionism was fascist, regardless of any scrupples its own Duce might have on the matter.—LB

Foreign words should be used with a bona fide knowledge of what they really mean. Fasces was the Latin term for a bunch of rods with an axle in the middle. Roman "lictors" used to carry them ostentatiously, to remind the citizens that if they don't obey orders they will be beaten, or their heads chopped off. Fasces was the symbol of coercive discipline, of the State's resolve and power to enforce obedience on all dissenters, no matter whether wicked criminals or honest conscientious objectors. Italian Fascism is an attempt to reaffirm the principle that the State has the right and the duty to coerce—and the actual power too.

Right or wrong, all this can have no application to Jewish social phenomena. There is no Jewish government, and no Jew can be administratively "coerced" to obey orders issued by any Jewish leader or committee of leaders. Jewish political organizations are voluntary associations and can be nothing else. Should one of them conceive the whim of imposing on its membership the strictest kind of "compulsory" discipline, that would simply mean that all its members chose to agree to this kind of game: all of them, for, if you or I suddenly cease to agree we can simply walk out of that organization and cannot be "coerced." When a minority of that membership say "We submit to the will of the majority," they simply mean that they voluntarily condescend to submit. The doctrine of Fascism is rooted in the opposite principle: the individual will be made to agree whether he agrees or not. In Jewish life this doctrine is simply unreal, as unreal as "depth" in a two-dimensional oil painting.

As to the very old principle that the interests of a nation should supersede those of an individual, a family, or a "class"—to describe this idea as "Fascism" is silly. This is everyman's view, including ninety-nine percent of all Socialists, probably also of all Communists if ever put to the test.

The really "Fascist" addition to this world-old idea is, again, only that thoroughness of coercion which Fascism applies to social relations. It refuses to rely on the workers or the employers' own patriotism: it simply commandeers all the workers and all the employers, treats them as battalions of the State, orders, forbids and punishes. This again, cannot be initiated in our Jewish life. When we Jews speak of "compulsory" arbitration in Palestine, what we mean is a free pledge by all concerned to renounce voluntarily any other method of settling industrial disputes and to accept (voluntarily) the arbitrators' judgment however unpalatable.

Whether such a covenant is a possibility (as I believe) or a dream (as pessimists affirm) is beside the point: the point is that this program is the reverse of Fascism. Fascism says to both Labor and capital: "I don't ask you to be patriotic, you may go on feeling selfish: but you will have to accept the State's ruling or go to jail—and even if you do go to jail, it won't help you, for the State's ruling will be enforced in your enterprise all the same."

There is, on the other hand, also this difference—that, while in Fascism any concrete form of "class war" is only verboten, in Zionism (where nothing can actually be "verboten") the very idea of "class war" is immoral. The national funds which support the proletarian Halutzim are being provided by the bourgeoisie. That bourgeoisie is being daily urged to leave the Galuth and come and build factories in Palestine, because there "you can be among your brethren." When a bourgeois starts a workshop in Palestine, he is being urged to employ expensive Jewish labor instead of cheap Arab labor—because "the Jewish workmen are his brethren."

All this is absolutely fair: they are brethren, and partners in the great enterprise of building the Homeland, and comrades in Zionist ideology:

brethren, partners, comrades in a sense incomparably more intense and more concrete than it can be said of capital and labor in any other country. That is why it is unfair and immoral to import "class war" ideas into Palestine—even though it cannot be "verboten."

Fascism is wholly and organically inapplicable to any aspect of Jewish life: it is therefore simply dishonest to call any Jewish party "Fascist." In many cases, it is even akin to hitting under the belt. In liberal or democratic countries Fascism is looked upon as patriotically subversive, governments have been known to take active measures for suppressing it by police action, and may have to do so in the nearest future with considerable severity. In view of all this, decent opponents should be very chary of stamping a Zionist party as "Fascist." It is just as indecent as calling Socialists "Communists," and likely to lead to the same kind of outside interference.

In countries like Austria, where the term "Marxists" is equally dangerous, we Revisionists have instructed our followers never to apply that term to left-wing Zionists, quite regardless of whether that would be scientifically true or untrue; and, though we officially disbanded our German branches when we decided to join the boycott movement, that wing of Zionists in Germany who share our Herzlian views also know that "Marxist" is a word never to be used in Polemics. In the "London Agreement No. 1" between the two executives there is a special paragraph banning this mania of describing Zionist opponents by names which may prove politically dangerous.

But the main warning I wish to convey is that there is also a much more important reason for discontinuing to use the term "Fascism" as a cuss word in Jewish discussions. Fascism is today the official doctrine of Italy, and Italy is one of those countries where Jews enjoy full equality not only politically but also socially. Such countries are not very numerous, and their number is, to say the least, not increasing. It is very unwise to insist on antagonizing one of them by turning to abuse a term and an idea which is so highly cherished both by its rulers and by its youth.

Nor is it quite fair. Whatever any few may think of Fascism's other points, there is no doubt that the Italian brand of Fascist ideology is, at least, an ideology of racial equality. Let us not be so humble as to pretend that this doesn't matter—that racial equality is too insignificant an idea to outbalance the absence of civic freedom. For it is not true. I am a journalist who would choke without freedom of the press, but I affirm it is simply blasphemous to say that it in the scale of civic rights, even the freedom of speech comes before the equality of all men. Equality comes first, super-first; and Jews should be the first to remember it, and to hold that a regime maintaining that principle in a world turning Cannibal does, partly but considerably, atone for its other shortcomings; it may be criticized, it should not be kicked at. There are enough other terms for cuss use—Nazism, Hitlerism, Polizeistadt, etc.—but the word "fascismo" is Italy's copyright and should therefore be reserved only for the correct kind of discussion, not for exercises in Billingsgate.

Especially, as it may yet prove very harmful. That government of the copyright is a very powerful fact, whose sympathy may yet ward off many a blow, for instance in the League of Nations' councils. Incidentally, the Permanent Mandates Commission which supervises Palestinian affairs has an Italian chairman. In short—though of course I do not expect street-urchins (irrespective of age) to follow an advice of caution—responsible leaders ought to take care.

"Georg Kareski Approves of Ghetto Laws: Interview in Dr. Goebbels' 'Angriff'"

Jewish Chronicle
London, January 3, 1936

Georg Kareski joined the German Revisionists after Hitler came to power, seeing them as the potential equivalent of the successful Nazis. Indeed the Nazis allowed only the "State Zionists" the right to wear uniforms, indoors.

After Jabotinsky declared in favor of boycotting Germany, he had to publically disassociate himself politically from Kareski. But as late as 1947, Kareski was made the chair of a Revisionist health fund in Palestine.—LB

The *Angriff*, the organ of Dr. Goebbels, has published a full-page interview with Georg Kareski, the Jew who has accepted office under the Nazi Government as Reich Commissioner for Jewish Cultural Affairs. Herr Kareski's answers to the first two questions put to him by his anti-Semitic interviewer are of particular interest:

(1) Question: "Do you know, Herr Director Kareski, that our Leader and Chancellor has, in justifying the Nuremberg laws, expressed the hope that through this secular solution a basis may be established for a tolerable relationship between the German and Jewish peoples? You, as a leading personality of the State Zionist Movement, have always defended a sharp division between the German and the Jewish peoples on the basis of mutual respect."

Reply: "That is so. I have for many years regarded a complete separation between the cultural activities of the two peoples as a condition for a peaceful collaboration and I have always been in favor of such a separation, provided it is founded on the respect for the alien nationality."

(2) Question: "What are your views on the situation created by the Nuremberg laws sofar as the cultural life of the Jews in Germany is concerned?"

Reply: "The Nuremberg laws of September 15th, 1935 seem to me, apart from their legal provisions, entirely to conform with this desire for a separate life based on mutual respect. This is especially so when one takes into account the order for separate school systems which has been issued previously. The Jewish school is an old political demand of my friends, because they consider that the education of the Jew in accordance with his traditions and his mode of life is absolutely essential."

"Kareski Again"
The American Hebrew
February 21, 1936

The ZVfD bitterly fought the Revisionists for the Nazis' patronage.—LB

The Nazi Commissioner for Jewish Cultural Affairs, Herr Hinkel, has given an important interview to the official Nazi newspaper, *Rote Erde*. Herr Hinkel began by enumerating the many "favors" which the Nazi regime has done for the Jews by establishing the special Jewish "Kulturbund" to look after their cultural interest. He then explained that owing to the shortage of special Jewish dramas, the Kulturbund was obliged to produce also non-Jewish dramas. It was unfortunate that this was necessary, but the Nazis were "generous" and did not make unnecessary difficulties for the Jews.

The most important part of the interview, however, dealt not with the Kulturbund, but with Zionism. Towards the end of the interview, Herr Hinkel said: "I have consciously allowed the Zionist movement to exert the strongest influence upon the cultural and spiritual activities of the Kulturbund because the Zionists as the 'Racial Jews' have at least given us formal guarantees of cooperation in acceptable form."

Since the German Zionists have never given such guarantees to Herr Hinkel, he could only be referring to Mr. Kareski as representing the whole of the Zionist movement. This has called forth a new storm among German Zionists who are now more determined than ever to draw a line of distinction between themselves and Mr. Kareski and let him appear to be the representative of Zionism in Germany. It is expected that the matter will come to a head in the near future, when Mr. Kareski, who is at present still convalescing, makes his first public appearance.

"Nazi Opinion of Zionism"
Palestine Post
January 29, 1936

Altho the romance between the Nazis and Kareski was almost too tender for mere words, eventually the Hitlerites realized that they had to deal with his ZVfD/WZO rivals, as under British rules, establishing an annual quota for immigration to Palestine, the WZO determined national quotas.—LB

Berlin, January 27

A Nazi explanation of why Zionists are favored in Germany has been given to the German press by Herr Hinkel, Commissar for Jewish Affairs in the Reich.

"We purposely favor the Zionists culturally because they are the only Jews who have given a formal and acceptable guarantee of cooperation with the Government," he said in the interview.

Since, actually the German Zionist Federation never gave such a guarantee, Herr Hinkel apparently refers to Dr. Georg Kareski as representative of the Zionist Movement. Dr. Kareski is associated with the Revisionist party.

This statement has called forth new protests on the part of Zionists, who are determined to differentiate between Kareski and the Zionist Movement.

"Dr. von Weisl Believes in Fascism"
World Jewry
London, June 12, 1936

For all his hostility to the leader principle, Jabotinsky knew that his movement's financial director once proposed him as the Revisionist Duce. Von Weisl supported Kareski. In 1936, on his own, he contacted the Mosleyites and proposed a mad imperialist alliance, Britain, Germany, Poland and Japan, and a Zionist state, against the Soviets, Arabs and the Asian colonial revolutions.—LB

The French newspaper in Bucharest, the "Moment," which is regarded as one of the organs of the Roumanian Foreign Ministry, has published an interview with the Revisionist leader, Dr. von Weisl.

The Revisionist leader accused the Zionist leaders of Socialist sympathies, and he declared that, although opinions among the Revisionists varied, in general they sympathized with Fascism, and they were strong opponents of Socialism and Communism.

He, personally, was a supporter of Fascism, and he rejoiced at the victory of Fascist Italy in Abyssinia as a triumph of the White races against the Black. He also asserted the Revisionists wanted to bring to Palestine, within the next ten years, 900,000 Jews from Poland, 300,000 from Roumania and 300,000 from Germany.

Finally, he stated that the Revisionists had no desire to colonize Jews in Abyssinia, and that, in his opinion, it would be well for the Arab strike in Palestine to continue for several weeks more, as by then the authority of the Arab leaders would be completely broken for a number of years.

VLADIMIR JABOTINSKY

"Letter to Plugat Betarim Civittavechia"

Selected Writings
U.S.A. – Undated

Like most Zionist leaders, Jabotinsky had a Hebrew name, Ze'ev, Wolf, but for the historians he is Vladimir. His pro-Italian policy bore fruit. Mussolini trained the first sailors for the future Revisionist state at his Naval School in Civitavecchia. He wrote his youthful followers there, laying out his hesitations re Mussolini, but in a way that only a mind reader would have been able to figure out that it wasn't a ringing statement of endorsement of Fascism's sacred principle of opposition to the working class.—LB

Betarim,

The serious step which you have taken in going to the Naval School in Civittavecchia will be of great importance. Whether for good or bad, depends on you. If you succeed in acquiring the love and respect of the Italian principal of the school, its teachers and pupils, you will pave a new path for the development of our people that will lead us, in the future, to the acquiring of a decisive position at sea. But if you do not succeed, you may come to one conclusion: that you will create a new source of racial hatred in a country which, up till now, has not suffered from this malaise.

This depends only on you, and the secret of success depends on that principle which you have already learnt in Betar—that is Hadar. There in Civittavecchia it will be a test for you whether you have learnt Hadar not only in theory but also in reality.

The meaning of Hadar is, first of all, tact. Do not forget, day and night and every moment, that you are a guest in a school, in the city and the country. BE NOBLE!

Do not grab the first bench, even if it is given to you. Learn the Italian language well; but do not place yourself in the position of a poor man who asks support from the State. If you have insufficient money, it is better that you leave the school—because the honor of our people is more important than your career.

Learn to speak quietly in school, in the street and also at your meetings—even in your rooms lest you disturb the peace of the people, of the city. When you walk in the courtyards of the school, or in the streets of the town, walk in twos and not in threes, lest you bar the way for the local townsmen.

Personal cleanliness of your clothing should be a commandment to you every minute of your life. You must shave every morning, and not even a hint of hair should remain on your cheek or chin. Every morning you must look at your nails to see whether they are clean. Remember that every stain is a stain for Betar and a stain for the whole of the Jewish people. When you work, your face, hands, ears and your whole body must be clean. Learn the work of the school diligently. Do not boast of your progress. Help your Italian friends with whatever you can. Do not intervene in any party discussions concerning Italy.

Do not express any opinions about Italian politics. Do not criticize the present regime in Italy—nor the former regime. If you are asked about your political and social beliefs, answer: "I am a Zionist. My greatest desire is the Jewish State, and in our country I oppose class warfare. This is my whole faith."

I hand over to you the honor of Betar on a very important front and I am sure that you will know how to guard it. You are Betarim!

Tel 'Hai,
Ze'ev Jabotinsky

"Supplement to *L'Idea Sionistica*, Number 8, Dedicated to the Betar Hebrew Maritime School in Civitavecchia"
March 1936

If you run with wolves, you don't have to howl. But wag your tail you will. An Italian Revisionist magazine would be past human for saintliness if it heeded any scruple of their Rosh Betar (High Betar) about the closeness of the two movements: "Giovinezza," the Fascist Party's lyrical anthem, "was sung with much enthusiasm by the Betarim" at the opening of their squadron at Mussolini's maritime academy. Indeed, Revisionist members of the Blackshirts' University Fascist Youth, were among the founding cadre of the future Israeli navy.—LB

The Inauguration of the new home of Betar's Maritime Squadron at Civitavecchia, March 29, 1936.

The ceremony, combined with the official inauguration of the school's 2nd academic year, took place on a truly Spring-like day, which contributed much to its great success.

The guests, who came from outside the base, numbered more than 100. Many of them were youth, who wanted to give the event a lively tone. They also wanted to provide a sense of fraternization with these brave young sailors.

The celebration, in its own terms, although of short duration, was one of self-communing, in order to appreciate better the magnitude of the partially completed work here, before our very eyes, to deepen our joy, to make us aware of what a great thing has been started here, with this significant Hebrew maritime squadron.

THE PARTICIPANTS

There were many notable guests: We will record some of them here, requesting the forgiveness of those we omit: Col. Fiore, Commander of the Port of Civitavecchia; Prof. Aldo Lattes, Assistant Head Rabbi, Commissioner David Fano, councilor of the Roman community, and Mrs. Fano, President of the A.D.E.I., Prof. Marco Almagia; Professoressa Maggi, Mrs. Ascarelli, Kurt Korniker, correspondent of the *Jüdische Rundschau*, Dr. Edmond Schaechter, President of the Austrian Zohar, Col. and Mrs. Mendes; Amadio and Mrs. Fatucci, representing the Directory of the Italian Zohar, Profs. Sciaky and Cohen of Florence, Mr. and Mrs. Maurizio Mendes of Rome. "Our Flag" of Turin, unable to send a correspondent, sent a telegram of congratulations.

ABOUT THE NEW SCHOOL

One representative of the squad, as well as Captain Fusco, the Director of the school, was to wait at the station for those coming by train. Others joined who came to Civitavecchia by car. And this was our first fine impression: Strapping young men with broad smiles, looking proud, wearing beautiful uniforms (if only their fatigues), knowing how to wear them; on the uniforms a Star of David stands out vividly, which encloses a Menorah, interlaced with an anchor; without hesitation, the young men obey and execute a perfect military salute, with broad smiles and happy and intelligent looks. Now there is an air of amazement among the guests. Their thoughts are apparent: Is the ghetto Jew finally going to disappear, once and for all? Or are they just a creation of a sick imagination? This pleasant thought, this doubt about the very existence in the future of the present-day ghetto, will not go away very soon. Friendships are made, and friendly feelings were directed towards the school-ship "Sara," during the very enthusiastic gathering.

A Betari on guard at the gangway, stands rigidly at attention as the guests pass by. Another is on the bridge, and is no less sharp, with his martial air, and the precision and perfection of his salute. The guests suddenly swarm all over the ship.

PROF. SCIAKY'S SPEECH

Listen to this: A whistle, some sharp commands in Hebrew, then the crew lines up. It passes in review before Col. Fiore, who looks satisfied. The participants take their seats, crowding around the Betarim, still at attention, and the ceremony begins. Mounted on the ship's anvil, Professor Sciaky speaks.

The orator underlines the great significance of the fact that young Jews today are in Italy to take the course being officially inaugurated: Jews who have come from the most diverse countries, even from those with sanctions. A sure sign of the people who first proclaimed the idea of justice to the world, and of the great injustice and injuries done to that people, who first gave the world the Law. And the similarity between the Hebrew national revival and the Italian is not without significance.

The speaker remembers that while Europe's better known politicians were ambiguous about the possibility of Italian unity, a Jew, Moses Hess, almost a century ago, in his "Rome and Jerusalem," predicted that the revival of Rome would contain within it the revival of Jerusalem.

Italy preceded Israel in obtaining independence. This was in the order of things. And today she has much to teach the Jewish people. It is here that our young men are coming to learn the maritime arts. They will have to live a hard life, a life of sacrifice. As the High Betar says, in a letter to the speaker, our youth will have to spend 10 years, their engineering diplomas in pocket, as simple sailors. But in that time the Hebrew merchant marine will be created.

The thought spontaneously occurs that in some very near future, it will be possible for the Hebrew merchant marine to reciprocate the cordial hospitality and the honor that today Italy is bestowing upon the Jewish people by welcoming its young men into this school. The Jewish people will not forget Civitavecchia. It will remember Italy with gratitude. It will remember Col. Fiore's constant aid in the hard work of laying the foundation for a Hebrew fleet, it will remember the work of Captain Fusco, who created this first base, and for whom the seriousness of his work, and his skill, have won him, not only the esteem, but also the friendship of the Rosh Betar.

The speaker concluded by turning his thoughts to Italy, to its head of government who, lighting the King's victorious reign, showed us the destiny of Italy, whose guidance bears signs of great Italy's valor and civilization. One thinks of the purity expressed by the Rosh Betar, chief and father of the new Hebrew youth.

A roar of applause greets the end of the brief speech, heard with total attention, not only by those on the ship, but by the numerous people on the pier.

THE HIGH BETAR'S MESSAGE
Then the squadron commander, A. Blass, reads the following Hebrew message from the Rosh Betar:

London, March 27, 1936

Dear Mr. Blass,

I beg you to transmit to the cadets at the Maritime School my thanks for having sent me the photo with the signatures. I am very delighted with this lovely gift, which will be one of the most beautiful ornaments here in my room at our new agency. If you receive this letter by inauguration day, I beg you to say to your comrades that my heart is with them at this very moment. Please believe that even while away from the official inauguration, I do not forget Civitavecchia. I know how hard your road will be after the end of studies, because we do not yet have a fleet. If destiny gives me sufficient strength to continue my struggle, I will fight along side of you, also, for this goal, but that is not important; with me or without me, I believe in your future.

I beg you to give my greetings to Captain Fusco: it is not necessary that I describe his character to you and the spirit of his nation. To all the instructors and their assistants, blessings and thanks.

My respectful greetings to the Mendes family, Messrs. Carpi and Sciaky, and to all my friends.

Tel Hai,
Z. Giabotinschi

THE RABBI'S BENEDICTION

The order—"Attention!" A triple chant ordered by the squad's commanding officer—"Viva L'Italia! Viva IL Re! Viva IL Duce!" resounded, followed by the benediction which Rabbi Aldo Lattes invoked in Italian and in Hebrew for God, for the King and for IL Duce, followed by a prayer for the Rosh Betar.

Remembering with suitable words, with this act he consecrated the naval school, making it not only a home, but also a temple, he blesses the Sefer Torah which has just been put back into the lovely Aron Ha Codesh, together with the necessary mezuzah for the school, gifts from Signore Amadio Fatucci of Rome.

"Giovinezza" was sung with much enthusiasm by the Betarim, still somewhat awkward with the Italian language. (The majority have been in Italy for no more than two months, others for much less time, and some even for a few days only), and the singing of "Besciùv Adonái," the official Betar hymn, close the ceremony.

The public again swarms into the ship, most not forgetting to partake of the refreshments offered by the school, demonstrate a distinct enthusiasm for the joyful Betar company, who give vent to their youthful exuberance, with Italian and Hebrew songs. (The "Black Front" is also heard.) The Betarim extend their cordiality to teaching the "hora" dance to all desirous of learning it. We confess that we don't know if Terpsichore is one of its enthusiasts, but we are. And we would want a few years, at least, consorting with the dancers. However it is not possible. And the only thing for us to do is exchange a few quick words with the Betarim on guard at the gangway and on the bridge, and temporarily substitute for them, so even they can at least try the vermouth and, for a few minutes, join the hora circle.

AT THE SCHOOL

The inauguration took place, at the base, then on board the ship. The naval school is a more stable place, i.e., more enduring: even when not on a cruise, the boat provides good accommodations for a part of the Betarim, making up, with its berths, for the insufficiency of hammocks on the base itself.

And the party of guests goes to the school after dinner and remains there up to the moment of departure.

The structure, which faces the sea, is wooden, but lacks nothing: from the bath (with tub) to the library, from the infirmary, the secretariat and the Commander's office, etc., etc. All is orderly, polished, inviting. There one breaths the air of the "Hadàr Betari" (Majesty of Betar). A vast clearing lies before the school, on it a mast, completely outfitted for military drills. The guests are housed here and after touring the building, there are scenes of cordial fraternization and merriment, with songs and dances accompanied by an orchestra (two violins and two guitars) which the cadets can boast of.

Some guests prefer more specific proof of the cadets' actual ability and entrust their lives to the new mariners, going for a turn in the boat. Upon their return, we see them so happy that we can infer that all went well.

PIONEERS OF THE HEBREW NAVY

Some visitors, new to this thing, wish to know the significance of the school within the complexity of the Jewish national movement. And Professor Sciaky satisfies them, explaining that the basic idea of Zionism is that of normalization of Jewish life and, therefore, the creation of the necessary organs of its development on its own land. Revisionist Zionism, has seen this demand as constructive, and has created, by the way, this school as a branch of the apolitical, athletic and military Betar activities. Real sacrifices are asked and will be asked of the cadets. They will be the first sailors of the Hebrew navy. Officers will, at first, have to be simple sailors, that is pioneers, as the first agricultural workers in Eretz Israel were pioneers. They will abandon comfort, neglect the careers towards which their completed studies gave them the right to aspire—and all this to bring about the settlement of the Hebrew people, giving them a position which it previously lacked.

The speaker was vigorously thanked for putting forward a lucid and thorough synthesis of the school's idealistic and practical reasons for being.

Soon afterwards, the guests returned to their homes.

FROM CIVITAVECCHIA
DR. BEN JAMMI

Correspondence on life in the Civitavecchia school can in no way be thought of as ordinary news. It must be the description of a process of transformation, of the struggle of young Jews against nature. It is the sound of a hammer striking an anvil where Jewish spades are being forged, a laboratory in which bent backs are being straightened, character is elevated, muscles hardened, and the spirit educated to the "Chibbùsh Haiam."

The pride of a people is its sailors; what people is not proud of them? They always serve as symbols of heroism and bravery. For thousands of years we dreamt of our conquerors of the sea, and these came when no one believed in it—unforeseen, unexpected.

Here in this little city on the Tyrrhenian Sea, something began to stir: here was found a man who declared himself ready to realize this dream of ours as a people; here was found the group of idealists from all parts of Europe, and—the dream has been transformed into a reality. The first Hebrew naval units were created.

I wish to dedicate this first article to the Commander and the Cadets.

Captain Nicola Fusco

To speak of the Jewish navy without citing captain Fusco's name would be the greatest absurdity. It is only to him, this tall, slim and always affable Italian captain that we owe so much. He, he alone, is the one who built, created and brought to such a dazzling result, the world's first Hebrew maritime school.

This is his work, his pride and joy.

I am not his biographer, and am not obliged to give you Fusco the whole man; nor am I the school's historian, who might give you a flawless image of the school's founder and director. Here I just want to present to you the Fusco that we students see and know.

He is a man who labors for the whole society. Wherever you wish, you may see his work and his spirit at work.

He is the director of the local Maritime School, captain of the Balilla and directs the autonomous group of foreigners at the Maritime School—our "ghedud."

All day long, we see him working for our "ghedud." Classes, reports, financial matters, ect. Where does he find time for all this? No one knows.

The pupils, arrived from abroad only yesterday, attend his classes, even when they understand hardly a word of Italian. He talks, teaching very complicated seafaring questions. I am thinking that all his efforts to make his words understood are in vain. But how I marvel when I am convinced that even the weakest students have understood! This is his art, his secret, He knows everyone by name, although he saw them only yesterday for the first time. If you want to know a pupil's character, Capt. Fusco will tell you at once. He is a brilliant psychologist—a cunning man, full of wit, thus intelligent and energetic. He admires Jabotinsky greatly—"don't shame your Mr. Jabotinsky, a man blessed by God," he says, to scold us.

All the pupils love him.

Besides Capt. Fusco, the principal instructor, the other teachers are:

Capt. Scalabrino
A man who is still very young, but nevertheless a sailor, very experienced in his trade. He is also an enthusiast for our cause, and his dedication knows no limits. He is very concerned that the students study and know everything, so that they may serve their people honorably.

Capt. Cervilini
A good and sincere teacher who relates to us like a father. He himself suffers along with our sufferings, and rejoices with us, like a baby. He teaches us rowing and signaling.

FURZI
I should dedicate a special chapter to this good Tuscan. He was the one who made it possible for us to speak and understand Italian. He grew so much into our circles that he is a part of us. I remember that when we began the Hebrew curriculum he came to me to register for the first course. He helps us at every opportunity.

In addition to the Italian personnel, there are Jews among us. The Commander of the ghedud is a marine officer, first class. He directs the Betar work at the school. Moreover we often have inspections and visits from sympathizers like Maurizio Mendes.

CADETS
This year there are 49 cadets—from Poland, Romania, Lithuania, Germany, Austria, Latvia, Hungary, Czechoslovakia, Tripoli and Rhodes. As you can see, a mixture of different peoples and countries. The mixture of languages forms a "Tower of Babel." A record—in all, 21 languages! A microcosm of

our settlement in the Diaspora. But it can also be seen that Hebrew unifies us all. Poland is the most represented, with 22 Betarim. Czechoslovakia with 9, Germany with 5, etc., etc.

Nevertheless they live well together. In off moments there have been clashes between persons of two different mentalities and educations. But at once the thought comes that we are Betarim and at once the conflict is resolved.

Our human material is extremely intelligent. The majority are university students and 30 of them belong to the G(ioventù) U(niversitaria) F(ascista), (University Fascist Youth—*LB*).

Among us are different specialists and even journalists. An interesting community of differing characters and customs. There is only one banner, only one chief, under whom we are forging and creating our colossal opus: A Hebrew Navy.

The school-ship "Sara 1" is our life, our different future.

EYES TOWARD THE SEA
VALS HAMEIR

Facing the catastrophic conditions in which people find themselves almost everywhere, some throw up their hands, look toward heaven, and await miracles. But it is centuries and centuries since miracles rained from the skies, and today they come only in the wake of huge effort and a great expenditure of energy.

Our generation has understood this: it is not the waiting but the will that creates miracles!

Life is hard, it demands many sacrifices. All of which makes us stop and think and, actually, prepares our consciousness for the task ahead, for the struggle on behalf of our holy cause: the regeneration of our people and the creation of our fatherland.

Thus, the psychology of the Jew has changed. Jews look toward nationhood. We have undergone a profound revolution of the spirit, of which we are proud, because we have made this revolution ourselves, and by ourselves alone.

Not long ago, we launched a new "Conquest of the Hebrew Sea!"

Hebrews and the Sea! How strange the words sound to the cultivated ears of many Jews! But for nationalists it is obvious: Palestine is bathed by the best-stocked seas in the world. The sea must feed us, it must be our strategic base.

This is logical!

Lovers of Deeds, we have accomplished this end; we have founded a maritime school, acquired a ship, towards the conquest of the sea-lanes. We have already generated seamen; today 25 and in several months another 50!

We are consciously advancing, our work is methodical, and we are creating the Hebrew navy. As it was in the beginning, when Hebrew sailors founded Carthage; as it was at the time of Solomon; and still earlier, when there existed a maritime Zebulon!

With the aid of the seamen that we are creating, our people will have a fountain of nutrition, our fatherland a base of defense!

That is our aim! And we will reach it for the grandeur of our people, for its future of freedom and of life in its fatherland!

"Opening of the Third Congress of the Jewish Communities of the Far East"

Ha Dagel (The Banner)
Harbin, Manchukuo
January 1940

World War ll is the modern American Trojan war. Arguably, the History Channel runs more footage on it than on any other topic. Americans, Jews, Chinese, are the white helmets; the Axis, Germany, Italy, Japan, always the black helmets. Jews hailing the Japanese conquest of Manchuria disrupts the natural, folk illiterate notion.

Ha Dagel is Hebrew, but beyond its name the journal was in Russian. The Jewish community were traders in an imperialist environment and Revisionism's militarism and adaption to the Japanese invaders seemed to many to be ideally suited to their bloodthirsty world.

However, there was a gross problem. Japan was Hitler's partner in the Anti-Comintern Pact, which made everyone in the world but them see the Japanese military as Asia's Nazis, slaughtering Chinese. Their finessing of their political contradiction is certainly a curio of the world's political literature.

There are petty linguistic obscurities in a Russian piece discussing Japanese and Chinese and Manchurian terms. But they will not effect readers' grasp of the article, which leaves no doubt as to the Revisionists' allegiance to the traitorous regime and the Japanese, with their Yamato and Van Dao "principles."

Readers will also see Japanese named as Manchukuo officials because the regime was so thin on Chinese support that Japanese frequently had to staff its bureaucracy.—LB

The third Congress of the Jewish Communities of the Far East opened cere-moniously on December 23, 1939, in the Commercial Assembly hall.

Among the honorary guests were representatives of the Japanese Com-mand and regional officers, and the head of the Emigrants Office, General V. A. Kislitsin.

The stage was decorated with the flags of Japan and Manchukou and a white-blue Jewish banner. A color guard of honor, from the "Brit-Trumpeldor" and "Maccabi" organizations, stood behind the presidium.

The presidium consisted of the Chairman of the Congress and National Council, Dr. A. I. Kaufman, representatives of the authorities, the chief of the Japanese military mission in Dairen, Colonel Yasue, a representative of the local military mission, Major Niimura, the Governor and the chief of the Kiova-Kay staff, Mr. Vay Huan-Chzgan, Vice-governor Mr. M. Genda, the head of a department of the Kiova-Kay staff in Bin'czyan, Mr. Imaiosi, K. I. Nakamura, a Kiova-Kay official, Mr. Katagiri, and honorary visitors: the sec-retary of the Executive Committee of the National council, M. G. Zimin, members V. M. Arkin, I. M. Berkovich, and M. M. Grossman, delegates from Harbin, M. I. Geiman, Ya. V. Zyskind, and H. Slutsker, a delegate from Shanghai, B. A. Kopeliovich, Yu. M. Beiner, D. Moris, D. Ye. Habinski from Tientsin, S. M. Groisman, and Ye. L. Kovner from Dairen, N. I. Kolyaditski from Mukden, Dr. V. M. Dubinski from Tsingtao, A. Ya. Strizgak from Tsitsihar and Hailar, A. G. Ponevezgski from Kobe, secretaries, etc.

Chairman Kaufman opened the Congress in Hebrew, the ancient Jewish language.

Then the audience rose as the "Brit-Trumpeldor" band performed the Japanese, Manchurian and Jewish anthems, while the standard-bearers held their banners aloft.

National Council Chairman A. I. Kaufman made the longest and most significant speech, devoted to the purposes of the Congress and its impor-tance. Dr. Kaufman emphasized that, while this Congress was convened due to the goodwill of the Japanese and Manchurian authorities, the Jews of the world faced heavy days, in connection with ruin of the Jewish center in Poland, and persecution of Jews in some countries of Eastern and Central Europe. Then he spoke on the refugee problem.

"The refugee problem is not only a Jewish issue, it should trouble the whole of mankind," the speaker declared, "and all countries should be involved in the fate of these people without a roof above their heads. The Jewish people have gotten used to appealing to humanity, relying on the great ideals bequeathed to the world by its prophets and now, in the abyss of its suffering, it trusts that the conscience of the world will wake up and a just solution shall be found. In Jewish history there have been many catastrophes, but the Jewish people always revived like the phoenix from the ashes. It will revive again after the current burdensome days."

The speaker was pleased to emphasize the fair and benevolent attitudes which Jews met in the countries of the Far East, guided by the Yamato and Van-Dao ideals, hence devoid of racial antagonism.

Further, Dr. Kaufman noted a number of important events and anniversaries: this year, the community in Kobe opened, the first in all of Japan, the community in Tientsin celebrates 35 years of existence, the Jewish community in Dairen will soon be 10 years old, the first Jewish city in Palestine, Tel Aviv, is 30 years old, and finally, its 900 years from Talmudist Rashi's birthday. The assembly welcomed each of these anniversaries with vigorous applause.

Passing to the significance of the Congress, Dr. Kaufman related that, "whereas the first Congress was a corner stone in the building of the Jewish community as a whole, and the second built the foundation of its organization, the current third Congress should finish the organizational period and systematize this work."

"I deeply believe in the Jewish national forces of the Far East. I believe that the governments of Manchukuo, Japan and China will understand the tragedy of the homeless, landless people and, together with that part of mankind living by the sacred principles of humanity, justice and equality, will enable the Jewish people to begin to live a normal life alongside with other peoples, so that, united with them, they can deal with the great issue of a peaceful commonwealth of the peoples. With this faith, I open the Third Congress of the Jewish Communities of Far East," Dr. A. I. Kaufman concluded. The Chairman's speech was greeted with a storm of applause.

Then he read a telegram from Rabbi A. M. Kiselev of Tientsin. The Rabbi expressed gratitude to authorities for their benevolent attitude to the Congress and prayed for the peoples of these countries.

Following that, Vice-Governor M. Genda read the greeting of Lieutenant-General Hasimoto, the chief of the Central Kiova-Kay staff in Dairen, with its subsequent translation to Russian.

General Hasimoto's greeting described the critical moment in Europe. He urged all to remain aware, after this Congress, of some very important political factors.

"Humanity disappeared in our century: A weak country is a victim of a strong one, and the principles of justice are broken. All of this is a result of the wrongful materialistic civilization of the West. Today, our empire, Manchukuo, aspires to impart to our people moral principles. With the help of the powerful Japanese empire, for eight years our state goes on its progressive way, and in this procession we are united with those peoples guided by similar principles. We view the Jewish people, who grievously suffer, in this light, as we do all other peoples, and I hope, that the work of this Congress will be the pole star for the whole Jewish people and will serve the dissemination of true morals, as well as creation of the new higher order in Eastern Asia."

The chief of the Kiova-Kay staff, Governor Vay Huan-Chzgan, explained the nature of the conflict between Japan and China, and noted that Japan and Manchukuo aspire to establish the basis of a secure peace in Asia. Some European countries, with self-interested purposes, try to prevent this. But their attempts are futile. No events are able to change the path of Japan and Manchukuo, direct to the new, brighter order.

"We deny any national antagonism, and consequently we cannot be biased against you," declared the orator to the delegates of the Congress, "and I wish that Jewry becomes further engaged in the work, making its contribution to the common concern of building in Asia. I am sure that today's Congress will serve this aim, and I call on you for cooperative, fruitful work, in a name of the Van-Dao ideals."

Then the chief of the Dairen military mission, Colonel Yasue, made a warm welcoming speech, in which he noted that the three-years of work by the Congresses not only have united Far Eastern Jewry, but also promoted the strengthening of its connection with Japan and Manchukou, and improved relations between world Jewry and these countries.

"Now the whole world experiences shocks, and the Jewish people, which doesn't have a motherland, is exposed to an ordeal unknown in a history," Colonel Yasue said, "and from my whole soul I express my sympathy toward the Jewish people. At the same time I take pleasure from realizing that, though Far Eastern Jewry, unfortunately, shares hardships with us, as a consequence of the military situation in East Asia, it nevertheless is relieved of a national ordeal, under the racial equality observed in Imperial Japan and Manchukou."

After further noting the great sacrifices which, for two and a half years, Japan and Manchukou have made, in the name of a strong peace in the Far East, Colonel Yasue thanked Jewry for its contribution to the common work.

"However, military action in the Far East hasn't stopped yet, the new structure is not complete, and consequently it is very desirable that the Jewish population of the Far East, and especially you, as the representatives of this population, assist us in fulfillment of this difficult task, even more actively, suffering together with us, these or other sacrifices. I hope fruitful work comes of the present Congress and further success in uniting the Jewish population of the Far East." Colonel Yasue finished his speech to the thunderous applause of the entire audience.

Then greetings from all the Jewish communities of the Far East began. Representatives of the following communities took the floor: From the Shanghai community, B. A. Kopeliovich, from Tientsin, D. Ye. Habinski, from Dairen, Ye. L. Kovner, from Tsingtao, Dr. V. M. Dubinski, from Mukden, N. I. Kolyaditski, from Tsitsihar and Hailar, A. Ya. Strizgak, and from the youngest community in the Far East, from Kobe, A. G. Ponevezgski.

S. S. Skidelski gave a greeting after the speeches of the representatives of communities. He noted the intensive development of the Manchukuo state and the positive circumstances in which Far Eastern Jewry exists.

One of the outstanding industrialists and philanthropists, L. G. Tsykman, also gave a salutatory speech. He said: "Gentlemen, delegates from the whole Far East Jewry. Let me welcome you on the occasion of your Congress. At the 1937 Congress, I also had the honor of welcoming you. Having expressed moral satisfaction regarding my industrial and public work, I then reported to you on the actual life situation here. Two years have passed, and I want to tell to you that now I feel an even greater satisfaction from this work, mainly because I see the fruit of my small contribution in the creation of a new and promising life for all the peoples of the Far East."

"Gentlemen, its not a secret that hundreds of tons of so-called anti-Semitic literature were sent to Japan, though there was no Jewish question there, to create popular Japanese hatred towards Jews, and, secondly to sow discord among the peoples of Manchukuo. The Japanese people has, more than once, itself felt the injustice of racial enmity. But it is free from this evil feeling of hatred towards other races and religions, and naturally hastened to distance itself from specific hatred of Jews and, in 1937, at the first Congress, in the lecture by General Higuchi, declared its attitude to the Jews and other nationalities."

"There are few countries now, where we, Jews, can freely live. I am happy to testify that Japan and Manchukuo belong among these nondiscriminatory countries, and neither friends nor enemies will push Japan and Manchukuo off their correct paths. I remember the words of one man, popular in Japan, directed to the correspondent of a foreign newspaper. 'Let us import from abroad only those ideas which correspond to the spirit and moral values of our people.' Knowing the people of Japan, I always believed that this false anti-Semitic propaganda would not bare fruit there, especially as it is not literature, but simply false vilification, in justification of immoral actions."

"Gentlemen, the men who sent you here are, in the majority business-people. Therefore I additionally want to touch on the economic part of life in our countries. You read in newspapers, and frequently hear about a new order which the authorities aspire to begin in the Far East. Let me tell you, in brief, from personal experience, what this new order turns out to be in practice, in life."

"Calmness reigns in the country, and schools, hospitals, roads and rail-roads are built. In places where one train per day plied earlier, eight passenger trains per day go now. Non-burdensome taxes, identical for all nationalities, were introduced. Agricultural schools, experimental fields, are organized."

Fertilizers are distributed to peasants. Periodically, peasants are gathered in special fields, where agronomists give the peasants advice and instructions for increasing crops. They build a lot of factories. The population earns money for itself, and begins to consume different goods. Previously, because of pover-ty, the many millions of people of our country gave away raw materials on the global market, and, by that, competed with farmers of other countries. Now, due to prosperity, the population itself consumes a significant part of the raw material, exempting the foreign market from pressure of local products."

"You observe what the sale of goods is now in the local market. Perhaps you remember how little fabrics, soap, sugar and even gramophone records were sold in the villages, and how much is sold now. The consumption of such products as sugar has increased for some years by six times, to 170,000 tons sold annually, from 30,000 tons in the previous period."

"I know that many are afraid of state control over some large enterpris-es. The manufacture of sugar, in which I have honor to participate, is also under state control and I can assure you that, contrary to other countries, the control is aimed at improvement of business and protecting it from chaos and ugly forms of competition. The norms used here are those completely protecting business people and consumers equally under the law."

"The man who sees huge growth of the country, and does not trust in the success, does not trust in himself."

"Gentlemen, you see how property rights are reliably protected here, that these rights are equal for all peoples and nationalities before the face of the law. Unfortunately we still experience unusual times, owing to which, the authorities had to introduce temporary restrictions regarding import and exchange, but these rules are identical both for the indigenous population and other nationalities."

"It is a big injustice to see in these temporary rules a desire to limit any-one's interests and rights. We should obey them completely, if we want to help the authorities with their great and noble task."

"We frequently read some people, asserting petty principles, overlooking the fact that, in this case, the future will be sacrificed. These people remind me of the one who dropped a coin in a lake, and then tried to drain the lake in order to get it. I can advise these people to take part in fishing and other trades on this lake, and then they will return their loss one hundred times, give work to the population, and keep the water for the fields."

"Gentlemen, you see what is going on in the world. You see that in Europe they have been at war for centuries, almost every ten years. They war because of prestige, because of ambitions and, as a result, the people are destroyed, ruined. We, the Jews, wander from country to country, during a war and without a war. Here, in the East, a new life is under construction."

"On the Eastern shore of the Pacific Ocean, a powerful industrial coun-try grows [Japan—LB]. In the future, it can become the same in the country on the Western shore of this ocean [Manchukou—LB]. Here, in this coun-try, free of hatred and racial enmity, we can construct a life and a quiet tomorrow. I welcome you delegates, and I wish you fruitful work for the common boon."

L. G. Tsykman's speech was listened to attentively and loudly applauded by the audience.

The Secretary of the National council, M. G. Zimin, read greetings from the Shanghai Ashkenazi Jewish community, from the chairman of the Dairen community, Mr. Rogovin, from Mr. Gurevich of the Peking community, from the naval attaché of Japan in Shanghai, Captain Inozuki, from Dr. Sudzuki.

The last greeting was from the famous Japanese Hebrew scholar, Professor Katsudgi. He spoke in Hebrew and was hailed by stormy applause.

Professor Katsudgi expressed his pleasure that he could speak Hebrew, which has a wonderful history. He spoke about the tempestuous storms abroad in the world. Certainly this Congress cannot decide all questions pressing on the life of the World Jewry, but the Jews should remember the precepts of their great prophets and keep their religion.

Professor Katsudgi finished by saying: "I am always glad to see the representatives of the Jewish people, and I shall always respect this ancient nation. I hope that the day is close at hand, when the banner of Judah will flutter proudly over an independent Jewish country, in Eretz-Israel."

Thunderous applause developed into an ovation for Katsudgi.

In a final word, the chairman of the National Council, Dr. Kaufman, declared that the authorities and Kiova-Kay always met representatives of the Jewish communities with benevolence.

"We shall build our state, Eretz-Israel, on the same basis, the commonwealth of the peoples, which is the strength of the Japanese and Manchurian peoples," Dr. Kaufman said.

THE DECLARATION OF THE CONGRESS

The Third Congress of the Jewish Communities of the Far East takes place in an extremely grave and tragic period for the Jewish people, when five million Jews in Central Europe suffer under political, national and economic yokes. The Congress calls upon Far Eastern Jewry to unite and mobilize all its forces, to act vigorous and help our brothers.

The Third Congress of the Jewish Communities of the Far East expresses its sharp protest against violence, prosecution, and persecutions of the Jewish people, its religion and principles, in a number of Central and Eastern European countries.

The Third Congress of the Jewish Communities of the Far East upholds the national viewpoint, asserts the right of each nation to an independent existence, and opposes antinational currents and movements in World Jewry.

The Third Congress of the Jewish Communities of the Far East knows that the complete solution of the Jewish question is possible only with the realization of the centuries-old ideal of the Jewish people, the Jewish state in Eretz-Israel.

With feelings of deep gratitude, the Third Congress of the Jewish Communities of the Far East acknowledges the humane attitude of the governments of Manchukuo, Japan and Northern and Central China towards the Jews, their needs and aspirations.

The Third Congress of the Jewish Communities of the Far East is glad to certify the equality of all citizens without distinction of religion and nationality, and the right of development of national culture of all nationalities, including the Jewish one, in Manchukuo, Japan, and Northern and Central China.

The Third Congress considers it necessary that this should be known to World Jewry, in Western Europe, America and all countries where Jews live.

The Third Congress expresses gratitude to Japan and Manchukuo, for recognition of the Jews here as a fraction of a unified Jewish people, and expresses the hope that all the communities in the Far East will have an opportunity to develop their initiatives according to the laws of their country of residence.

The Third Congress of the Jewish Communities of the Far East welcomes the Great Empire of the Rising Sun's aspiration for the establishment of peace and a new order in East Asia, and expresses the hope that the hour is near when the language of bayonets and the rumble of shells will break off, and under the wise leadership of Japan, all the peoples of East Asia will begin peacefully building.

The Third Congress of the Far Eastern Jewish communities calls on the Jewry of the Far East to actively participate in establishing the new order and in building East Asia, guided by the principle of struggle against the Comintern, in close collaboration with all nations.

THE CLOSING OF THE CONGRESS

At this point the celebratory session was over. Then the honorary visitors and the delegates of the Congress were invited to tables gracefully laid by ladies from the Jewish community. Wines, hors d'oevres and fruits were offered. At the supper, a "buffet table," the delegates, members of the Council and visitors exchanged their impressions.

The second session of Third Congress was held on the morning of December 24th, in the presence of the chairman and all the members of the Executive Committee of the National Council, as well as all the delegates at the Congress. Representatives of official organizations, including K. I. Nakamura and Mr. Fukuyama, the secretary of Colonel Yasue, were present as honorary visitors.

At the opening of the second session, Dr. A. I. Kaufman told of new telegraphic greetings received from the Kobe Jewish community and from the biblical Christian church "Kiova-Kay Holiness." The late Bishop Nakada used to be the leader of this church.

The program was: 1) Election of the Congress presidium, 2) The report of the Executive Committee, and 3) Reports from localities. The following were elected unanimously: Chairman Dr. A. I. Kaufman, Vice-presidents Ye. L. Kovner and G. Moris, and Honorary Secretaries, M.G. Zimin and A.G. Ponevezgski.

Dr. Kaufman devoted a brief word to Bishop Nakada, who recently died in Japan. The orator emphasized the constant special concern of Bishop Nakada towards the Jewish people. Those present paid homage to the memory of Bishop Nakada.

Then Dr. Kaufman went to the program topics.

The report of the Executive Committee of the National Council, submitted by Dr. Kaufman, was approved, and then the reports from communities began. After a number of reports, the chairman closed the session and announced that the third session would hold in the evening of the same day.

The third evening session was devoted to reports from three large communities: Harbin, Shanghai, and Tientsin, and also a general debate.

During the session, the President of the South-Manchurian Railroad kindly gave delegates sets of books and albums, five perfect items, devoted to Manchukou and the work of the South-Manchurian Railroad. At the urging of the Chairman, the Congress expressed deep gratitude to the President of the South-Manchurian Railroad for the interest rendered. Then reports of the three above mentioned communities were read. The report of the Harbin community described, in passing, Betar's work in Harbin and the recent celebration of the ten year anniversary of the Brit-Trumpeldor organization in our city.

At this point the third session ended.

The fourth and fifth sessions were held in the morning and evening of December 25. The following issues were considered: Refugee problems, the communities' activities, culture and education. A resolution was approved, that it was necessary to organize Hebrew-language schools in each community.

Social, political and Palestinian problems were also considered. During the lecture on the Palestinian problem, Dr. Kaufman proposed that those present should pay homage to the memory of the people who had been lost in the struggle for restoration of the Jewish state in Palestine.

The estimate of the National Council as 9,000 Gobi was approved. The sixth session of the Jewish communities of the Far East was held to accept the final editing of resolutions.

The resolution on the General statute was presented:

The Third Congress of the Jewish Communities of the Far East considers it necessary, and charges to the National Council to work out a common statute for all of the Jewish Communities, in accordance to the laws of each country.

The second resolution says: The Third Congress of the Jewish Communities of the Far East considers necessary and orders to all the communities to make obligatory registration of whole Jewish population within each region.

The third resolution was approved in its latest form: The Third Congress of the Jewish Communities of the Far East considers it necessary for the communities' normal functioning to have a strong financial base in each community, resulting from the obligatory imposition on all the Jews in each region of taxes without determination of the rates.

Then the Congress approved the following resolutions on religious, cultural, and educational problems:

The Third Congress of the Jewish Communities of the Far East considers it necessary for each community to have special functionaries for the execution of religious services.

The Third Congress of the Jewish Communities of the Far East proposes to the National Council to regard it as obligatory to organize special Hebrew schools.

The Third Congress of the Jewish Communities of the Far East calls all the Jewish communities to follow the appeal of the National Council of the Jews of Eretz-Israel to require obligatory Bible study.

Z. Ye. Slutsker suggested that a percentage of the community tax go to national cultural centers in Palestine, for example for the Academy of Sciences, Yeshivas, etc. After a correction by the chairman, the following resolution was approved: Taking into account the enormous significance of Eretz-Israel as the spiritual and cultural center, the Third Congress of Jewish Communities of the Far East suggests to each community to provide support for all the Jewish cultural organizations in Palestine.

According to the proposal by D. Ye. Habinski, the delegate from Tientsin, one more resolution was approved: The Third Congress of the Jewish Communities of the Far East authorizes the National Council to submit to the authorities a petition about granting to Jewish communities' rights as local representative units, subordinated immediately to the local administration.

GREETINGS FROM COLONEL YASUE

At the beginning of the fifth session, the chairman translated greetings from Colonel Yasue, who could not present at the session because of urgent matters. Colonel Yasue wished complete success to the Congress in its work and sent his regards to all the delegates. The chairman informed the delegates that, on behalf of the Congress, he would send Colonel Yasue their gratitude for his continuous benevolent attitude, and wish him all the very best in his private life and in his work for the benefit of Japan.

On Betar in Tientsin.

During one of the sessions, the Tientsin delegate, Mr. Habinski, in his lecture, recognized the extremely useful work which was made by Tientsin Ken Betar during a flood. Mr. Habinski said that people from Betar worked without fear and favor. The municipal authorities of the English and French concessions also recognized Betar's work.

CELEBRATORY CLOSING OF THE CONGRESS

The last session of the Third Congress of the Jewish Communities of the Far East was on the evening of December 26.

As well as the delegates and members of the National Council, the following were at the session: the representative of the head of the Special Sector of the Japanese gendarmerie in Harbin, Major Sazava, the head of the military mission in Dairen, Colonel Yasue, the head of the Special Sector of the Police Department, Mr. Furutani, and other representatives of the authorities, press, and public.

At the beginning of the sixth session Dr. A. I. Kaufman moved to select a place for the next Congress. D. Ye. Habinski proposed Tientsin. Ye. L. Kovner preferred Dairen. The proposal of the chairman to solve this problem immediately before the next Congress was approved.

Then delegate from Harbin, Ya. V. Zyskind, on behalf of all the delegates, proposed to elect Dr. Kaufman as chairman of the National Council, and I. M. Berkovich, M. M. Grossman, and M. G. Zimin as members of the Council. General applause of the delegates approved the election.

Then Dr. Kaufman gave a parting speech. First he recognized the benevolent attitude of the powers towards Far Eastern Jewry and proposed expressing gratitude to the central governments of the countries where the delegates came from, especially the governments of Japan and Manchukuo.

General applause greeted his words. Like applause met expressions of gratitude to the military mission in Harbin under the guidance of General Hata and Major Sazava, to Colonel Yasue, whom the delegates hailed with a standing ovation, to the Harbin Police Department and its representative, Mr. Furutani, to the organizations Brit-Trumpeldor and Maccabi, that carried the color guard of honor at the celebratory session.

Afterward Dr. Kaufman proposed to send greetings from the Congress to American Jewry, sacrificing for Polish Jewry in these hard days. In conclusion, the chairman asked the delegates to relay the best regards to their communities, and he thanked the local press in the name of the Congress.

After that, B. A. Kopeliovich, Ye. L. Kovner, and Z. Ye. Slutsker made speeches. The last gave his in Hebrew. On behalf of all the delegates they expressed great gratitude to that untiring public worker, the chairman of the National Council, Dr. A. I. Kaufman, and emphasized the gratitude of all of Jewry towards the Japanese authorities.

Mr. Beiner expressed gratitude to the Japanese authorities, and especially to Colonel Yasue, which was again met with applause. V. M. Dubinski spoke about the unity displayed by the Congress.

In reply to these speeches, Colonel Yasue gave a talk, which was translated by his secretary, Mr. Fukuyama. Colonel Yasue indicated that the people of Japan and the Jews were among the most ancient races, and supposed that some interaction between the races existed in a far past, but was broken later. He expressed confidence that new contact between these two races would initiate friendship between them.

"The significance of all three Congresses, which I attended," Colonel Yasue said, "is the foundation of concord and friendly cooperation between the two nations. Gentlemen, you should transfer to your electorate the mood of cooperation of nations, characteristic of the Congress. I wish you happiness and success."

At the closing, the chairman of National Council, Dr. Kaufman, once again recognized the great significance of the Congress and addressed the delegates with the following words:

"Gentlemen, send greetings to all the communities and allow me to close the Third Congress with our national greeting, 'Shalom.'"

"New Palestine Party: Visit of Menachem Begin and Aims of Political Movement Discussed"

Letter to the Editor
The New York Times
December 4, 1948

Few recalled Albert Einstein's prior racist monkey chatter in 1948. For the world, his theory of relativity was the mysterious key to the universe, from beyond the farthest star to the Atom bomb, which the broad public knew he proposed to Roosevelt, for fear that Hitler might otherwise invent it first.

Being attacked by such an authority was indeed like unto being hit by an A-bomb. It became impossible for Begin to recruit even politically naive American Jews on the basis of their raw Jewish nationalism, aroused to Himalayan proportions after the Holocaust. Their sympathies went over to the Laborites, who they saw as the Israeli version of their idol Roosevelt's New Deal, and their trade unions.—LB

To the Editor of *The New York Times*:

Among the most disturbing political phenomena of our time is the emergence in the newly created state of Israel of the "Freedom Party" (Tnuat Haherut), a political party closely akin in its organization, methods, political philosophy and social appeal to the Nazi and Fascist parties. It was formed out of the membership and following of the former Irgun Zvai Leumi, a terrorist, right-wing, chauvinist organization in Palestine.

The current visit of Menachem Begin, leader of this party, to the United States is obviously calculated to give the impression of American support for his party in the coming Israeli elections, and to cement political ties with conservative Zionist elements in the United States. Several Americans of national repute have lent their names to welcome his visit. It is inconceivable that those who oppose fascism throughout the world, if correctly informed as to Mr. Begin's political record and perspectives, could add their names and support to the movement he represents.

Before irreparable damage is done by way of financial contributions, public manifestations in Begin's behalf, and the creation in Palestine of the impression that a large segment of America supports Fascist elements in Israel, the American public must be informed as to the record and objectives of Mr. Begin and his movement.

The public avowals of Begin's party are no guide whatever to its actual character. Today they speak of freedom, democracy and anti-imperialism, whereas until recently they openly preached the doctrine of the Fascist state. It is in its actions that the terrorist party betrays its real character; from its past actions we can judge what it may be expected to do in the future.

Attack on Arab Village

A shocking example was their behavior in the Arab village of Deir Yassin. This village, off the main roads and surrounded by Jewish lands, had taken no part in the war, and had even fought off Arab bands who wanted to use the village as their base. On April 9 (*The New York Times*), terrorist bands attacked this peaceful village, which was not a military objective in the fighting, killed most of its inhabitants—240 men, women and children—and kept a few of them alive to parade as captives through the streets of Jerusalem. Most of the Jewish community was horrified at the deed, and the Jewish Agency sent a telegram of apology to King Abdullah of Trans-Jordan. But the terrorists, far from being ashamed of their act, were proud of this massacre, publicized it widely, and invited all the foreign correspondents present in the country to view the heaped corpses and the general havoc at Deir Yassin.

The Deir Yassin incident exemplifies the character and actions of the Freedom Party.

Within the Jewish community they have preached an admixture of ultra-nationalism, religious mysticism, and racial superiority. Like other Fascist parties they have been used to break strikes, and have themselves pressed for the destruction of free trade unions. In their stead they have proposed corporate unions on the Italian Fascist model.

During the last years of sporadic anti-British violence, the IZL and Stern groups inaugurated a reign of terror in the Palestine Jewish community. Teachers were beaten up for speaking against them, adults were shot for not letting their children join them. By gangster methods, beatings, window-smashing, and widespread robberies, the terrorists intimidated the population and exacted a heavy tribute.

The people of the Freedom Party have had no part in the constructive achievements in Palestine. They have reclaimed no land, built no settlements, and only detracted from the Jewish defense activity. Their much-publicized immigration endeavors were minute, and devoted mainly to bringing in Fascist compatriots.

Discrepancies Seen

The discrepancies between the bold claims now being made by Begin and his party, and their record of past performance in Palestine bear the imprint of no ordinary political party. This is the unmistakable stamp of a Fascist party for whom terrorism (against Jews, Arabs, and British alike), and misrepresentation are means, and a "Leader State" is the goal.

In the light of the foregoing considerations, it is imperative that the truth about Mr. Begin and his movement be made known in this country. It is all the more tragic that the top leadership of American Zionism has refused to campaign against Begin's efforts, or even to expose to its own constituents the dangers to Israel from support to Begin.

The undersigned therefore take this means of publicly presenting a few salient facts concerning Begin and his party; and of urging all concerned not to support this latest manifestation of fascism.

Isidore Abramowitz, Hannah Arendt, Abraham Brick, Rabbi Jessurun Cardozo, Albert Einstein, Herman Eisen, M.D., Hayim Fineman, M. Gallen, M.D., H.H. Harris, Zelig S. Harris, Sidney Hook, Fred Karush, Bruria Kaufman, Irma L. Lindheim, Nachman Majsel, Seymour Melman, Myer D. Mendelson, M.D., Harry M. Orlinsky, Samuel Pitlick, Fritz Rohrlich, Louis P. Rocker, Ruth Sager, Itzhak Sankowsky, I. J. Schoenberg, Samuel Shuman, M. Znger, Irma Wolpe, Stefan Wolpe.
New York, December 2, 1948

ABBA ACHIMEIR
"Diary of a Fascist"
Herut (Freedom)
Jerusalem, March 18, 1949

Abba Achimeir flagrantly ran a column, Diary of a Fascist, in the Revisionists' Palestine paper. He had his squadristi, the Brith Ha Biryonim, the Union of Terrorists, styled on the sicarii, dagger-wielding assassins during the Judean revolt against Rome.

Their outspoken line—but for his anti-Semitism, Hitler was a role model nationalist—was too much for Jabotinsky, who instructed Achimeir that "To find in Hitler some feature of a 'national liberation' movement is sheer ignorance."

After the Holocaust, Achimeir was constantly cited by the Revisionists' oppenents as the prime example of their fascist past. His defense here, "I did it, but hey, it wasn't so bad when I did it, and look what you did," convicts himself and the party whose newspaper he was writing in.

As you will see, his article sprays countercharges about incidents, in Palestine and in the Tsarist empire, that he thinks convicts his critics of being as bad, maybe worse, than him. To annotate some of his points would require another book to deal with obscure matters far removed from the accusation against him, that he was a Jewish fascist in full regalia in the Hitler period. That meant, post-Holocaust, that he was politically certifiably mad. Just keep your eye on the prize: what does the article say about Achimeir and revisionism and fascism?

In any case, his references re the "Holy Gun," refer to June 20, 1948, when the Irgun tried to land a ship full of guns for itself. The Israeli army, i.e., the Haganah, used cannon to sink it, and killed Avraham Stavsky, among others, ending the Irgun's existence as a separate force.

Numbers 25: 1-15 has Zimri murdered by Aaron's grandson, after one hell of a pissed off God ordered Moses to slay everyone bowing to their shiksa girlfriends' heathen gods. Zimri brought his Midianite before ol' Mt. Sinai Mo, and everyone took pity, "weeping before the tabernacle of the congregation." So Phinehas ups and javelins the two of them, "So the plague was stayed from the children of Israel."

To Achimeir, as fanatically opposed to mixed marriage, and as ready to do some cutting as Phinehas, Zimri is the ultimate sinner wearing an air of injured innocence.—LB

A.

The Prime Minister's response in the Knesset was not a Prime Minister's speech. It was a typical speech from a head of a party, with a clear typical totalitarian orientation. It was not a diplomatic speech "that most of the nation desires his respect," whether it was justifiable or not. In the presence of the non-"Histadrut" members of the Knesset, representatives of foreign governments, and representatives of the international press—our Prime Minister dealt with "cleaning the dirty laundry" of Mapai and Mapam. The Prime Minister went beyond a strict bounds taken from Russian culture that said "taking the garbage from the house to the outside world is not allowed." Yet, the Prime Minister did it with malicious intention and suggested that the non-Histadrut members get use to this kind of Histadrut Executive Committee language.

In this particular speech, the spiritual solemnity of a Prime Minister was not revealed, but what was? A parliamentary demagogue. And the despair is great: in the presence of the Israeli parliament (a real parliament), the Prime Minister recalls past episodes, not the "Segera" version, but the version from his homeland, this is the version from the period of the endless "Discussions," "the Kroujeki," the "Byrji" of "the year 1905."

To Mr. D. Ben-Gurion is attributed the motto "from the class to the nation." It was one of his declarations that he widely proclaimed, and that we got so accustomed to hear. However, all of his Prime Minister's speech was imbued with the spirit of change from nation to party—and the action came before the talk. The Prime Minister is responsible to the party's hierarchy, which begins with the Prime Minister's position and ends with the security officer of the lowest office. Mr. D. Ben-Gurion opens the history of Zionism with the "Segera" event. Indeed, in this regard Ben-Gurion is not the only one so dealing with its contents. The late Berl Katznelson used to begin the story of Zion with the Kineret strike. And in this sin, the sin of "the story of the Creation of the World begins with Me," other sinners besides the Histadrut sin.

There is a deep abyss between different socialist factions. Communism on one hand, and more moderate socialism on the other hand, that, prior to Hitler, was symbolized by the German Social-Democrats (SD) and now—by British Labor. Against any Communist apparatchik stands a nightmare by the name of Trotsky. Woe to any Communist apparatchik that the Secretary accuses of being a Trotskyite. And another nightmare, frightening to a SD-Laborist apparatchik, has the name MacDonald (meaning, of course, not the American representative in Kiryah, but the late British Prime Minister). This MacDonald Dibbuk is very strong in Ben-Gurion's soul. It has already caused many disasters, including the "Holy Gun." Without the MacDonald obsession (Mapam has substituted the Italian Sargetti for the British MacDonald), Mr. Ben-Gurion wouldn't have made his demagogic Knesset speech—a speech that did not honor either the Knesset or the speaker.

B.

The Prime Minister went even further. In the course of his discussion and personal accounting of the "naysayers," he wasn't satisfied with personal scandals regarding the not-'our friends' group. With the "magic" of his tongue, the Prime Minister reached the level of the "stage magician" dealing with one person who doesn't have the honor of being a Knesset member. For over ten years now, this man has been guided by the light of ancient Gideon's wise younger son in the Book of Judges 9: 7-15. The Prime Minister, in his ecstatic discussion, recalled a writer of articles titled "Diary of a Fascist." A secret is revealed to readers: The Prime Minister meant your obedient servant. And this remark, out of the mouth of a typical 1905 "Byrji" member, is the occasion of this short article.

The Prime Minister succeeded in publicly shaming the movement to which your humble servant belongs: "There is a fascist among you, God forbid." After hearing this condemnation, we were all amazed. Is "fascism" the author of this article's only public sin? There was a time when Mr. D. Ben-Gurion and his fellows publicly blamed the writer for the murder of Dr. Arlosoroff, (May the Lord revenge his blood!). Why did the former contain his "magical" oratory, and base it upon the fascist "splinter"—and not upon a heavy beam, such as the murder's details? This reminds us of Israel's haters, who shout about Jews being usurers, but omit that they use the blood of Christian babies.

C.

Before Pontius Pilate, the Roman Governor of Judaea, sentenced the Galilean to be crucified, he asked him "What is truth?" The Governor did not get an answer from Jesus. That's because there are "damned" questions, to which the seeker may get not one but a dozen answers. And, if you receive a dozen answers to your one question, it is as if you have received none.

As to the question, "what is fascism?," the seeker may get at least a dozen answers. It all depends on who you ask. If it were asked of a Histadrut apparatchik, he would answer, without hesitation, "The Herut movement is fascist." Very well. And, if you asked a member of the Israeli Communist Party (Maki) the same question, you would get the following: "Fascism in Israel, that's Mapai." And Jewish communists from Warsaw, Budapest, Bucharest or Sofia will agree, including in fascism the Zionist movement and Mapam as well. One question. Plenty of answers. Because there are many interviewed. (A member of Maki thinks Mapai is a fascist movement and Mapam is a Trotskyite movement.)

And if you would ask the author of this column: "What is fascism?"— he asks you half a dozen questions in return: Is National Socialism fascist? And today's regimes in Spain, Portugal, Argentina, South Africa? What was the character of the Pilsudski regime in Poland prior to the war? And DeGaulle, Churchill? Who do you prefer? The Socialist Bevin or the fascist Franco? And you would end your half dozen questions with a bitter remark: The existing fascist regimes did not turn their weapons towards Jerusalem and did not disturb the city, as did the socialist regime. And while the labor government caused the "Struma"—during the war, Franco's government allowed thousands of immigrants to Israel to cross the Pyrenees. (We add this remark with no intention whatsoever of defending the Spanish regime.)

In 1928 (!), your devoted servant published four-five short essays in Ittamar Ben-Avi's *Do'ar Ha Yom* [*Today's Post*]. These had a common title: "Diary of a Fascist." Only the title was fascist in these short articles. These essays had no content of fascism, unless we would accept our enemies and our excommunicators' assumption, regarding Jabotinskian thinking—that it is fascism. It has been 20 years since the publication of these essays—and not just any 20 years. Your obedient servant was then a young journalist. In fact he was on a crossroad and the shots from particular basements were still echoing in his ears. Not only people (especially youth) remind us of the butterfly in their political shifts, but also political movements. The worm turns into a cocoon and the cocoon—to a butterfly. There is a difference between Fascism in the year 1928—and Fascism 10 years later, after British diplomacy threw Mussolini into Hitler's hands. In regard to Fascism, not only the humblest of Israeli writers, but also a writer of worldwide reputation, by the name of Emil Ludwig, hailed it. Italian Fascism went downhill. And what was the destiny of British Socialism? Didn't it open with Owens, the Chartists and the Fabians and end up with slaughtering in Hebron and disrupting Jerusalem? And didn't the labor movement in Zion open with A. D. Gordon and end up with the famous sentence, with some collaboration and "the Holy Gun?"

D.

A few months after the publication in I. Ben-Avi's *Today's Post* of these short essays with the miserable title, the paper came to be directed by Ze'ev Jabotinsky. The writer of these columns was summoned to a meeting with the new editor. Jabotinsky expressed his opinion regarding Fascism, among other things. The following is a summary of what he said. First of all, he declared himself politically a son of the 19th century. The worship of the leader makes him sick; he doesn't want to discuss to what degree Fascism saved Italy from civil war; he doesn't want to get involved with the internal affairs of other nations; the Italian or the Russians' internal political regime is their nation's concern only, and we should be aware of ideological intervention. Of all the nations (except Israel, of course) the Italians are my favorites: it is the least anti-Semitic nation of them all, and I spent the happiest years of my life in Italy.

Jabotinsky concluded his conversation with the author of this essay with the following remark: "I've never given an order to anyone. I 'ask' you sir, not to be an assimilant, as is the Zionist 'Left' that uses terms taken from foreigners."

So said Ze'ev Jabotinsky. And now something about Zvi Feinberg. (May the Lord revenge his blood!) A few of us haven't forgotten Grishke yet (that is the nickname we gave him). He published a book about Mussolini. Right when the war broke out, Zvi volunteers and gets killed on the Egyptian front, when Mussolini's army tries to pave the way to the Nile Valley.

In the modest autobiography of your devoted servant there is, among other things, the period before the war with the Third Reich. Young men in Israel took the red flag with the swastika down from the German consulates in Jerusalem and Jaffa. (In the second operation, one fellow was outstanding, and a few months later, he became very famous. His name was Avraham Stavsky. [May the Lord revenge his blood!])

These men, meaning the Brit Ha Biryonim. had organized the embargo on all German imports. (Mr. Y. Lichter especially excelled in this operation.) What was the Histadrut Executive Committee involved in back then? What was this "Zimri" in Zion involved in? He was dealing with "Transfer"—with propaganda for commercial relations with the Third Reich. In the Zionist Congress in Lucerne (1935), Mr. Ben-Gurion was very enthusiastic (so he reported) about the Transfer.

Who are the fascists in Zion, if not the ones that take credit for the Transfer and collaborating with Bevin's secret service?

PART IV

The World Zionist Organization and Nazism During the Holocaust

STEPHEN S. WISE
"Letter to Franklin D. Roosevelt"

Carl Voss

Stephen S. Wise, Servant of the People

Rabbi Stephen Wise headed the American Jewish Congress during the Hitler era. In August 1942 he received information about the Nazis' new gassing program. The State Department asked him not to reveal the news until it was verified, and he kept silent, as he tells Roosevelt here, for 88 days about what needed no such verification.—LB

To the President, the White House, Washington
December 2, 1942

I do not wish to add an atom to the awful burden which you are bearing with magic and, as I believe, heaven-inspired strength at this time. But do you know that the most overwhelming disaster of Jewish history has befallen Jews in the form of the Hitler mass-massacres? Hitler's decision was to exterminate the Jewish people in all Hitler-ruled lands, and it is indisputable that as many as two million civilian Jews have been slain.

I have had cables and underground advices for some months, telling of these things. I succeeded, together with the heads of other Jewish organizations, in keeping these out of the press and have been in constant communication with the State Department, particularly Undersecretary Welles. The State Department has now received what it believes to be confirmation of these unspeakable horrors and has approved of my giving the facts to the press. The organizations, banded together in the Conference of which I am Chairman [Joint Emergency Committee for European Jewish Affairs], feel that they wish to present to you a memorandum on this situation, so terrible that this day is being observed as a day of mourning and fasting throughout the Jewish world. We hope above all that you will speak a word which may bring solace and hope to millions of Jews who mourn, and be an expression of the conscience of the American people.

I had gathered from the State Department that you were prepared to receive a small delegation, which would include representatives of the American Jewish Committee, the American Jewish Congress, and the B'nai B'rith. It would be gravely misunderstood if, despite your overwhelming pre-occupation, you did not make it possible to receive our delegation and to utter what I am sure will be your heartening and consoling reply....

Department of State Memorandum of Conversation

May 19, 1944

Only one Zionist group understood that rescue had to be their priority during the Holocaust. Irgunist Peter Bergson realized that the U.S. announcement of the gassing meant that they had to push Roosevelt to act. Ben Hecht, author and scriptwriter of Front Page, *the classic '30s newspaperman book and film, wrote a pageant,* We Shall Never Die, *bringing it into a full Madison Square Garden, March 9, 1943, and toured it to California.*

Kurt Weill orchestrated the musical accompaniment. Edward G. Robinson and other film stars worked on it. A Trotskyist journalist complained that it was too pious and memorial. Indeed recordings of it sound ponderous to later ears. But that was the state of show biz political consciousness at the time. They did the best they could think of.

The WZO forces were forced to organize a Garden event, to head off their rivals. Instead of uniting with Bergson, they pressured auditoriums in Pittsburg and other cities, who refused to rent to the pageant. Purblind hostility culminated in Nahum Goldmann of the World Jewish Congress, the international equivalent of Wise's AJ Congress, going to Washington to demand action—against Bergson, not Hitler.

The WZO element did nothing to pressure Roosevelt to loosen rules restricting '30s German-Jewish immigration, and were incapable of self-starting in the time of castastrophe. The Irgunists, as terrorists, understood, at least for a time, that they had to act, in this case, to mobilize public opinion, or Roosevelt would do nothing.

In his later years, Bergson broke with Zionism, becoming a major voice in the chorus of its Israeli critics, and a vital source of information on America during the Holocaust. Goldmann never broke with Zionism, but his remorse for his role in that era is recorded in a later document herein.—LB

Department of State
Memorandum of Conversation
Confidential

Date: May 19, 1944
Subject: Attitude of Zionists Toward Peter Bergson
Participants: Dr. Nahum Goldmann, Chairman of the Administrative Committee of the World Jewish Congress; Mr. Murray, NEA; Mr. Alling, NEA; Mr. Merriam, NE; Mr. Wilson, NE

Copies to: Jerusalem, VD, WRB (Mr. Warren) and Justice (Mr. Nemzer)

In the course of a discussion today on Zionist affairs, Dr. Goldmann referred to the accounts appearing in the press of the establishment of a "Hebrew Embassy" by the "Hebrew Committee of National Liberation" under the aegis of Peter Bergson. Dr. Goldmann gave Mr. Murray a copy of the statement which the Zionists had issued to the press in this connection. He said that the activities of Bergson and his colleagues had been a matter of the greatest concern to the official Zionist leadership and that it distressed him to see Bergson received in high places and given facilities by this Government. The entire matter, he said, was a gigantic hoax which Bergson and his group were perpetrating on the more guileless members of the Jewish community, and he drew particular attention in this connection to the fact that Bergson's committees are especially active in Chicago and Los Angeles. In other words, Dr. Goldmann said, the chief support of this group came from persons who had a less close connection with or knowledge of international affairs or of the Palestine problem, and this was true of non-Jews as well as Jews. He asserted that Bergson's activities had not resulted in the rescue of one single Jew or in the saving of a single Jewish life, and he said that now that the War Refugee Board had been established and had absorbed a great deal of the rescue work, Bergson and his associates had developed this "fantastic notion" that they were a government-in-exile, representing the stateless Jews of occupied Europe and the Jews of Palestine, which latter they regarded as being under occupation by the "hostile" forces of Great Britain. Dr. Goldmann characterized this reasoning as complete nonsense, and he said furthermore that the group in question in no way were representative of Jewry either in Palestine or abroad. He pointed out also that the distinction which Bergson now drew between the "Hebrew nation" and the American or other assimilated Jews of the world was undoubtedly devised in order to attract the financial support both of non-Zionist Jews and of non-Jews. He continued that the Zionist leadership had had many discussions with Bergson and his associates during the time they had been evolving their present ideology and that he had finally broken completely with Bergson, whom he now regarded as no longer a Zionist in any sense of the word but as simply an adventurer.

The thing which concerned the responsible Jewish organizations, Dr. Goldmann declared, was the fact that Bergson and his colleagues were free to go about the country collecting large sums of money for which they did not make any accounting and giving the impression that they were engaged in a vast humanitarian work. He alluded to the fact that Bergson and his associates were in this country on temporary visitors' visas and he also mentioned their efforts to obtain draft deferments. He added that he could not see why this Government did not either deport Bergson or draft him.

Mr. Murray replied that these were matters which were handled by different Government departments, and he made it clear to Dr. Goldmann that there was no disposition on the part of the Executive branch to support or assist Bergson or his associates.

Dr. Goldmann recalled that Eri Jabotinsky, a member of the group, had recently departed for Palestine and Turkey by air with the ostensible purpose of engaging in rescue work on behalf of the War Refugee Board. He said that he did not see how this could contribute in any way to the rescue of Jews from the Balkans, since the Jewish Agency representative in Turkey, Mr. Barlas, was the only person in Turkey who had the right to allot certificates for entry into Palestine and in addition had facilities for engaging in clandestine activities in occupied Europe which Bergson's group did not possess.

A discussion then ensued as to various aspects of Bergson's activities, including the inquiry which the Foreign Agents Registration Section of the Department of Justice is conducting with a view to determining the liability of the various organizations involved to register under the Foreign Agents Registration Act. Dr. Goldmann said that he was quite familiar with this Act as he himself had registered as the representative of the Jewish Agency, and he did not believe that Bergson's registering would in itself curtail his activities. What was needed, he asserted, was for persons in authority to have the facts laid before them and they would then see the light and desist from supporting Bergson or paying any attention to him. Dr. Goldmann mentioned the remaining members of Bergson's committee and declared that he had never heard of most of them, which he cited as showing that their claim to be representative of any element in Jewry was all the more ridiculous.

Dr. Goldmann said that Rabbi Wise while recently on the Pacific Coast had been present with Bergson at a large meeting and had questioned Bergson about his activities until the latter had admitted publicly that none of the funds which they had collected had been sent out of the country or had been employed for any purpose other than to finance the purchase of additional advertising space in the newspapers. In spite of this, however, many misguided persons continued to contribute being attracted by the prominent names appearing in the list of sponsors of the various committees and their avowedly humanitarian aims. With regard to the sponsorship of these committees by members of Congress, Dr. Goldmann said that he and other Zionists had often discussed the matter with various Senators and Representatives, with the result that almost all members of Congress, except Representative Will Rogers, Jr., had severed their connection with Bergson. This was true even of Senator Johnson of Colorado. He predicted that within the next few days Senator Wagner would issue a scathing denunciation of Bergson and that an additional several representatives, including Congressmen Celler and Dickstein, would make a public attack upon him. Insofar as Representative Rogers was concerned, he said that the Representative was a complete fanatic on the point and that he and Mrs. Rogers harbored a great admiration for Bergson which no amount of persuasion had been able to shake.

Insofar as other branches of the Government were concerned, Dr. Goldmann said that today he had addressed a letter to Secretary Morgenthau pointing out that Bergson's committee intended to float a million-dollar bond issue to be redeemed in 10 years by the "Hebrew nation." He said that in addition he would try to arrange for a group of prominent Jews to call personally on Mr. Morgenthau to expose the background of Bergson's activities. He mentioned the support which Bergson had been receiving from the War Refugee Board, and he said that he had discussed this several times with Mr.

Pehle, the Executive Director of the Board, who had taken the position that Bergson's Emergency Committee to Save the Jewish People of Europe had inspired the introduction of the Gillette-Rogers Resolution, which in turn had led to the creation of the War Refugee Board. In one of their meetings with Mr. Pehle, Rabbi Wise had gone so far as to inform Mr. Pehle that he regarded Bergson as equally as great an enemy of the Jews as Hitler, for the reason that his activities could only lead to increased anti-Semitism. Dr. Goldmann said that only yesterday he had again seen Mr. Pehle and had told him that unless the War Refugee Board disavowed Bergson it would be necessary for the World Jewish Congress to denounce publicly the War Refugee Board. Mr. Pehle had agreed to break with Bergson, but Dr. Goldmann added that if this should not take place, it would be difficult for the Zionists to press the matter in view of their obvious interest in the board's activities.

Further on this point, Dr. Goldmann said that recently Mr. Ira Hirschmann, the War Refugee Board's representative at Ankara, who is now in this country, had appeared at a reception which Bergson's Emergency Committee had given in New York City and he ventured the opinion that this fact alone was worth $50,000 to $100,000 to the Committee in additional contributions.

Mr. Wilson inquired as to Bergson's purpose in all this activity, and Dr. Goldmann expressed the opinion that it was purely a question of personal ambition on the part of a group of irresponsible young men who had to leave Palestine because the British authorities were aware of the true nature of their activities, and he asserted that their connection with the Irgun Zvai Leumi was well-known.

Mr. Murray assured Dr. Goldmann that there was no question of the Department's recognizing Bergson or any of his colleagues or organizations in any official capacity whatsoever.

YITZHAK GRUENBAUM

"About the Holocaust and About the Reaction"

Speech at Zionist Executive Meeting,
February 18, 1943
*Bi-Mey Hurban ve-Shoah (In Time of
Destruction and Holocaust)*
pp. 62–70

Yitzhak Gruenbaum had been a leading Polish Zionist before emigrating to Palestine. As head of the WZO's wartime Palestinian Rescue Committee, he defended himself against his many critics in this speech.

In his book, From Diplomacy to Resistance, *Yehuda Bauer, a Zionist scholar, described him well. Gruenbaum's mood "turned to utter despondency. He and some of his close associates thought that nothing could be done to save Europe's Jews, and that money sent to Europe for escape, resistance or rescue would be wasted." They went through the motions of rescue, but only "in order to be able to say after the war that everything possible had been done."*

From that perspective, hear Gruenbaum's speech as more than a bit like a mad scene in an opera.—LB

The bloody holocaust that came upon European Jewry is most horrible. Had we wanted to compare it to one of the disasters in our history, we would have to go back to the days of the Mongols and their assault on ancient Asia, Eastern and Southern Europe. This holocaust began, not as it has come to be thought here, in the summer of 1942, but in 1941 with the beginning of the war between Germany and the U.S.S.R. The progress of the German army in the part of Poland conquered by the Russians on the basis of the agreement between Germany and Russia, in Lithuania and Latvia and Western Russia, inhabited by millions of Jews, was accompanied by the murdering of Jews with unprecedented cruelty.

We have received information about these murders from Russian sources and, only lately, we have details about slaughtering Jews in Riga and in Latvia generally and in different cities in Moldavia, Bukovina and Bessarabia. And then—I would like to say, out of sorrow—that, not only in Eretz-Israel and not only in the Jewish world, but in general, that public-opinion was not very shocked. It was as if massacre in time of battles was the natural thing, the way it has to happen. In Eretz-Israel, the climate was of people who themselves were saved from holocaust, since it was clear that had the Germans conquered Russia, they would have entered into the Middle East, and then we would have been victims. We were lucky that, instead of us, the victims were Jews from Russia, Jews from Latvia and Lithuania, Jews from Eastern Poland and Rumania. They were the victims and their number most certainly was hundreds of thousands. And articles were written in those days about these horrors—were certainly received by sighs, but no conclusions were drawn, based on this horrible information.

In the first half of 1942, the German authorities began to systematically act against Jews. On the one hand, they began to deport the Jews of Western and Central Europe to the east, to Poland. And, on the other hand, in Western Poland, in the same part that was attached to the Reich, they started to cleanse the country of Jews. There was only one region left, Silesia, that includes the Dombrowa Valley, that didn't get hurt; there, the situation of Jews was better than in any other region in Poland in general.

How did this difference come about? It is hard to say. In this region, most Jews are working. In mines, in factories, in big workshops, established in order to satisfy the army's needs, and this seems to save most of the Jews from the destiny of the Jews in other regions in Poland.

In the same period, we got terrible news about horrible acts in Klodowa, Kalisz district, and other horrors in these places. These things were published in all the newspapers, articles have been written, but no organization called for any action whatsoever. It is worth mentioning. It is not possible to say that our public—in Eretz-Yisrael and in the diaspora, in America and England—did not know about these terrible acts. Maybe we did not know the details, but the general idea was known.

Maybe most people did not want to believe the information. In articles of the press, in columns, it was established that maybe the information was exaggerated, but something—and something horrible—was happening in Poland.

The public didn't move; and, let me emphasize, the extent by which most of the people in the Yishuv {Jewish community} in Eretz-Ysrael did not move then. Me and my friends from Poland, we dealt with little things, concerning the situation of Poland's Jews and their refugees, and we faced several examples of indifference and of unwillingness to pay attention to all of these horrors.

That is the way it was up to the summer of 1942. Then lots of information about the massacre in Poland started being received. Information started to arrive about mass deportations, accompanied by murder, from Western Europe to Poland. We didn't yet know all the details, but the horrible general picture was known.

Not once have we spoken about the events, not one article has been published in "The World," columns and articles were written in other newspapers, not once meetings were gathered and the things were made public in them—the Yishuv did not budge, did not move.

And when I then asked myself, and when I ask myself even today: why did such a thing happen, why did the Yishuv not budge, did not move then, the same Yishuv out of which we now hear so many and severe accusations, that the bloody deeds were concealed from it, I have an answer. I know that now, in a time in which each and everybody in the Yishuv thinks that he has to blame another if the latter does not scratch the wounds as strongly as he would have wanted, my answer will not be accepted. But in my opinion, there is no other answer. I do not suspect them, the people of the Yishuv, that they are capable of indifference in the face of the horrors and atrocities such as those that happened in Poland, but then—in those days the Yishuv was fearful about its own destiny. Unrest, fear overtook the Yishuv concerning the German attack in Libya and in Greece, concerning their victories in both places, that threatened our destiny here in this country, upon which depends the rest of our hopes.

Let me note here one fact, which in my opinion is very important. In July, horrible information about the bloody deeds in Poland arrived in New York, and our friends put together a very big meeting in Madison Square Garden. There were read letters from Roosevelt and Churchill, in which, for the first time, sympathy was expressed for the Jews who were suffering for being Jews. Before that, the suffering of the Jews was passed over, and when Churchill spoke about the suffering of the people of the countries that were enslaved by the Germans, he didn't mention the Jews. After everything that happened in Poland in the first half of 1942, the suffering of the Jews started to be talked about specifically, and also they started to be condoled, it was announced in front of us and in front of the entire world, that the criminals will be punished.

After this gathering, when they started to speak significantly, publicly, in this way, the author, Shalom Asch, composed a prayer, and published it in Hebrew in "Ha Doar." In this prayer, of the sort of "out of the depths I have cried unto thee," he turns to God concerning the saving of the Yishuv in Eretz-Yisrael—and Asch is not an official Zionist. He is the poet of Polish Jewry, and all his soul's roots are involved with it. And this edition of "Ha Doar" was full of articles and information about the massacre in Europe, but it starts with Asch's prayer to save the Yishuv in Eretz-Yisrael. Does this not prove, that the danger that was seen facing the Yishuv was frightening the nation's soul more than anything else?

In the second half of 1942, Poland turned into the field of slaughter for European Jewry. All the people that were expelled from France and Belgium, the Netherlands and Austria, Czech-land and Yugoslavia and Slovakia, all of these, on arrival in Poland, disappeared and their whereabouts are not known.

The French Red Cross in Paris is incapable of telling the relatives of the deported, what happened to these Jews that Laval handed over to the Germans. The same goes for Jews of Slovakia, for Jews of Germany, and other countries. And at the same time—in the second half of 1942—started what is officially called in German the "evacuation" from different towns of Poland, and the traces of the "evacuated" have disappeared too.

For a long time we didn't know the details, we knew only the general picture, which we got from different sources—Polish sources and our sources in Geneva and in Istanbul. This information was general, and the extent of the terrible events and the horrors was not known. They talked about hundreds of thousands of massacred, about 200,000 to 700,000. They even talked about a million, and about a million and a half.

Such differences in the figures did not, of course, strengthen the credibility put in them, but it was clear that there is something terrible going on in Poland, without any precedent. At the end of the summer, a message arrived that Czerniakov has committed suicide. Now we know that not only Czerniakov put an end to his life. Many Jews of the Jewish intelligentsia, lawyers and medical doctors, took his path. The names are still not all known, but the information is very reliable. And then we published articles, we had memorials, in which we talked about the situation.

I myself said at that time: I know Czerniakov. If he did what he did, it is that he did not have any alternative. They wanted to compel him to sign an order that he could not sign without seeing himself as a bastard. Now we know, from Polish sources, what the order was. He had to sign an order according to which 6,000 to 10,000 Jews a day were to report to a place that the Germans chose, to be sent to an unknown place. In Warsaw they knew that this meant to death's lap. He did not want to sign such an order and chose death.

We then asked Ehrenpreis in Stockholm and got some answers, which perhaps confirmed the information and perhaps did not. Now we know: Ehrenpreis simply did not dare send more clear telegrams, because telegrams from Sweden to Eretz-Yisrael pass through Germany. And most likely would be stopped, if he spoke clearly.

And here we arrived at the moment in which—to me at least—it was clear, that whatever happened in Poland is beyond the beyond, and, together with my friend Ries, we sent telegrams to our representatives in America and London. It was—if I am not mistaken—at the end of September, or the beginning of October. We demanded that they protest and act. They answered us—both from New York and from London—saying that they are doing whatever they can.

The information became broader and broader. All expellees to Poland were also slaughtered—the Jews of Germany, the Jews of France, the Jews of Belgium, and so forth and so forth. It seems as if the Germans do not want, or are afraid, to kill the Jews of Western Europe in their own countries, and are transferring them to Poland, where they actually slaughter them.

When I said this to the Polish envoy, Professor Kott, he jumped up, hurt, and asked me: "So, you think the Germans do that because the Poles' attitude towards Jews is so much more accommodating to extermination?" I said to him: "Sir, I know that many Jews were saved from death by the help of Poles who have hid them. But I also know that no public reaction had been made in Poland in sympathy for the Jews; and in the time—I do not know if this fact is absolutely true—that the Jewish workers in Lodz (Lizmannstadt) went on strike because they wanted to take away their wives and children and send them to an unknown place—the Polish workers did not help them, and kept on working."

Now we know that there are internal Polish documents, appeals by Poles in Poland to the Polish Government-in-Exile, in which atrocious deeds and massacre of Jews are reported, and they demand that the Polish Government react to the horrors. The documents' authors remind the Polish Government that, after the Jews would be finished with, they will start exterminating Poles. In the last documents, which are already published, there are reports about the beginning of the horrors that are committed against Poles.

There is one thing in this whole picture, that I cannot get rid of, the feeling of sorrow and sore pain that it awakes in my heart. By fate, we met men and women who had arrived here from Poland, at the end of autumn. They gave us detailed descriptions about what happened there. From them, we know that Jews went to slaughter without any one of them having in his heart the spirit to stand up for the defense of his life. I read some Polish documents, in which this is being emphasized, that the Jewish masses did not find in their souls the courage for defensive action, out of desperation, and this although they knew that there was no saving from death.

One of the survivors that arrived in Israel, a very intelligent woman, relates that a group of women stood in one courtyard, facing squadrons of soldiers ready to shoot at them. The number of soldiers and policemen wasn't high, and in the courtyard, apart from that group of women, many other groups were waiting their fate. And lo!—she said—"I wanted to shout: 'what are we waiting for, let's do something, let's assault them, isn't it so that we know that we will die anyway.' But the words did not come out of my mouth, something grabbed me at my throat." At that moment, the commander of the soldiers called to her: "disappear" and she ran away. The commander got information that she was a Palestinian citizen, and that she was on a list of women about to be exchanged for German women—and this commander had, apparently, human feelings, and did not bury the information in his pocket, and did not kill this woman as many others had been killed in similar events.

One man told me—let me tell just this one more, I shall report no more details of the atrocities—and he belongs to the active Zionists, he had some rights because he was a professional, and he waited for a certificate to leave Poland to come back to Eretz-Yisrael. The certificate was delayed, and one moment—at the eve of his getting the certificate—he came back to his house, and saw that both of his children were walking with other children to the train station, surrounded by a powerful German guard. He started to run after them. They called to him in Hebrew: "Dad, save us", but he couldn't save them, neither did he save his wife. After they took away his wife and children and sent them to a place where no one returns from, he got his visa. And now, here he is, and told me this.

It seems that by the end of October, general systematic slaughter stopped. There is not one day without the murder of a Jew, but mass slaughter has stopped. It seems that the annihilation units, in German, Vernichtung-Kommissionen, as the Jews called them, already finished their actions, they don't move anymore from town to town, and they no longer choose Jews for extermination and expulsion.

Why do I say extermination and expulsion? There is this information that a train, loaded with Jews from Warsaw, arrived at Sosnowiec and Bedzin, in Silesia, meaning that Jews that were expelled from Warsaw and other towns were not all sent to death. It is possible that the younger are sent to work on the home front.

In the middle of November, a new order was published—we got it from Istanbul and from Geneva—according to which, Jews are to be concentrated in 55 places. Among these, ghettos in big cities and entire small towns, which are supposed to turn into Jewish townships. That is: the non-Jewish population would be made to leave, make room, for Jews. During November and December, this concentration should have been completed. It seems that this order doesn't hurt Jews working for the war effort. These have to settle down in their working-places, in huts near the working-places, sometimes with their families, sometimes without their families. There is information, according to which, it happens that these Jews were transferred to these huts with their families, but when they went to work and came back, they did not find their families in their apartments, they did not find their children. They were sent out of these places and disappeared.

Gentlemen, if you take the list of these towns, the townships that are supposed to turn into Jewish townships, you will find towns and townships, in which the percentage of Jews was maximum 20 or 30 percent. It means that 70-80 percent of the non-Jewish residents of these townships will have to leave their places, make room for Jews.

You can describe to yourself, what feelings it would awake in hearts of Poles and in hearts of Ukrainians, who will be forced to leave their places for the Jews, and they also do not know where they will go and what their destiny will be in the new places. It isn't clear from this version of the order, whether the German authorities, helped by local police, will evacuate the natives, in order to have places for Jews, or they have to go of their own free will. I doubt if they will go of their own goodwill, but we do not know what happened in Poland in these months. The latest information is from October. Whatever has happened in these two months, starting in mid-November, we don't know, and it is evident that something happened, and I shall not be surprised if, within some time, we will get horrible information on a process of Jewish concentration in those specific 55 spots.

All these horrible deeds cost the Germans very little. No one defended himself. Nothing exceptional happened in Poland, owing to these horrors. Thousands, myriads of Jews waited quietly, out of some horrible apathy, in courtyards and squares, to be led to train stations, to be loaded onto freight cars, their floors covered with wet limestone, and the doors shut down and all the cracks sealed.

The Poles say—I am not sure if it has been translated and published in our newspapers—that in one place many Jews were at a loss, and they ran onto the cross which stood in the middle of the square and shouted for the messiah to save them. No one has been saved. All of them were lost.

This is the picture in general lines. The time will come when we will know all the details, and among the details, things that will awaken—I do not know whether in all of you, within me in any case—feelings of bitter shame without parallel. I didn't think that Poland's Jews wouldn't defend themselves in such cases, that there would not be one leader to awake them, to die defending themselves.

Yes, I know that in 1939 and 1940 the Germans were working with a fixed plan. They have the science, they are programmatic, they have the machines, and, first of all, they killed the Jews' souls, murdered all their spirits, humiliated them, crushed them down to dust. People, whose souls get killed, can't stand up for the soul that has been killed, that has been murdered, except on two or three occasions, about which the truth isn't clear, there is no information about self-defense. As for myself, I can't console myself. Our education for defense, since the time of the pogroms in Russia, our Zionist education, the Socialist education, was not there for the Jews in this time of horror and atrocity.

We face the question: what should we do? And the first thought arises: first of all, we have to do everything that we can, in order to stop the slaughter, and save. What we were not able to do in the time of Rommel's attack, was possible after Rommel started to withdraw, and the situation at the outskirts of Stalingrad changed. At the same time, the allies started to talk differently.

I have no doubt that, had the situation in the front not changed for the best, no one would have talked to us, for better or worse, about this matter. In the previous war, they hushed up the Armenian massacre—to hush up the Jewish massacre, this isn't so very difficult.

But here—let me talk about this side of the picture as well—here, there is only one treatment, that is universal to every disaster, to every catastrophe. First of all, we start to attack the leaders, they, of course are guilty. The Jewish Agency is guilty, the Zionist Executive is guilty, the National Committee is guilty, for it is clear and known that had we not wanted, that had we not cried out—we have this belief in the voice of Jacob, that this voice can do everything—had we cried out, had we demanded, everything possible immediately would have been done to save, to help. And, if they didn't do anything—deduce of it, that's because we did not cry out, we did not make any demands, we did not utter the voice of Jacob.

I do not want to destroy these illusions. It is OK for the Jews. Who will they cry to? They can demand that I resign because of everything that has happened. Can they actually demand that from Roosevelt, from Churchill? And when they say in some newspaper that I am an anti-Semite, it is because they know that it will hurt me, in that they also find a bit of consolation, but, if they say that Churchill is an anti-Semite, I don't know whether it would hurt him.

We had in front of us the question of rescue, of help, and we started the actions. The free diaspora in South Africa, in England, followed the Yishuv. We have received information that on February second, a big general gathering will take place again, in Madison Square Garden, to demonstrate for a second time about what is happening in Europe.

The governments moved as well. A declaration has been published, not private letters of Churchill and Roosevelt, but an official statement from the United Nations, threatening judicial procedures against everyone involved in the slaughter. We were happy with this declaration. Earlier we could not get such a declaration. But it is clear that it cannot stop the slaughter, it cannot save even one Jewish soul. Its purpose is to put fright and fear in the Gestapo people, and the German authorities. I let myself doubt whether it actually had this effect of fright and fear, that would compel them—the German authorities, and even the authorities of Rumania and Slovakia—to stop the acts of extermination.

From the German press, and from the press of those nations whose governments collaborate with Germany, it is possible to see that they have no fear. There are somehow signs, although it is hard to detect them, that something is moving, although not out of the fear made by the declaration, but because the United Nations have begun to win. This apparently undermines the belief in the Germans' final victory, and it starts to give signs that we may be able to exploit, if we dare.

I don't want to get into all the plans, demands, schemes, that have been proposed to us by word-of-mouth and in writing. Among these there are some that it are possible, and we need to dwell upon. There are some among them, which are not worth spending even one moment. And one thing is characteristic in all of them: we do not ask ourselves, not at all, what is the real attitude of the Allies? For several months already, the Polish Government demands retaliatory acts. It demands that Germany should systematically be bombarded, not only places of strategic and military importance. And it— the Polish Government—does not succeed with this demand. It proposed that the Polish Squadron would take care of these things, and they did not let it. Because there is a strategic war calculation. The Poles say to us: "We talk with the British, but we cannot move them from their stances. They are not used to punitive-retaliation acts. Maybe you"—they say to us—"maybe you, the Jews, will be able to influence; go, give it a try." Mocking the poor.

And lo!, for example, to rescue Jews, especially women and children, from the conquered nations, it was necessary that neutral nations give them a shelter, that warring nations open their gates to those who escape. When we propose to demand this, through our friends, we are told: "You have to be more considerate of their stands, of the danger that revolves around them if they make a try at such rescue activities. And some say: "Don't touch this thing, After all you know that no one wants to let Jews enter South Africa, the United States. Do not put our friends in such a difficult trial." And the public cannot accept, and resign itself to understand, all these calculations, it does not understand them, it does not want to understand them.

I doubt very much though, that, through our demands and outcries, it is possible to achieve the stopping of the slaughter, to achieve rescue. If the slaughter will stop—it will be thanks to Russian victories, and British and American.

And the same goes for help. Of course it is always possible to find some crack, some hole, through which it is possible to give help. But we are not talking only about helping our friends. When I think about the destiny of Jews that have concentrated in the 55 sites, it is clear to me that our help should be help to the masses.

The Joint sits in America, in 1941 it took care of help to Poland, and in 1942 it stopped, and I don't know if there is any way to move it, to renew its help, and find holes and cracks, to give help.

With regard to all that is happening to Jews in Europe, the International Red Cross situation resembles its situation in the time of the Armenian slaughter. It can do almost nothing, because they do not let it enter countries conquered by the Germans.

It seems that in these last days, a crack has been opened; but there is no answer to the need to provide for the masses. We have to make use of every crack and every hole to provide help. But anyone who wants to comfort himself in this help and its size—may he be comforted, I can't be.

Meanwhile a mood has begun to sweep over Eretz-Yisrael, which I think is very dangerous to Zionism, to our efforts for redemption, to our war of liberation. I do not want to hurt anybody, but I can't understand how is it possible that such a thing could occur in Eretz-Yisrael, something that never happened abroad. How is it possible that, in a meeting in Jerusalem, people would call to me: "If you don't have enough money, you should take the assets of Keren Ha Yesod; you should take the money from the bank, there is money there."

I thought it obligatory to stand up before this wave. In the past, comrades in Eretz-Yisrael accused me of "Sejm Zionism." But, in the hot days of elections to the Sejm (Polish parliament), we put Eretz-Yisrael at the top of our aspirations: We convened meetings for the benefit of Keren Ha Yesod. But here, in Eretz-Yisrael, nobody paid any attention to these actions of ours—and created this term of disrepute, "Sejm Zionism," that has us allegedly evading real Zionism.

But these days in Eretz-Yisrael, things are said: "Don't put Eretz-Yisrael at the top of your priorities, in such a difficult time, in an hour of catastrophe and destruction of European Jewry." I do not accept such a saying.

And when some asked me: "Can't you give money from Keren Ha Yesod to save Jews in the Diaspora?," I said: "No!" And again I say no. I know that people wonder, why I found it necessary to say this. Friends teach me that, even if these things are right, there is no need to reveal them in public, in such a time of sorrow and concern. I disagree. I think we have to stand before this wave that is pushing Zionist activities into the second row. Have I said this to glorify my tenets? And, because of these things, people called me an anti-Semite, and concluded that I'm guilty, for the fact that we don't give ourselves completely to rescue actions.

I am not going to defend myself. The same as I'm not going to justify or defend myself, if they would blame me for murdering my mother, so I'm not going to defend myself in this case. But my own comrades did not have to abandon me in this battle, and then even comfort my soul later: "If you were connected with any political party, we would have known how to put the reins on you." I think it necessary to say here that Zionism is over everything.

Whenever the Jews underwent a disaster, our ancestors saw the footsteps of the Messiah. Our history does not extol the pleaders that arose in times of catastrophe and destruction, and found cracks and holes, straightforward and winding paths, tricks and ruses, and saved whatever they saved. But history extols the Messiahs, that made heroic efforts for the redemption of the nation. Our nation exists by virtue of these Messiahs, who tried to redeem but did not redeem. And from those days on, there was no structure built which resembles this, which we have built in the last 50 years.

The last few months, I stood in debate with a person who said "The Zionists want to give only that which can be spared from the efforts and resources needed for building Eretz-Yisrael for the rescue of the diaspora in conquered Europe." And he asks: "Will you not stop the work in Eretz-Yisrael, at a time in which Jews are being murdered and slaughtered by hundreds-of-thousands and by millions, at a time in which there is a need to concentrate all the efforts for their rescuing? Do not establish new settlements, do not engage yourself in building the country, disburse the money for needs of rescuing and helping the downtrodden diaspora."

But, if Zionism is not above all, the answer to all these demands can only be positive. If Zionism is not the central point of each and any era, in time of catastrophe or in usual times, then the answer may be only positive. Hence it is necessary to take all the money of Keren Ha Yesod, and use it only for this goal: rescue and help. Rescue and help need plenty of money, not only demonstrations and screaming.

On June 19, 1942, it was decided within the Executive, after long discussions, that we have to proclaim a special fund for the help to the Jewish refugees from Poland, in the U.S.S.R. We were supposed to start working immediately, but, in July, Rommel arrived at the outskirts of Alexandria, and then began the mobilization-fund activities, and the committee that was supposed to take care of collection of money for helping the refugees has not been established. And I ask you—what should we have concentrated on, at that time: the mobilization-fund or the collecting of money for the help to the refugees? We concentrated on the mobilization-fund. Now there are Jews among us, whose conscience is not clear because of this, who do not give themselves an account of their mood in those past days, and they justify themselves and say: "We didn't know, the information was hidden from us."

Who didn't know? Who disguised the information? In the Zionist gathering convened by Keren Ha Yesod, I dwelt upon the atrocities happening in

Poland and in other countries of conquered Europe. I described the horrid picture, as was known to us in those days. What came out of this—the mobilization-fund, the Keren Ha Yesod collecting?

Could we have spoken at that meeting about other collections? Why are people coming now, with accusations of disguising the information, of not alerting them about rescue activities? These people do not want to confess that their own hearts were incapable of comprehending the horrid descriptions.

I dare to tell you that, even in Warsaw nowadays, such demands would not be made public. There, in Warsaw, they know that the only and last hope is solely in Eretz-Yisrael. If we manage to succeed, we have rescued a whole nation. If we do not manage here and, even if we will rescue whatever we can rescue in the diaspora, we will save for a life that we do not need to describe, here, what kind of life it is, even in the best days.

I said these same things in the Zionist meeting. I said it later, when anxiety for the destiny of the Yishuv arose. Then they accepted the things. But then, when spirits quieted, and anxiety for Eretz-Yisrael's destiny had stopped or weakened, accusations began.

I wish to end with some suggestions. Of course it is incumbent upon us to continue all action for the sake of rescue and not neglect one opportunity that can be used to stop the slaughter. We have to demand retaliation-activities, associate our forces and our influence with the forces and influence of those Poles who demand this. Let us not be frightened that we will not be received nicely when we will demand these actions. Let us not be afraid of being told that we are "Shylocks" and so on. We have to tell to all these kindhearted people, that had even a small percentage of all that happened to us, happened to the people of their countries, all these moralists, all these quackers, would be furious and would demand punitive-retaliation activities. But, since the thing did not happen to them, only to the Jews—they are moralizing.

We have to demand alternative compensation, we have to demand that the gates will be opened; and we must not be considerate of the position of this or that master among those who hold power, of this or that friend of ours, nor should we be considerate of his fear that his political position will be undermined because of our pressure upon him. At least it will be him telling us that he cannot fulfill our demand, not we saying that he cannot do it, hence we should avoid demanding. Secondly, we have to exploit every possibility, every crack and hole, to be of help to the tortured people. In my opinion, my comrades have made little amendments to my proposition, we should have created a special operation that will take care of everything that can be done in order to rescue and help. Someone has to devote himself to this matter. The operation, which will be the tool for this work, should be turned over to him. We need to proclaim a funds collection, which will make available to us the many means needed for help and rescue. We need to decide in which form we will manage this collection.

I would like to once more emphasize that we have to do whatever we can to help and to rescue, as much as it is possible to rescue. We need to use all our influence and all our forces, in order to bring about a change in the situation of the Jews of the conquered countries in Europe, as much as it will be in our ability. At the same time, we also must guard Zionism. There are those who think that this should not be said in the time of catastrophe which came upon us, but, believe me, lately we see worrisome phenomena in this respect. Zionism is above all. This has to be proclaimed whenever a catastrophe diverts us from our war of redemption in Zion. Our war of redemption does not arise directly from the very fact of a catastrophe, and does not interlock directly with actions for the benefit of the diaspora in the time it exists—and this our disaster. This situation does not exist for any other nation. We have two areas of action. Theoretically they connect and interlock, but they are actually two separate areas of activity, and sometimes they clash with one another. And it is incumbent upon us—especially in times like these—to hold to the supremacy of the war of redemption.

"Rabbi Michoel Ber Weissmandel's Personal Story: Part III"

Jewish Guardian
Summer 1986

Michoel Weissmandel was one of the outstanding figures of the Holocaust era. An Oxford student when the war broke out, he returned to his native Slovakia as the representative of the Agudat Yisrael, then an anti-Zionist Orthodox movement. He was the first to demand the bombing of Auschwitz. Captured, he sawed his way out of a moving train with an emory wire, broke his leg, and continued to rescue Jews.

His post-war book, Min HaMaitzer (From the Depths), *written in Talmudic Hebrew, is a gripping narrative and a powerful indictment of the Zionist and assimilationist leaders in Palestine and the West.*

He had bribed a Nazi official and temporarily stopped the deportation of Slovak Jews to Poland. He reasoned that money from Jews in the Allied world could be used to stop or slow down the death of more Jews, and he pleaded for help, getting a singular answer.—LB

At that time there were already many needs for the money: to bribe those who enacted the decree and the police in all the cities in Slovakia. Money was needed for the three work camps in Sered, Novoky and Vihena in Slovakia, which were the basis for rescue work. Money was needed for those fleeing to Romania and Hungary; for those who fled from Poland through our country to Hungary and Romania, even though at the time there were not as many as in the following months; and there was a need for money for thousands who had no livelihood.

Also at that time, there was that fearful situation which I spoke of earlier which required that money and items worth money be sent to those exiled from our country who were still in the first exile in Lublin before being killed in the extermination camps. It was still possible to live a day-to-day existence by bartering money and items for food from the Poles. We explained that their aid alone we needed thousands of dollars. I wrote in detail after our Rov wrote in general.

I went to Pressburg where Mrs. Fleischman, of blessed memory, spent hours writing flattering and obsequious letters to Sali Meyer of the Joint and the Agency in Switzerland. She also wrote a personal letter to one man by the name of Nathan Schwalb of whose efficiency and devotion she constantly spoke.

In a few days the messenger returned empty-handed without even a letter. They told him to say that they had no time then and when another messenger arrived there, they would write. We were dumbfounded, as if the house had fallen on us. Mrs. Fleischman began to say that "Uncle Sali Meyer is an old and cautious man. It is necessary to write again and to send a copy to Silberstein who heads the Congress; the jealousy between Silberstein and Meyer will result in action. It is also necessary to depend mostly on the Agency and especially on Schwalb. Perhaps because this is such an important matter someone needs to travel immediately to America or to England or perhaps to Eretz Yisroel."

I wrote a desperate letter in the name of the rabbis. We sent messenger upon messenger and alarming letters in which we cried and begged. Meanwhile, the seven weeks passed, and we asked Hochberg to tell Wisliceny that the messenger had an accident on the way and broke his legs and was in a hospital in Switzerland. He let us know that he would be well in three or four weeks time and would return. So Wisliceny extended the time limit.

Finally, the day of salvation arrived. The messenger returned with a letter to the home of Reb Binyomin Shlomo. I was there, and I opened the letter with trembling hands. There were only a few words written by Meyer, and in summation the whole terrible letter said, "There is no money." Several reasons were given for this:

1) The sum of $50,000 is a huge sum for a small state such as Slovakia, and the budget which Slovakia received last year from the Joint was only several thousand dollars.

2) Your stories claiming that this year you need more money, and the letters you have gathered from the Slovakian refugees in Poland are exaggerat-

ed tales. This is the way of "Ost-Juden" (Eastern European Jews), who always demand money.

3) Presently there is no legal avenue to send even one penny, because our organization's money was contributed from America, and there is a law there forbidding dissemination of their currency in enemy countries.

4) It is possible to make a monthly allotment, as was done before the war in Hungary. However, this can be done only by consent of the Joint and must take the form of a payment against a debt incurred before the onset of the war.

There was another letter in the envelope, written in a strange foreign language which at first I could not recognize. Then I realized that it was Hebrew written in Roman letters, and it was written to Schwalb's friends in Pressburg. It took up a page and a half. It is still before my eyes, as if I had reviewed it a hundred and one times. This was the content of the letter:

"Constantly to be before us that in the end the Allies will win. After their victory they will divide the world again between the nations, as they did at the end of the first World War. They then unveiled the plan for the first step, and now, at the war's end, we must do everything so that Eretz Yisroel will become the State of Israel, and important steps have already been taken in this direction. About the cries coming from your country, we should know that all the Allied nations are spilling much of their blood, and if we don't sacrifice any blood, by what right shall we merit to come before the bargaining table when they divide nations and lands at the war's end? Therefore, it is silly, even impudent, on our part to ask these nations who are spilling their blood to permit their money into enemy countries in order to protect our blood—for rak b'dam (only with blood) shall we get the land. This is in respect to everybody—but in respect to you, my friends, Atem taylu, and for this reason I am sending you money illegally with this messenger."

After I had accustomed myself to this strange writing, I trembled when I realized the meaning of the first words which were, "only with blood shall we attain the land." But days and weeks went by, and I did not know the meaning of the two last words. I finally realized that the words "Atem taylu" were from "Tiyul" (to walk) which was their special term for "rescue." In other words: You, my fellow members, my nineteen or twenty close friends, get out of Slovakia and save your lives, and with the blood of the remainder—the blood of all the men, women, old and young and the sucklings—the land will belong to us. Therefore, in order to save their lives it is a crime to allow money into enemy territory; but to save you beloved friends, here is money obtained illegally.

It is understood that I do not have these letters, for they remained in Slovakia and were destroyed with everything else that was lost. There were many people at the home of Reb Shlomo at the time the letters arrived, a few of whom are still alive today. They all remember well what they saw and heard at the time—the anger and crying over what their eyes and mine saw written in these frightening letters.

Mrs. Fleischman and her friends, although they were leading Zionists, did not know Hebrew. Months later when their anger was magnified toward those active in public service in the free world, due to their indifference concerning our debts to those evil men who held our lives in their hands, I reminded them of the letter to make them understand that their question was an answer and not a question. If the question is why were they not sending money, the answer was that they were insane—and the letter was proof that this was so.

They brought the letter and I translated it for them. It was like a flash of lightning in the dark of night, showing them how deep the chasm was, as revealed in the clear words of those destroyers. They, too, wrung their hands in bewilderment regarding their question arose. There is a limit between blood and land—a very decisive boundary—when blood shall be the price of the land, and when land shall be the price of blood. If there is no nation without a country, there certainly is no country without people, and where are the vibrant Jewish people if not in Europe? Who is insane enough to place his thought and effort on land to the complete neglect of the people?

Several weeks after this meeting, the schedule for deportations began again in Slovakia. As always was the manner of these evil people, they tried to frighten us in order to extract the ransom money. With great haste, we wrote a weeping letter to Zurich. Mrs. Fleischman still had the words of the friend Nathan dancing and penetrating before her eyes. How can anyone in the land of peace and plenty preach wisdom and counsel patience to those in the land of despair? And Mrs. Fleishman (may G-d avenge her blood) wrote this:

"We are only asking for money, which can be lost and can return; but human life, when it is lost, never returns. Therefore I will conclude with the teachings of Nathan—don't forget the most important matter."

The situation was frightening. The deadline of seven weeks Wisliceny had made conditional was over at the end of Av 1942, and the deadline for all excuses and postponements also had arrived. I forged a letter from Switzerland with the fictional name of Ferdinand Roth, the same imaginary official of world Jewry mentioned above. He wrote to his nephew that he was very sorry that his illness was keeping him hospitalized longer. If it were only possible he would write himself, but he did not know his address. He asked that he not go, but that he should wait another two weeks and at most three and he would come to visit. On the strength of this letter and the explanation given through Hochberg, Wiliceny again agreed to extend the time limit.

Meanwhile, we sent letter upon letter by way of diplomatic messengers hired with great difficulty and danger. Letters pleading and swearing, letters crying and cursing, begging the Joint, the Congress and the Agency and any agency with money to have pity on us. It was obvious that the Allies would overlook the sum of $50,000—for of what importance was it? Even if they did not ignore it, how did their laws bind us? It is the Jewish religion which rules over Jewish blood—the law of the Torah which decrees that you shall not stand by idly as your neighbor is being killed. But all our cries were to no avail.

Holocaust

We still hoped that the money for the general necessities would arrive any minute. We could not perceive how money could be refused those exiled to Poland who were dying by the thousands from starvation and lack of everything. For even before the deportations were stopped in Slovakia—after the first shipment of goods was sent to Poland, hundreds of letters were received with news of enough suffering to melt a heart of stone. We sent dozens of these letters, originals and copies to those leading the community in Switzerland. We reasoned that if we, who had no means of livelihood, were giving our savings and treasures upon which we depended for food and to save our lives, certainly those in the free world would send much money, as much as we asked and was needed. Certainly they would do so immediately, for they were only appointed over the money of the Jewish people, collected in synagogues in America and other free countries. They were not giving their personal belongings. On the contrary, they were being paid and honored to allot this money.

How were we to know that there were two refutations to this reasoning: that of the "Western Jew" who is assimilated and that of the nationalist "Zionist?"

How were we to know that the Western Jew, the member of the Joint, would refute the basis of our reasoning and tell us openly, "There is no urgency there and no room for getting excited—there is no blood and no tears, only the conniving of the 'Eastern Jew' in order to get undeserved money? Everything is false, this is only the well-known ploy of fearful tales of the schnorrer from Poland, district Lublin. We won't be impressed by these letters. We already know the crooked way of the Eastern Jew with which he extorts the good money out of the pocket of the Western Jew who is honest and straight."

How could we dream that the Zionist nationalist member of the Agency would say, "Of course, it is an urgent time? But the urgency is not there in exile, not with your blood or tears. There is something more urgent: 'building the land.' Of course, there is room for reasoning as to what is more and less important, but your blood is less important. Spill it in joy, for it is unimportant, and with it we will buy what is more important. With it the land will belong to us."

Even if we had already seen their rebuttals written black on white, we felt that it could not possibly be true. This is only an old cantor, an old poet bachelor. The address was incorrect. They need only one more letter to clarify things. Mrs. Fleischman will write gently, and I harshly, on the matters and they will immediately open the gates of money for the rescue of the Jews remaining in Slovakia, and to save our Jewish brothers exiled to Poland and those living there."

JULIAN KOSSOFF
"Full Version of *Perdition* to be Published"
Jewish Chronicle
London, November 27, 1992

In 1987, Jim Allen, a leading British TV playwright, wrote a stage play, Perdition, *based on incidents in* Zionism in the Age of the Dictators. *Days before opening, it was driven out of the theatre by Zionist intimidation.*

It backfired. Allen and director Ken Loach were too well-known to be isolated. Allen, Marion Woolfson and I debated the play and the history behind it, on nationwide prime time TV, against Zionist Sir Martin Gilbert, the Churchill family's "official" historian, rabbi Hugo Gryn and Dr. Stephen Roth, chair of the British Zionist Federation.

We won. The Zionists admitted that the public felt that they had taken away its right to see the play. But they then resorted to using Britain's notorious libel law against Allen.

Decades ago, the U.S. Supremes basically said "don't waste everyone's time with libel suits. If you're a political figure, folks can say anything about you." But British law still works back-asswards in double reverse. Someone can sue a writer for libel, and the law works against the writer until his innocence is established, often at huge expense.

Schwalb, now known by his Hebrew name, Dror, sued Allen, who found Schwalb's letter in my book and put it in his play. Allen had to publish Perdition *in expurgated form, with a blank space where a character quoted the letter.*

Eventually there was a judicial day of reckoning and the Zionist hustle failed. Better yet, the play was restaged, to enor-

mous publicity, with reviewers proclaiming its honesty and humanity.—LB

The collapse of a libel action has allowed the controversial anti-Zionist play *Perdition* to be published in full for the first time.

The play, due to be reissued this week, was at the center of a major storm in 1987 when its planned performance at the Royal Court Theater was cancelled after angry protests from the Jewish community.

Written by left-wing British playwright, Jim Allen, the play alleges that Zionists collaborated with the Nazis.

The publisher, Pluto Press, omitted several pages from the original text because of a libel action which was brought by Nathan Dror, a senior figure in the Israeli Labor Federation, who headed the Jewish rescue committee in Switzerland during the war.

He brought the action against Mr. Allen for references to a letter quoted in *Perdition*, allegedly written by Mr. Dror during the Second World War, which claimed Jewish deaths would help justify the foundation of a Jewish state.

The action, heard in the High Court in London, collapsed due to lack of evidence.

Anti-Zionist Israeli writer Uri Davis, who is acting as consultant to Pluto Press, said: "This marks the end of attempts to suppress the play."

Mr. Davis said the debate created by the play had helped a "consensus to emerge" which showed "you could be an anti-Zionist like Jim Allen without being an anti-Semite."

Meanwhile, Dr. David Cesarani, director of the Wiener Library, who was involved in the original campaign against the play, commented this week: "Critics of Israel established their credibility in the peace movement long before Jim Allen's tawdry piece of propaganda..."

DR. REZSÖ KASZTNER

The Report of the Budapest Jewish Rescue Committee— 1942–1945

Schwalb's letter was an incident in Allen's play, which focused on Laborite Rezsö Kasztner (aka Rudolf Kastner), head of the Zionists' Rescue Committee in Budapest during the extermination of most of Hungarian Jewry. In 1946, the real life Kasztner wrote a Report to the WZO on his activities. He appended two letters from an American diplomat, as defense against accusations that he collaborated with Adolf Eichmann.

In 1953, the Israeli Labor government, on Kasztner's insistance, prosecuted a Hungarian pamphleteer for libeling him, calling him a collaborator. But the judge found that he had cooperated with Eichmann, and then, after the war, gone to the defense of a war criminal he had dealt with.

Kasztner appealed, but was assassinated in 1957, before the Supreme Court's decision. When it came down, in 1958, they ruled, 3-2, that he wasn't guilty of collaboration because, as one judge wrote, "There is no law ... which lays down the duties of a leader in an hour of emergency toward those who rely on leadership and are under his instructions." But they voted 5-0 that he had indeed perjured himself on behalf of a Nazi.

Subsequent research, presented by Shoshana Barri (Ishoni) in the Journal of Israeli History *(1997), reveals that Kasztner tried to help seven murderers escape punishment:*

"We may conclude that Kastner turned the war criminals with whom he had negotiated during the war into purer indi-

viduals in his own mind, in order to be able to live with himself.... Certainly the Jewish Agency knew of some of them [testimonials—LB], while with regard to the others the picture is less clear. Yet archival sources suggest the probability that the Jewish Agency was aware of them all."—pp. 141, 145.

Israel not yet born, there was no Jewish representative on the Nuremberg War Crimes Tribunal. The Jewish Agency saw Kasztner as being uniquely acquainted with so many prime murderers that he could testify and, in effect, be their representative to the court:

"What appeared possible in 1946-1948 in the American zone of occupation [in Germany—LB] and in correspondence which took place behind the scenes, was perceived as astonishing in the Israel of the 1950s, in a trial in court. Kastner's testimony on behalf of Becher was already known to members of the Jewish Agency in the late 1940s, but they could not admit this and stand behind Kastner (even insofar as basic knowledge was concerned) in the period of the trial and thereafter, for fear of public backlash."—p. 151.

The enormity of the Nazi crime, 5 plus going towards 6 million murdered Jews, made the WZO's pre-war and Holocaust strategies of accommodation and utilization of Nazism unacceptable, politically and psychologically in the post-Holocaust era. World Jewry was reading novels like John Hershey's The Wall, *about heroic Zionist youths who resisted in the Warsaw Ghetto. And Zionism's own military prowess in 1948 contrasted sharply with Kasztner's behavior, including getting three Zionist parachutists, sent to organize resistence, to surrender, in the interest of preserving Kasztner's deals with the murder machine.*

In any case, Kasztner's German manuscript is 188 pages, single spaced, far too long for complete inclusion here. In excerpting the provisional translation (I am donating a copy to New York's Center for Jewish History libriaries) two concerns were uppermost in mind.

1) To be fair to him, by letting him defend himself.
2) To give readers a clear picture of what happened in Hungary.

Like most people defending themselves, "he doth protest too much." Once edited, Kasztner, a lawyer, capably defends himself, showing the difficulties confronting Hungarian Jewry in 1944, when Germany marched in and took over what had previously been an ally.

Hungary had already put young Jewish men into slave labor battalions attached to the Hungarian Army. There was no possibility of serious armed Jewish resistance. But everyone involved knew that Germany was certain to lose the war. The point was to help people escape, hide, etc.

Kasztner wrote so Zionist leaders could understand him. However, as many readers will not recognize the Palestinian "Grand Mufti" of Jerusalem, Amin al-Husayni, let me introduce him.

He tried to get rid of the threatening Zionist colonizers by allying himself first with Mussolini, then with Hitler. After the war, he was seen as a major war criminal for mobilizing Muslims in the Soviet Union and Yugoslavia to fight on Hitler's side against the Red Army and Marshall Tito's partisans. They, not the Zionists, insisted on putting him on the wanted list.

For more information on him, readers are referred to chapter 8 of Zionism in the Age of the Dictators.*—LB*

FOREWORD

pp. 1-2:

The Budapest Vaadat Ezra Vö-Hazalah (Help and Rescue Committee, known as the Vaadah in the following) hereby submits the following report about its work....

This report is a summary of the most important points of this work. Some things will seem paradoxical to outsiders, they may seem incredible and unbelievable. These were crazy times. These events often seemed to us, who were involved in them, as unfathomable and eerie. They were not understandable by normal rules of human behavior....

How was it even possible to receive a present of Jewish lives from the SS?... The fact is that the annihilation of Jews slowly stopped in the summer of 1944.... Hitler did not change his perspective.... But from the middle of 1944 on, the Administrator of this total death sentence, the almighty SS head, Heinrich Himmler...began to doubt this was the right way to go. We had gradually discovered this fact. The threads of our negotiations led to him.... As a palpable proof of this change, 318 Hungarian Jews from Bergen-Belsen, were allowed to leave for Switzerland on August 21, 1944....

pp. 3-4:
From Chaim Arlosoroff's Transfer Agreement, between Palestine and the Third Reich (1933) until Hitler's collapse, more than one attempt was made by the Jewish side to mitigate the harshness of anti-Jewish measures by way of direct negotiations with Nazi leaders. Local attempts by Jewish leaders in various countries of occupied Europe to save Jews from deportation through these negotiations led to no permanent solution, and were a means for the German annihilation machine to extort the last of Jewish fortunes.

The first successful attempt to go this way was undertaken by the Jewish Rescue Committee in Bratislava. In March 1942, the leaders of this Committee, Rav Weissmandel, Ing. Steiner and Gisi Fleischman, tried to induce the German bureaucrats to halt the deportation of Slovakian Jews, by paying a ransom. The German in charge, SS Captain Wisliczeny, declared that, after the deportation of 55,000 Jews, he was willing to forego the deportation of the remaining 25,000 Jews for $50,000 (in dollars), $2.00 for each life. They were supposed to come from abroad. But they did not arrive, or at best very slowly. Wisliczeny waited many weeks for the negotiated sum, then he sent his own demand for payment: he again shipped 3,000 Jews to Poland. After that, the money arrived, and the deportations stopped....

pp. 5-6:
The plan, which we worked out immediately after the occupation, was partly based on the earlier plan in Bratislava and counting on various possibilities, included the following points.
1. Organization of the active and passive resistance movement.
2. Negotiations with the Germans over the renunciation or the postponement or the diminishing of the annihilations.
3. Cooperation with Hungarian elements against the German pressure.
4. Hiding of Jews through installation of shelters and distribution of false papers.
5. Organization and guidance for escape routes to Romania and to Tito's partisans. (Mainly Polish and Slovakian refugees, who are equal to such an undertaking.)
6. Appeals to the International Red Cross and to neutral embassies for protection and aid.

The negotiations with the Germans succeeded, as mentioned, on an economic basis. We proposed to them, directly after the occupation, to abolish the erection of the ghettos and deportation of the Hungarian Jews, in consideration of a certain amount of money. We hoped to at least gain time by this maneuver.

The German Commissioner and leader of the Judenkommandos (Jews-Commandos—LB), the infamous Adolf Eichmann, rejected our plan after some hesitation. Later, he thought the 2 million dollars we offered him was insufficient.... Finally Eichmann declared that he did not need money, and that he would not stop the deportations. He declared himself willing to let all the Hungarian Jews live, in exchange for needed war materials for Germany. One million Jews in exchange for 10,000 trucks, that means 100 human lives for one truck. That was the proposition with which Joel Brand, a member of the Vaadah, brought with him to Istanbul on a German courier plane. On this proposition hung the last hope of a community sentenced to death, who could only be saved if a miracle should occur. This wonder did not come to pass.

Not only was granting these perverse German demands refused, but no effort was made on the western side to exchange these impossible demands with other means, or to make propaganda with these demands.

pp. 9-10:
More than a quarter of a million Jews were liberated by the Allies in the various concentration camps when Germany collapsed.

These liberations did not happen automatically with the Allied victory. The Jews in the concentration camps had to be kept alive first in order to be liberated.

During the last months of the war, this question was the continuing focus of heated discussions in the highest SS circles: should one let the few remaining Jews live or not? The radicals, Kaltenbrunner, Müller and Eichmann took the position that the preservation of the rest of the Jews would not change anything. They were insufficient as an alibi. Against it, this would only free many people bent on seeking personal revenge from the German people.

Other high-ranking officers, amongst them our negotiating partner in Budapest, Kurt Becher, as well as the well-known Schellenberg, suggested to Himmler that letting the Jews live would be a gesture, on which one might base an eventual special peace offer to the British.

As a result of our negotiations, at the end of November 1944, Himmler ordered the cessation of gassing in Auschwitz. From then on, according to his orders, Jewish lives were to be respected. This order was only partly obeyed. Even though gassing stopped in Auschwitz, other methods were used in other camps. Eichmann, supported by Kaltenbrunner, and his traditional methods, tried with all of his might to sabotage Himmler's new course. The battle between the radicals and the moderates ended only with Germany's collapse. It was one, but not the only reason contributing to the terrible conditions found in Bergen-Belson and the other camps. Besides Eichmann and Kaltenbrunner's sabotage, the war also played its part. The Allies through the bombardment of the German transport system, which in itself was a work of organizational art, had succeeded, by the end of February 1945. Nothing in the Third Reich worked anymore. It was impossible to think that the Germans could overcome their transportation difficulties and supply the camps with food....

PART I—THE JEWS IN HUNGARY
pp. 6-7:

Slovakian and Polish refugees in Hungary

In February 1942 the first waves of Polish refugees arrived in Hungary.... In March 1942 they were followed by hordes of Jews from Slovakia.... The presence of thousands of Polish and Slovakian Jews in Hungary presented several problems which had to be dealt with without delay. The refugees had to be housed, and as most of them were without resources, had to be financially supported. They needed documents to be able to go into the streets or to work. As legal papers were hard to come by, falsified papers were obtained. About 3,500 were arrested by the Hungarian authorities and interned. (Garany, Kistarcsca, Ricse.) Through this they became "legalized" and were therefore able to receive care from both central offices of the Reformed and Orthodox.

But what should be done with the great majority? Advocate Stern refused to supply the necessary money. He thought that by helping several thousand illegal refugees, he would endanger the existence of all of Hungarian Jewry. Fearing reprisal, the leaders of Keren KaYemeth and Karen HeYesod refused to release the sums already collected for Palestine, but which could not be sent, for this purpose.

A few leading Zionists and a few wealthy Orthodox took over the job of caring for and defending the refugees. Illegal money was collected, and conveyed by trusted men to the refugees, organized in groups. Papers were supplied, bunkers prepared, and apartments organized, where the arriving refugees could spend the first few nights, and receive their first sustenance....

pp. 8-9:

Formation of the Vaadat Ezra Vö-Hazalah Bö-Budapest

In Autumn 1942, we received the first letter from Istanbul, through Springmann's mediation. It was brought by courier and was signed by Ruth Klüger. In this way, our Zionist friends in Istanbul transmitted to us the first modest sum of money. They sent a message from Palestinian Jewry: "Help the refugees! Help the Polish Jews!"... The organization for the rescue of Jews from Poland to Hungary—this undertaking, named in our code "Tijul" (excursion), was headed by Joel Brand....

p. 15:

Connections with Istanbul and Switzerland

As already mentioned, connections with Jewish organizations abroad started at the end of 1942. Through two breaks, it was possible for us to end our isolation, and to reach connections in the free world. One way led to Istanbul, where the Jewish Agency's aid organization, under the direction of Chaim Barlas, had their headquarters. In Switzerland, it was Nathan Schwalb, the HeHalutz representative and, later on, through his contact, Saly Mayer, the Joint representative in Switzerland, who supplied us, with the help of diplomatic couriers, with the financial help to continue our aid and rescue work.

pp. 17-19:

A strange offer from the German Army

...Twenty-four hours later, on March 14, 1944, Winniger informed us, in strict confidentiality, that the occupation of Hungary by Germany was near. He could or would not give us the exact time.... At a conference called immediately after Winniger's message, attended by Otto Komoly, Dr. Joseph Fischer, Dr. Ernest Marton, Hillel Danzig, Moshe Schweiger, Joel Brand and Dr. Kasztner, we came to the following decisions.

1) Alert Istanbul immediately.

2) Ascertain what the intentions of the Germans are towards Hungarian Jewry, through the Bratislava committee, which has connections to SS officers.

3) The Haganah, the Jewish self-protection instrument, has to be immediately activated.

In relation to these last two points, some remarks are proper here. Some anticipated events make it understandable why the Haganah refused to do anything in the first three to four months after the occupation.

a) Since the end of 1943, the necessity to take proper measures to organize a self-defense unit, and the urgency to activate it, was clear to the responsible Zionist leaders. The Vaadah was prepared in every way to establish a responsible organization. However, many reasons postponed the actual forming of this unit. The split up of Zionist life in Hungary, the battle between parties, which very often became very vehement, long unproductive discussions, etc., were responsible for the planned decisions not being speedily and energetically carried out.

b) Dr. Moshe Schweiger, who Palestine named as the Haganah leader, and who was acceptable to all parties, was arrested by the SS, several days after the occupation.

c) Istanbul declared in February that some Palestinian Haganah officers would be sent. They arrived in Hungary in the middle of June. Their timely arrival probably would not have changed the course of events, but could have influenced the Zionist youth movement's conduct. When the expected officers, Hannah Szenes, Perez Goldstein, and Joel Nussbecher arrived in Hungary, the deportation of the provincial Jews was almost complete....

PART II—THE GERMAN OCCUPATION—March 19, 1944
p. 6:
The Sztojay Government and the Jews
In the first days of the occupation, members of the Vaadah and the Zionist leadership met in various places. We tried to orientate ourselves in the new political situation, and to find eventual points of support for a political defense. We asked ourselves: How far can and will Sztojay withstand the presumptive German pressure on the Jewish question? We made plans, we divided the lists. Otto Komoly took it upon himself to contact Hungarian politicians, and to ask the Christian churches for assistance. Moshe Krause was ordered to put himself under the protection of the Swiss embassy, and to ask the neutral diplomats to intervene. The job of working on the "German line" was assigned to Joel Brand and myself....

p. 8:
Why no revolt? ...And Jewish internal life?
It is already a historic banality that the Hungarian Jew was a long dead branch of a tree. This really only concerned Budapest's Jews. They showed a careful indifference towards the Jewish fate. They were lifelong individu-

alists, with often conscious and consequently suppressed feelings for community and instincts. Therefore often brittle and decadent, tired, more interested in the lighter side of things. How could such a crowd of individualists be spurred on to heroic leanings? Especially when everyone clung to the hope that personally one just had to mark time, while the Russians near the border, and an invasion by the Allies is due. But an armed resistance, even if not prematurely discovered, would only be an excuse justifying total annihilation.

So it was in Budapest. So it was in the large city, where the individual could disappear more easily.

The provinces, (especially the Jewish multitudes of Carpathian Ukraine and the southern regions) were isolated from the capital. They did not grasp the meaning of events, with the breathtaking tempo of the erection of the ghettos and the deportations.

What did we do before the occupation, so we would not be surprised by events? Otto Komoly, a decorated Captain from W.W. I, contacted the organizations of former Jewish officers and war veterans. He explained the Polish tragedy to them. He proposed the formation of a resistance organization to them. They didn't even want to listen to him.

The numerically small Zionist troop nucleus, the youth, therefore remained completely isolated in the spectrum of Jewish life, completely isolated in their resistance effort. They could not act on their own. They wouldn't dare to try it on their own. They could not take upon themselves the responsibility that, later, it would be claimed that anti-Jewish decrees were instituted because of "irresponsible Jewish actions."...

pp. 10-12:
The first contact with the SS. "The preservation of the Jewish substance."

The appearance of Wisliczeny as head of the Budapest Judenkommandos, awakened the hope that direct contact with the SS could be reached, similar to what was done in Slovakia. Joel Brand and Dr. Rezsö Kasztner undertook the job of finding out if it would be possible for the Judenkommando to negotiate on an economic basis, and thereby introduce a "diplomatic" maneuver, to avoid the threatened ghettos and deportations, or at least postpone them....
Thereupon Wisliczeny received Brand and Kasztner on April 5, in Winniger's private residence.... We posed the following questions to Wisliczeny.

"Is the Judenkommando willing, and if so, under what conditions,
a) To spare the lives of Hungarian Jewry?

b) Not to put them in ghettos?
c) Not to deport Hungary's Jews?
d) To allow the immigration of Hungarian Jews, who were in possession of visas and entry permits to foreign countries?"

Wisliczeny answered as follows:

"There can be no discussion between us as to whether the Jews should wear the star or not, or if they should or should not retain their commercial or other positions. We naturally do insist that the Jews influence in all spheres be radically reduced. But we don't insist on placing them into ghettos, or on deportation. This possibility could occur only when this would be ordered, over our heads, directly from Berlin."

"We can discuss the preservation of the Jewish substance between ourselves."

"As far as immigration is concerned, I must ask for instructions from my superiors. Personally I don't believe that our high command would be interested in immigration in limited numbers. But if you should work out a plan for the immigration of at least one hundred thousand Jews, we would try to influence Berlin to make it possible."

As payment, Wisliczeny asked for 2 million dollars; as a sign of "good will," that we had the capacity to do this, a 10 percent or $200,000 advance in Pengö within a week. (Schmidt and Winniger demanded a 10 percent commission on this sum for the Army, and another 1 percent for themselves.)

The $200,000 had to be converted on the "black market." This amounted to six and a half million Pengös.

We declared that the requested sum would have to be obtained from foreign countries. It would only be possible to make this payment if:

1) The Jewish organizations in foreign countries accepted the German demands.
2) Would have the opportunity to bring the requested sum to Budapest. Only then could payments be made in monthly installments, under the condition that the Germans would live up to their part of the agreement....

p. 13:

After the conversation with Wisliczeny, a discussion took place in Samuel Stern's apartment, in which the conversation with Wisliczeny was closely analyzed. Present were: Ernst Szilagy, Samuel Stern and Karl Wilhelm. The results of the meeting with Wisliczeny seemed very meager to those present, as his promises, apart from the emigration, were unclear and uncertain. Nevertheless the assemblage could not decide to reject Wisliczeny's financial demands completely. It was decided to pay the first installment, to keep the connection alive, hoping to gain some time in this way.

Samuel Stern took it upon himself to raise the six and a half million Pengös, which was not an easy chore, as the congregations' coffers were empty. He invited the wealthy Jews singly to his house, calling upon them to make their contributions to the rescue work. After this troublesome effort, which lasted several weeks, he was able to collect 5 million Pengös.

The rest was covered by the Vaadah, partly by using foreign bill of exchange reserves we received for Tijul and the Haganah....

pp. 20-21:

A List of 600 Human Beings

At the same time Otto Komoly made the following notes in his diary. Long conference with Zionist leaders. Impossible to put together a list of 600. Six hundred names out of 800,000.

Otto Komoly and Ernst Szitay had to be trusted with putting this list together. The committee of party stewards of the Palestine Office, found it necessary to consider personal and party motives, which made this an agonizing, delicate impossible job. The task, to put together on one list, only 600 names, in which Zionists and non-Zionists, Jews from the capital and Jews from the provinces, Polish and Slovakian refugees had to be considered, presented severe problems for Presidents Komoly and Szilagyi, even though they were not bound by party considerations.

The compilation of an Alijah was never an easy job even earlier. Budapest was for years a city of refugees. Regarding Alijah, she was to a certain extent the center of east and middle Europe, she sheltered first-class human material, Zionist and non-Zionist, fighters and partisans from Poland. To divide the few certificates justly has always been an unsolvable task.

This time it was a matter of life and death....

pp. 21-22:

SS against Army

...Eichmann, the leader of the Judenkommandos, who had remained in the background until then, now had Joel Brand come to him. At this meeting, which was an important turning point, the Leader of the Judenkommandos opened the meeting with the following words:

I have made inquiries and found out that the Joint is able to make the payments. (After his experience in Austria and Czechoslovakia, everything that hung together Jews and money was synonymous with "Joint.") Naturally I know about the conferences between Krumey and yourself, but these are only trifles. Now I give you the big chance to save one million Hungarian Jews. I hear that Roosevelt, in a radio address, gave voice to his fears for the lives of the Hungarian Jews. Now I will give him the opportunity to do something for them. I do not need money. I do not know what to do with it. I need war materials, especially trucks. So I have therefore decided to let you travel to Istanbul, so that you can transmit to your friends there, this generous German offer. I will transfer all Hungarian Jews to Germany, they will be collected at a certain point. I'll wait two weeks for an answer from Istanbul. You'll immediately return from Istanbul, to bring me your friends' answer. If the answer is positive, you can take the whole million Jews away, as far as I'm concerned, but if the answer is negative, you'll have to suffer the consequences.

Eichmann spoke in sharp, short, commanding sentences. Brand tried to convince him that it would be easier to conclude this business if the Germans would give up their deportation plans.

"I can sell the Hungarian Jews only to Germany," Eichmann declared....

pp. 23-24:

The psychological preparation of a deportation

...In every ghetto, at the same time a collection point for the deportation, therefore as close as possible to a rail line (industrial or tile factories) one was convinced, until the last moment, that the transports were not crossing the country's border. Hungarian police and gendarmes, and SS personnel "secretly" told the leading Jewish personalities the names of the Hungarian towns to which the transports were supposed to go. Doctors, pharmacists, and engineers were promised special treatment. The warnings, which the Vaadah sent to many provincial ghettos, partly through the self-sacrificing bravery of the Halutzim, partly through the few sympathetic Hungarians willing to help, was 1) to encourage escape, 2) to appeal to them to refuse to enter the cattle cars, were unsuccessful. Even then, no one was ready yet to believe us....

pp. 24-25:

Between Budapest and Theresienstadt

During our talk with Wisliczeny and Krumey, we repeatedly pleaded to make it possible for us to establish contact with the Jews in Theresienstadt, to supply them with financial help.

To fulfill our plea, Eichmann ordered Captain Klausnitzer to travel to Prague and Theresienstadt. In Prague, Klausnitzer gave the money, $10,000, to the local Jewish Elder, Dr. Franlisek Friedmann, (a known Zionist, married to an Aryan wife, who was allowed to remain in his position, and who administered the Theresienstadt finances). In Theresienstadt he gave a letter to the Jewish Council. In it, we sent greetings to the friends in Theresienstadt from the Yishuv and American Jewry, and expressed the hope that there would be help for some of them to make Aliyah.

In a May 23 letter, Dr. Franlisek Friedmann thankfully confirmed the receipt of the $10,000, given him by Klausnitzer, which he will use towards the betterment of living conditions in Theresienstadt. In another letter written in Theresienstadt, on May 8, the leaders of the Jewish Council described life in Theresienstadt in suspiciously cheerful colors. The letter bore the signatures of Dr. Franz Cahn, Dr. Erich Munk, Dr. Paul Epstein, Engineer Otto Zucker, Dr. Reich Oestreicher and Gard Körbel. All of them were sent to Auschwitz, four months later, by Eichmann.

Brand's Trip to Istanbul, Fiasco of a Mission

Brand, alone, negotiated with the Germans from May 8 to the 17th. I was excluded....

p. 26:

The negotiations between Brand and Eichmann moved in a strictly "business" frame. Goods on one side, Jewish lives on the other. It was self-evident to Eichmann that a strong Jewish influence could be put on the Allies, especially on the Americans. They would therefore be willing to make any sacrifice to save the lives of a million Jews. Politics only entered the talks when Brand expressed doubts that it would be possible to procure trucks in Istanbul.

"You can assure your friends," Eichmann said, "that we will not use the trucks on the front, but will use them in the hinterland. At most, there is an outside chance, that in case of an emergency, they would be used on the Eastern front."

What was the hidden meaning of Eichmann's remarks?

What was behind these suddenly generous offers on one side, and the absurd demands on the other? Were they lunatics or clumsy plotters, who would make such proposals?

With the Istanbul trip, our initiative to arrange for a discreet human trade affair became an international matter. The Germans believed that Hungarian Jewry was a valuable pawn. They were determined to get the most out of it. They admitted to us "that after five years of war, there is a scarcity of certain articles in Germany." They needed the equivalent in merchandise, they wanted to get this from the Allies, their enemy, to strengthen their own war potential. They even went so far as to be ready to stop the Jewish extermination. They risked their offer being refused and being exposed as blackmailers. What were they really pursuing? Only economic or also political goals? Were they really willing to give a new direction to their Jewish policies?

We in Budapest could only presume what was happening. For a long time, we could not get a clear picture of what kind of cards the SS was dealing....

pp. 27-29:

Negotiations in Budapest on a new basis

After Brand and Grosz left for Istanbul, I reported with Hansi Brand (Joel's wife) to Eichmann. We knew that we were facing the main stage manager of the Jewish destruction. But the possibility to help was also in his hands. He, and he alone, ruled over life and death. We spoke to him openly about the cruelties in the ghettos and the deportation trains.

We asked him why the people selected for immigration were not brought to Budapest from the provinces, as Krumey had promised. We told him that, under such circumstances, successful negotiations abroad were in doubt.

Eichmann gave us a discourse of more than an hour. He referred to his actions as Commissar of Jewish affairs in Austria and Czechoslovakia. He spoke about his lost sympathy for the Zionists. He stiffened when we came to concrete questions. He said:

1) If it happened that, in lower Carpathia, 90 people were packed into one cattle car, it happened only because the Jews in that region had so many children, and children don't need much room. Also the Jews in that part of the country were less demanding. In other

regions fewer people would be put into the cattle cars.

2) He would investigate what happened to the transfer to Budapest of the people we had requested. He declared that he did not receive any list from us.

3) There was absolutely no chance that he would suspend or stop the deportations. We should not think that he was stupid. Because, if he would stop the deportations, nobody abroad would negotiate with him. We should be more forceful with our negotiations in Istanbul. He cannot be fooled and his patience has its limits.

We telegraphed Istanbul on the same day: "The deportations will continue!" We wanted to let our friends know that time was of the essence. They should act quickly.

At a second discussion, on May 22, Eichmann confirmed permission for the group of 600 to emigrate. However, he declared that the way down the Danube to Constanza was out of the question, as this way would lead to Palestine by way of Istanbul, and he would not permit emigration to Palestine. The group should travel to Africa, by way of Germany, occupied France and Spain.

Again I claimed the Prominents from the provinces, and gave him another copy of the list.

Eichmann promised to "follow up" on this matter.

In the next days, further telegrams arrived from Istanbul. Brand reported that he was holding promising discussions. Various delegates of the Jewish Agency, the Americans and British officials were on their way to him.

pp. 31-32:

The interference of the Hungarian Gestapo

...I called on Eichmann immediately after I was released from jail. I showed him the telegrams I had received from Istanbul, and asked him to suspend deportations until after we received the wording of the interim agreement. Eichmann refused and declared "There is no slowing down. Matter of fact, I'll proceed with full steam."

I again claimed the Prominents from the provinces, and this time Eichmann seemed to yield. He declared he would send a telegram ordering that the people in question were to be brought out of still existing ghettos in Transylvania (Szatmar-Nagyvarad, Kolozsvar, Marosvasarhely, etc.) We waited many days for the arrival of these transports. But all Dr. Joseph Fischer, chairman of the Jewish Council in Kolozsvar, could inform us about was that the SS had received orders from Budapest to put a special transport together. (Eichmann knew that Klausenberg was especially close to us.)

On the morning of June 3, Eichmann sent for me and declared:

"I cannot let any Jew be brought to Budapest right now! I must now go to Jarozs, Minister of the Interior. He will surely ask me what kind of business the SS had concluded with the Baron Weiss family. (Becher's notorious agreement, by which the 54 factories of the Weiss conglomerate were turned over to the SS. In exchange, 40 members of the Weiss family were able to get to Lisbon.) Did you know of this agreement? Jarosz will now make me pay for this mess. Why me? Endre will ask me, what kind of new business we are undertaking with the Jews, when we now bring Jews from Siebenburgen to Budapest. No, I will not do it."

"But you promised me. You always told me that you always keep your word. I know that you telegraphed to Klausenberg on this subject...."

"Yes, but I canceled the order yesterday by telegraph. Is this all clear? Now I have no time for you."

Once outside, it took a while until common sense overtook the powerless rage and desperation. I drew the balance of our "negotiations."

In the beginning, we tried to circumvent or postpone the deportations. The Germans promised, and we paid them for it. We requested emigration, they agreed. To this end, they promised 300 prominent people were to be sent to Budapest from the provinces. More than 300,000 have already been transported to Auschwitz, and it hasn't been possible to rescue one of the 300. In Istanbul, they offered to free one million Jews, but they deny us the release of 300, even now, as negotiations on this offer are going on in Istanbul.

Up to now, Eichmann had nothing but excuses. Once he claimed that we had delivered the list of the prominent people to the wrong place. Another time, someone forgot to give the order telegraphically, and the ghetto was "evacuated." Again, the lower echelons "did not follow orders." And now, Eichmann declares that he will not keep his promise. Not even towards the small group. As I acknowledge this fact, we will be accomplices in the deportation of these people, which we had tried so hard to save. We thereby reached the low point. We cannot continue this way.

I went to Eichmann's deputy, Herman Krumey, who was also our negotiation partner. I told him that I was forced to inform Istanbul about the senselessness of any further negotiations. I then went to see Klages. Klages, who always insisted that this trade had to be "clean and clear," promised, as well as Krumey, to intervene with the "chief."

PART III—THE FIRST GERMAN CONCESSIONS
p. 1:

"Zionist Conspirator"

At 11 o'clock Eichmann returned to his office. I immediately called upon him. His secretary said that Eichmann did not have time for me. I waited in the corridor. After about half an hour he sent for me. His close staff, Krumey, Wisliczeny, Hunsche and Novak were standing behind him. Klages had just left the room.

"You can get a chair for yourself!"

Eichmann began to shout. I kept quiet, one has to wait until these ravings are finished. Its clear to me where the play is leading to. It doesn't only concern the rescue of a few hundred Jews from the provinces. If Eichmann cannot be forced here and now to back down, then the Vaadah, who had put their chips in this game of roulette with human lives on the German number, was a much of a naive loser as so many of us in occupied Europe. The millions already paid were then a foolish delusion. The loser in this game can be called traitor.

"What do you actually want?" Eichmann finally started the conversation.

"I have to insist that our agreements are fulfilled. Will you bring the people selected by us from the provinces to Budapest?"

"When I say no, it remains no!"

"Then there is no sense to confer any further as far as we are concerned." I make believe that I am getting up.

"Your nerves are shot, Kasztner, I will send you to Theresienstadt so you can recuperate. Or would you prefer Auschwitz?"

"That would be useless. Nobody else will replace me."

"Understand me once and for all. I must rid the provinces of the Jewish dirt. No arguments and no tears will help."

"Then our discussions with Istanbul will also be useless."

"What do you want with these few Jews?"

"It doesn't only concern them. The Istanbul matter is in bad shape, while you force the deportations. You must deliver proof that you are serious about your offer. What do these few Jews mean to you?"

We continued this way for an hour....

pp. 5-6:

Some points to understand this problem

On June 9, Eichmann declared that "if I don't receive a positive answer within three days from Istanbul, I will let the mill work in Auschwitz."

In sessions of the Vaadah and in deliberations with Jewish leaders, we thoroughly consider the situation. It was asked if there was any sense in negotiating with the Germans, or if it would be better to admit the hopelessness of our efforts and understand the full consequences.

However, we cannot come to a conclusion because of the Vaadah's other work.

The connection with the Judenkommando offers a certain protection for the members of the Vaadah from the Germans, as well as the Hungarian Gestapo. Active traffic developed in our often changing apartment. Polish and Slovakian refugees reported to receive help and support. Hundreds of Hungarian Jews asked for intervention. The Zionist youth leaders visited us daily. Organization and financial support of Tijul, necessitated a central place, with an unhindered flow of people.

This collection of Jews around our apartment was now all too obvious. Against the denunciations of neighbors, landlords and informers, the Judenkommando, paradoxically, provided a certain, if often only hypothetical, protection for our illegal work.

Finally, the question remained, if the military development, the Allied invasion (which made the Germans tremble, and they hoped with all their hearts that it would not happen) would open the way to make this help possible.

We could not look into Eichmann's cards. But we had to tell ourselves: if Eichmann receives us at all, makes small concessions, if Wesenmayer, the German Ambassador, intervenes for us with the Hungarian government, it seems unthinkable that they are doing it on their own responsibility or for their own entertainment. Behind or above them, there has to be a higher German tribunal which protects them, and that might be able to develop other plans for us.

If this is so—we continued in this train of thought—the action should be continued. If the hopes concerning Istanbul will not make it possible to save all of Hungarian Jewry, we must try to at least protect some of them from the gas chambers.

As far as Eichmann is concerned, we will maintain the assertion that negotiations abroad will, in time, be successful. If this, alone, will not be enough to continue with the action, we will try to obtain more money, gold and valuables from Hungarian Jewry, and offer this to Eichmann. We thereby create an "interim solution." Time will be gained, and with that, maybe, also human lives....

pp. 9-10:

Hitler's obligations towards the Mufti

In the course of further negotiations with Eichmann, we brought to the agenda the question of the transport to Palestine. We demanded that this group could be led to Istanbul via Romania.

Eichmann energetically refused this group traveling to Palestine via Romania. He claimed:

a) We must see to it that publicly the character of the deportation remains intact.

b) He cannot allow that the group should go directly to Palestine. He had no desire to agitate the Arabs against Germany. Besides that, he was a personal friend of the Grand Mufti, to whom Germany had made a pledge that no European Jew should reach Palestine.

Eichmann said the group should spend several weeks in Strasshof (Vienna), and then travel by way of occupied France to Lisbon, and from there sail to North Africa. What happens to the group later is none of his concern.

Eichmann finally declared that he was ready, on the basis of our previously submitted lists, to bring additional groups from the provinces to Budapest.

Pengö and jewels instead of trucks

The Vaadah now concentrated their efforts on raising the 5 million Pengös. For this reason, 100 places in the transport had to be offered to those people who were able to supply more valuables and greater amounts of money. The great majority of Hungarian Jews had obeyed the law, and had turned their mobile wealth over to the Hungarian government. But there were still Jews who had hidden assets.

The discussions with the applicants for the "places for sale" were held in the Jewish Congregation building by special committee under the leadership of Otto Komoly, Engineer Richard, Hansi Brand and Sulem Offenbach. The return remuneration for the 100 places was not enough.

We had to raise the number of the "paying ones" to 150. In the truest sense of the word, a battle was waged over these places.

The Jew, who was trembling for his own life and the lives of his family, lost all sense of money. They implored Komoly and the other members of the committee with their offers.

This tragic generosity made it possible for us, not only to continue the action, but the raised valuables covered the steadily growing expenses for the

Tijul, etc., for many months. Jewish wealth, which would have been completely destroyed, either by dispossession, devaluation, plunder or deportation of the owner, was therefor able to be used in the service of the community....

p. 11:

Eichmann demanded that I supply help in the organization of the transport to Austria.

We were again faced with the difficult dilemma which ran like a red thread through our work: should we leave the selection to blind chance? Or should we try to influence it.

This question, surely the most terrible one which was placed on our human conscience, was made more difficult by the fact that it did not only concern selection of individuals, but also of whole towns.

Should we take pains to take part in these decisions?

We did do it, tried to do it. We told ourselves that, as holy as every human being is to a Jew, we must at least strive to save those Jews, who, all their lives, worked for the Zibur (Community). Also the women whose husbands were assigned to "work camps." Care also had to be taken that children, especially orphans, would not be annihilated....

p. 13:

Two trains were changed

... Local influences counted at the place and on the spot, the arbitrariness of the ghetto leaders, their gold, their power. Someone on the outside cannot imagine how such a letter and such a list works at the place of execution—the ghetto. How it's first only known in the closed circle of the prominent ones and their following, and then in some wondrous way, works its way down to the general public. And how suddenly everyone is informed. Nobody knows what it's all about, yet everyone knows. Twenty, thirty, forty people will be called, one answers. The others hide, pulls his wife and children to him by force, he will not go. He is afraid, emotionally confused. They advise him, stay! And he doesn't go.

The other one, who didn't read, and wasn't called, he wants to go. He cries, pleads and threatens. With fist and teeth he accomplishes his goal in a wondrous second. And he goes....

p. 18:

The Palestine Transport

The day on which our "Aliyah" was to start came ever closer. The group had not been completely assembled. We weren't sure if it would or would not happen. Meanwhile we haggled with Eichmann about the number of participants. Under the title "Inclusion of the Klausenburger group," an increase of 1,000 was achieved. In consideration of the large number of Prominents brought from the provinces, he then gave his permission for a further 200. On the day of departure, the officially allowed number of participants was 1,300....

pp. 19-20:
Especially among the Polish refugees, sharp opposition reigned against the transport plan. "Aliyah in the form of deportation!?" "To trust the promises of the SS?" The Polish refugees, with all their experiences, thought it was crazy.

A decision had to be made, the responsibility for the start or non-start had to be taken. The Vaadah unanimously decided to let the transport leave.

Even though there was no precedent, that the Nazis would let a group of Jews travel to a neutral country, it was our deep conviction that it would be successful this time. And, as family members of the Vaadah were also on the train, many among the Polish refugees and the Halutz youth gave up their opposition and joined the group....

pp. 21-22:
A Noah's Ark: The composition of the transport for abroad
The departure of the group was set for June 30. We once again had to compile a "first" list. The available 1,300 places were distributed to the following categories—in a way set by the Vaadah.

1) Orthodox (refugees and Budapesters. Compiled by Philip Freudiger).
2) Polish, Slovakian, Yugoslavian refugees (according to their own lists).
3) Prominent Neologes (list by Samuel Stern).
4) Zionists, certificate owners (by recommendation of the Presidium of the Palestine Office).
5) Halutz youth, Hungarians and refugees: Dror Habonim, Makkabi, Hazan, Hashomer, Hazair, Noar Hazioni, Mizrachi Akiba (according to their own list).
6) Revisionists (by recommendation of Revisionist leader Gottesmann).
7) Paying persons, whose contributions supplied the exchange money to pay for the whole transport.
8) The rescued ones from the provinces.
9) Outstanding Jewish personalities from the ministry, science and cultural life.

(A committee under the leadership of Otto Komoly and Ernst Szilaggi invited the spiritual elite of Hungarian Jewry to be part of the transport. Despite the large crowd, we insisted that this category was correspondingly represented. Numerous writers, scientists, doctors and artists refused the invitation, evidently out of mistrust about the fate of the transport. In this way, we succeeded in saving, among others, the lives of Dr. Leopold Szondi, the world famous psychologist, Bela Szolt, one of Hungary's former publishers, X-ray specialist Dr. Franz Polgar, internist Dr. A. Braun, oculist Dr. J. Hamburg, architect Zoltan Gara, pianist Thomas Blum, the opera singer, Desider Ernsler.)

10) Orphans. A group of wards of Budapest orphanage, as well as 17 orphans from Poland. Their case was in the hands of Dr. Georg Polgar, the outstanding leader of the Jewish Welfare Office, who also was on the transport.

The distribution of the relatively few places among the various categories, whose representatives fought bitterly for their people, presented a merciless chore for the Vaadah. We made every effort, in the face of our monstrous responsibilities, to fill them as consciously as possible. The group represented a miniature crosscut of the Jews living in Hungary at the time. Those who, in the past, earned the respect of Jewry, were honored with special consideration.

Additionally, many personalities in the former public life in Siebenbürgen brought from Klausenberg to the Columbus Camp, could be saved by this action. Some should be named here. Drs. Theodor and Joseph Fisher, Joel Teitelbaum, the world famous Hasidic Rabbi, who was a strong opponent of the Zionist movement. With the exception of Otto Komoly and Dr. Rezsö Kasztner, who remained in Budapest to continue the work, the following personalities left with the transport: the presidium of the Hungarian Zionist Association, the collaborators of the National Fund, also some collaborators and members of the Vaadah: Ernst Szilagyi, Moshe Rosenberg, Joseph Weinberger, Ede Morton, Dr. Sarah Friedlander, Dr. Elizabeth Kurz. Some more outstanding Orthodox personalities, some deserving Neolog Rabbis, supplemented the picture....

PART IV—THE BATTLE CONTINUES
pp. 4-5:

The Jewish Councils in Hungary

It is possible to mention here, briefly, the role of the so-called Jewish Councils played in Hungary and especially in Budapest. Naturally, the purpose of these lines is solely to record and note problems. It isn't time yet to form a final judgment about these institutions, with this hated name, which was forced upon European Jewry by the Nazis, or the people who played a role in this. Only when tempers cool down, can impartial outsiders try, from a respective distance, to weigh the elements of an activity—when almost any negative or positive appearances in the decline was skipped over, in the distorted generalizations of Jewish public opinion.

The controversy about the Jewish Councils were known to us in Budapest, long before the occupation, through the stories told by Polish, Slovakian and Austrian refugees. Born out of the bottomless misery, thought of in the beginning as a return to a form of the life of the middle ages, of an internal autonomy, which would also provide a certain protection from external pressure, the Jewish Council finally became an instrument in the mechanics of annihilation. From this point in time, the sinister problems of the Jewish Councils began to show up. Does it function, can it comply, can it accelerate the process of liquidation? If it refuses to obey, it brings about sanctions against the community, without assurance of having stopped the liquidation process. Between the two extremes, was a path of other steps, depending on the elasticity of the people, which make up this group, or on the strength of the temptation they are exposed to.

Almost every place in Europe, the Jewish Councils went the same way. Bit by bit, they were made to comply. In the beginning harmless things were demanded. Valuables, wealth, apartments, replaceable property. Later came the personal freedom of the people, and in the end, bare life itself, whereby it was the duty of the Jewish Council to determine the order, who sooner and who later. One sacrificed to Moloch in a certain order of value, following a set criteria. A cruel hierarchy started: age, merit, achievements. Personal considerations came to the foreground, degree of relationship, sympathies, even interests. It was a slippery road, which almost always led to the abyss. Everywhere the Jew was facing the same problem, shall I—or whoever—be the traitor, in order to, here and there, be a helper, or even a savior. Or should I desert the community, and turn them over to others? Is the escape from responsibilities not also something of a treason? And if I take a post, where are the borders that I cannot cross? For the price of self-destruction, suicide or execution at the hands of the hangman, or to rid myself of an unbearable responsibility? The borders, the line between self-destruction and treason is almost impossible for human power to draw. It is no wonder that, where ever there is still a Jewish community, this question always would come up. That demagoguery also comes into play here, is almost a natural occurrence. To judge the Jewish Councils in retrospect, from testimony of witnesses, from actions and documents, surmounts in difficulty almost everything else that earthly judgment can accomplish....

pp. 8-9:

Hannah Szenes, Nussbecher and Goldstein. A greeting from Eretz Israel
Early in the morning, several hours after the departure of the Palestine transport, Hungarian Counter-Espionage arrested Hansi Brand, Salem Offenbach, Engineer Andreas Biss. Mrs. Biss and Dr. Rezsö Kasztner. The background of the arrests, and their relation to the Jewish tragedy must be told. Therefore, it is not possible to avoid it, in anticipation of future events.

As already mentioned, the Jewish Agency made plans at the beginning of the year to send three officers of the Jewish Brigade to Budapest. Their mission: to actively aid in the preparation of an armed resistance and self-preservation, and to pass on reports to the Allies....

pp. 9-10:

The first to arrive was Hannah Szenes. She crossed the southern border and was immediately turned over to the Counter-Espionage Office by a Hungarian Administration officer who was supposed to be dependable and on the Allies' side. She was brought to Budapest. The others, who did not know of Hannah Szenes' fate, turned to the same confidential agent, gave him their radio transmitter, and continued on to Budapest. They did not know that Counter-Espionage agents traced every one of their steps. They arrived in Budapest—with false papers—around June 20, and rented a room in a small hotel.

Their first visit was to me.

We were old friends. At one time they belonged to the Habonim youth movement in Siebenbürgen, which I led for several years. It was an experience, to meet after such a long time and under such circumstances. We talked and agreed to meet again tomorrow.

The two were to join the youth movement and start their work immediately, separate from us, so that we would not endanger each other. For coordination and contacts, respective opportunities would be arranged.

We didn't know that the reason why the Gestapo and Hungarian Counter-Espionage, which worked closely with them, let them move around freely was to find out where their connections would lead....

On the following day, as they came to the Jewish Congregation offices to make their first contact with the youth leaders, one noticed the presence of agents in the halls. The two tried to disappear. Nussbecher called on us later and was lodged in a private residence....

pp. 10-12:

Now the officials decided to arrest us. It happened on the day after the transport departed. We were brought to Hadik Barracks, the notorious Hungarian Counter-Espionage center. We were questioned: "Where is Perez Goldstein?"

To answer this question was not easy for any of us.

Only four weeks earlier, we were extracted from the falsified paper affair by the Germans. (Mrs. Brand is still carrying scars from this torture.) In the meantime, our responsibilities regarding rescue work grew considerably. The Aliyah group had just started their problem-plagued trip. The process of our various projects, their adoption by Kurt Becher, and also with Eichmann, hung in the balance.

Now to be involved with the entire Vaadah in a military espionage affair!!! There seemed to be no escape from this trap.

The question was repeated: "Where is Goldstein? I ask you for the last time. If you keep quiet, the other one, Nussbecher or whatever his name is, will be shot in 10 minutes."

"Give Mrs. Brand and myself time to think. Release us for several hours. My friends remain here as hostages. We will be back within a few hours."

Mrs. Brand and I went to the Columbus Street camp and conferred with Perez Goldstein. He had to make a decision now. He took only a few minutes. His decision: "I'll announce myself."

Hannah Szenes, Goldstein and Nussbecher remained under arrest. We tried for months, in vain, to obtain their release. After three months, it seemed that the day had finally come, when we would be able to free them. It was October 14, a Saturday morning. I negotiated with Military Commander Otah, the Secretary of War's personal secretary, about various questions, in an atmosphere which pointed towards Hungary's possible break with the Axis. The last thing on the Agenda was the matter of the three Jewish parachutists. We again asked for their freedom. Otah agreed. In a few days, Nussbecher, Goldstein and Hannah Szenes should go free.

Several days?

The next day, Horthy was a prisoner, Franz Szalasy, the Prime Minister. The two Jewish soldiers were deported. Nussbecher was able to escape from the moving train. It was a jump: his parachute training was put to good use.

Perez disappeared without a trace. Hannah Szenes was shot to death.

Their mission remained unfulfilled. But the support of the battling

(Palestinian) Yishuv that they brought to us, the personal example of their bravery, the wonderful spirit of their solidarity, which was manifested in their sacrifice, remained a permanent example and force in our work.

p. 12:

An Internal Assessment

... 3) Hungarian Jewry merely mounted sporadic efforts to resist. On the whole, they were passive, to the point where it bordered on lethargy. Besides the negative results, there were also some of a positive nature.

    a)   The rescue of about 17,000 Jews from the provinces to Austria.

    b)   The departure of the "Aliyah group," even though less quantitative than qualitative, can be counted as having a political meaning, and can be considered a positive....

pp. 19-20:

Dr. Schwartz and Himmler's agent

...Visibly irritated, Eichmann informed me on the same day that he had received orders from Himmler, to permit part of the Bergen-Belson group to travel abroad. The order was for 500, but there was no fixed number. It could be a little more or less. He would see to it. He would only give the order for their departure after a definite time was set for the meeting between Becher and World Jewry.

Concerning the selection of the 500 people, I was to instruct the "Jewish Elder" of the group, correspondingly. For this purpose, Krumey, who was going to Bergen-Belson to accompany the group, would take a letter by me with him. (I wrote to the group-leaders, that the 500 places should be filled proportionally, according to the various categories.)

But what would happen to those left behind in Bergen-Belson? Eichmann declared that they could follow the others within several weeks. But he would only give permission if Joel Brand returned from Istanbul before that time.

"I'm not used to permitting Jews to emigrate in German courier planes."

I finally asked him if members of my family were allowed to come along. "But naturally," answered Eichmann.

He had no power to defy Himmler's orders. He had to let the group go. He got his revenge by not keeping any point of the negotiated agreement....

pp. 32-33:

318 Jews from Bergen-Belsen leave the Third Reich

On August 19, at 15:30, we started our trip to Switzerland.... The list of the released ones was to be compiled in Department IV B of the SS main office in Berlin, alphabetically and according to age (possibly so men of military age are not used against Germany). My various suggestions were taken into consideration by Krumey. But all of my relatives and Brand's family were kept in Bergen-Belson as hostages, on Eichmann's orders.

Anyway, the first step was taken and 318 persons were released. They were the first large organized group, not only from the small group in Bergen-Belson, but from the great mass of Jewry languishing under Hitler's yoke, to cross the border of a neutral state, before the eyes of the whole world.

It was August 21, 1944 when the group was brought to Basel, from the small German border station.

PART V—THE INTERVENTION FROM ABROAD
pp. 13-14:

A difficult digression from the Axis

... In August the Vaadah started to make preparations and work on precautionary measures for various eventualities regarding the upcoming events.

Above all, connections between the Vaadah and the individual resistance groups that were forming was intensified. At various times, we made money available to them to buy arms and ammunition. The groups of Haluzim still remained in Budapest, prepared for the possibility of an armed confrontation with the Germans in the streets of Budapest.

The possibility was there. It should have been a sublime feeling, to fight side by side with the Hungarian resistance movement and, with gun in hand, sweep out the German tyrant, and take revenge for the destruction of provincial Jewry. But what would happen if the Germans should gain the upper hand? Would there still be a pardon for the remaining Jews? And what would be the Vaadah's position if the Hungarian uprising was successful and the Germans had to leave Budapest? Particularly, should I follow Becher because of the rescue work, which we hoped would deal with the entire German-held territory, and regarding our Jews in Bergen-Belson, which we could not abandon to their fate? Or should I, together with all my friends, remain in Budapest where, if a revolt occurred, there would be enough for us to do during and after liberation? If I remain in Budapest, would the Swiss negotiations still continue, and if yes, could we depend on the readiness of Mr. Saly Mayer to involve himself?

Above all, our work in these weeks had been concentrated on these problems, which seemed most urgent.

1) Continuation of the Bergen-Belson group's trip.

2) Securing the lives of Budapest's Jewish children. (After the annihilation of provincial Jewry, they, together with 15,000 from Austria form the only reservoir of Hungarian Jews.)

3) The liberation of the Palestinian parachutists....

PART VI—THE SEIZURE OF POWER BY THE ARROW CROSS
pp. 25-26:

The Commander of Auschwitz is against the foot march

Having been invited by Becher, on November 16, high German guests arrived in Budapest, the head of the Waffen SS, Colonel-General Jüttner, accompanied by Krumey, and Auschwitz Commandant, Lt. Colonel Höss. On the road between Vienna and Budapest, they witnessed the dreadful foot march. Corpses piled along the road, exhausted people, made a very painful impression on the German gentlemen.... Jüttner imparted the order to the Budapest Judenkommando to immediately discontinue the foot march....

p. 26:

On November 21, Eichmann arrived in Budapest, after a temporary absence....

p. 28:

Five days later, Eichmann reinstituted the death march. There was nothing left for us to do, but to try and aid the marchers with provisions, which would give them the strength to survive this difficult march. Thanks to the collective effort of the Swedish Red Cross, the International Red Cross (Division A) and the Swiss Embassy (Vadasz-Utca), it was possible to supply the Jews concentrated in Alt-Ofen, and those already on the march, with provisions and medicine.

The management and organization of these transports was conducted on behalf of our side by the Communist youth leader, George Aczel. He was one of the connecting links between the Vaadah and the Hungarian resistance movement, in which the Communists played an important part. It was often quite possible for him to smuggle provisions and medicines into the tile factories, pretending to be an agent of the International Red Cross, and he also had opportunity to repeatedly supply provisions to the marching people. At the same time, Aczel was our connection to Ferenczy and Lullay, with whom direct contact was no longer possible....

p. 29:

The Vaadah and the Hungarian resistance movement

... Directly after the Arrow Cross takeover.... A joint committee was formed, a plan was formulated to organize, in conjunction with the Hungarian army in Budapest, a resistance movement against the Germans.

The connection between the Vaadah and the resistance movement became ever closer. The left wing of the Zionist youth worked with the Socialist and Communist youth groups.

A leader of the Hungarian resistance movement and leading member of the Communist Party, who presently plays an important part in the life of the Hungarian state, found safety in our bunker. We issued him a pass, prepared by Becher (but without his knowledge), which made it possible for him to take part in resistance preparations. Through his mediation, we were able to supply the resistance movement committee with large sums of money for the purchase of weapons and ammunition....

p. 33:

Respect for Jewish lives?

... Before we parted, Eichmann had a last word for me: "Your family is slated to leave from Bergen-Belson with the next transport for Switzerland. You will also be at the border. They will escape me. I rather will detain your family at Bergen-Belson."

It was our last discussion, it was Eichmann's last pressure on me. I told him immediately: "I will only go to the border when my family is allowed to go with the group." I assured him that I would return under any circumstances. "Yes, but you know," replied Eichmann, "Brand assured me too. But look out. If you also remain abroad, there will be no more pardon. Your Jews will become acquainted with my vengeance."

It was stirring, how Eichmann clamped on to me....

PART VII—HOW THE BUDAPEST GHETTO WAS SAVED
p. 2:

New difficulties abroad

...Ketlitz, who had been expelled from Switzerland, joined us on our return trip. He swore he would revenge himself on Saly Mayer and the whole action. A heated debate now broke out over the text of the telegram to Becher. Ketlitz thought it could mean Becher's head if Himmler should find out that the whole action was a sham. The best thing now would be to tell the truth. The debate continued well into the night, by which time we returned to Bregenz. With all my might, I tried to convince Krell and Ketlitz that it would not be in Becher's best interest if he should receive a negative report. A negative telegram would expose him to the radicals, especially Eichmann and would be completely senseless. On the contrary, it was their duty to cover up for their chief, Becher, and to gain time. I argued further that it was clear that the difficulties on the Allies' part were only temporary. To blame for this are the foot marches, the liquidations in Slovakia, and the fact that the group from Bergen-Belson had not departed yet. A clear explanation on the part of the Germans about the handling of the Jewish question had to be forthcoming. Then the "business" would proceed.

SECTION 2 —SAVING OF THE REMAINING JEWS IN GERMANY
p. 16:

Wisliczeny's Tales

...So that something is done in the meantime, I make the following proposals:

1) Organize a transport of hidden Jews from Pressburg to Switzerland.
2) The train with the unemployed Jews from Vienna should also be sent to Switzerland instead of Theresienstadt.
3) A number of prominent Hungarian Jews are held as prisoners at Mauthausen. It would make a good impression on the Allies if these prominent prisoners were sent to Switzerland.

Becher: "What do you offer me for a transport from Pressburg?"

I tell him that it is possible to obtain various textiles, as well as some cooking oil. I will supply the trucks and gasoline for the transport. Saly Mayer answers that he first wants to talk to the Red Cross delegate about the clothing. By that time, winter will be over. March 3, 1945. The first lists of Hungarian Jews working at the border are received by Krumey's office. He agrees to send several hundred to the Vienna Jewish Hospital for a week of rest.

This plan did not come into fruition due to the Russian army's rapid advance....

pp. 29-30:

Kramer delivers a report. The capitulation of Bergen-Belson

...Hamburg is Becher's birthplace. Before we depart, he wants to show me the destroyed city. He takes me on a tour of the city. For minutes, the car travels between burned-out houses, through streets where no people can be seen because no home is occupied any more. The port presents the same picture of destruction. "And I am sure you must know," Becher says, clearly alluding to the destruction, "that German mothers and small children have also given their lives by the thousands during these air raids."

I remark that the war wasn't started by R.A.F. attacks.

Becher takes me for a walk in a very large park in Ludwigslust, which is connected to the Archduke of Mecklenburg's castle. He discusses the military situation openly.

"If we lose this damn war," Becher starts his statement, "I hope the Allies will have enough insight to appreciate our efforts and achievements. They must realize that this was only possible because I found the necessary support for my work in Himmler. If Mr. Saly Mayer would have behaved differently, if he had at least would have made more promises, I believe we could have achieved more. You have no idea how awkward Himmler's position was lately, due to the measures he took in the interest of the Jews and political prisoners such as Leon Blum, etc. I hope the time will come soon, when I can talk about this more freely."

As far as the military situation allows, he will visit other camps in my company, and take similar actions as in Bergen-Belson. "On all accounts," the following camps are to be visited: Oranienburg, Ravensbrück, Buchenwald, Dachau, Mauthausen, Theresienstadt.

We leave Ludswigslust at 2:45 PM. Above, low flying British planes accompany the retreating, beaten German army. Destroyed trucks in the streets, burning railroad cars in the train stations. The collapse takes on a tangible form.

We arrive in Berlin at 5:15 AM. At 9 PM, in my apartment, located at Fasanenstrasse, I hear on the radio, Stalin's Order of the Day: Vienna has been occupied....

p. 31:

April 15, 1945. At 10 PM, as the sirens announce the visit of the bombers, Becher's driver enters, and drives me to his apartment through the completely blacked out city, which is gradually illuminated by the colored tracers of the British planes. With the sound of the exploding bombs and the anti-aircraft guns in the background, Becher reports about his conference with Himmler.

"Himmler has been appointed by Hitler as Commander of the Eastern Front. He barely sleeps two hours daily and is swamped with agendas. He can't receive you.

"Regrettably, I have to report that people have been carried off from the camps, despite the orders given. I believe Kaltenbrunner has a hand in this.... Another report informed Himmler that the Russian prisoners of war and the Eastern laborers, who had been left behind for the Allies, had been armed by them and used against us. There are also reports that they are terrorizing

German civilians in sinister ways. It was suggested to Himmler, not to leave any Russians alive for the Allies.".…

p. 32:

Theresienstadt

The SS Command building is situated behind a red brick wall, which surrounds this fortress, built by the Empress Maria Theresa. A rope is stretched across the middle of the street, designating the beginning of the Ghetto. A Czech soldier walks back and forth in front of the cord. Behind the cord, walk star-wearing inmates of Theresienstadt.…

p. 34:

A theater performance was organized. On the expressionistic stage, boys and girls in Czech peasant costumes sing excerpts from "The Bartered Bride" by Smetana. A wonderful baritone and a somewhat tired alto add to the performance. These are children deported from the then Protectorate to Theresienstadt. Two artists from various Czech theaters and the Director of the Prague National Theater also took part.…

pp. 35-36:
April 19, 1945. Arrived in Switzerland.…

Himmler's disappointment

April 20, 1945. Repeated discussions with McClelland, Saly Mayer and Nathan Schwalb in Geneva. A final discussion with Becher is considered superfluous by them. On the 28th, Himmler, against Hitler's will, offered the Third Reich's capitulation to the Anglo-Saxons. In the search for contact points, he has made further concessions to Count Bernadotte during the last weeks and also permitted Jewish transports to Sweden.

On April 19, Himmler received, through the mediation of his Swedish doctor, the Swedish Jew, Mazur, representative of the World Jewish Congress, and listed his "accomplishments." (The concessions arranged by Becher.) He was already "disappointed" then, but what he said, wasn't only retrospective justification.

Among other things, he said:

"I left 450,000 (?!) Jews in Hungary, and what thanks did I get? The Jews in Budapest shot at our troops. I surrendered Bergen-Belson and Buchenwald without a fight, and received no thanks for that. I also left Theresienstadt undefended. As to refraining from forced evacuations, and the capitulation of the camps to the Allies is concerned, I will try to do my best. Last year, when I permitted 2,700 Jews to go to Switzerland, it was written that I was providing an alibi for myself. I don't need an alibi. I have always done what seemed right to me, for my people. I didn't become a rich man in the process."

RECOLLECTIONS
pp. 1-2:

After our parting in Berlin, Kurt Becher only visited Mauthausen. He brought the Commandant the order to surrender the camp to the Allies without a fight. Then he freed Dr. Moshe Schweiger and took him along. (Suspected of participation in the 1939 attack on Hitler, Schweiger was known to have been arrested by the Gestapo when the Germans entered Hungary.) Becher wanted to start his trip to the Swiss border in Dr. Schweiger's company. But the way was blocked by Allied forces. Before his arrest, near Bad Ischl, by the Americans, Becher turned over to Dr. Schweiger, a considerable amount of valuables which had been collected by the Vaadah, which had been the economic basis of the action. (When he accepted these valuables, Becher said that he wouldn't deliver these, unless his superiors forced him to do so.)

Dr. Schweiger gave the valuables to the American army's Intelligence Corps for safekeeping. The valuables turned over by Becher were estimated at several hundred thousand dollars. It will be the job of the Jewish Agency Executive to direct the use of the valuables. They will be put into the service of the Jewish community for a second time.

Immediately following the German surrender, American officials wanted to send the Bergen-Belson group from Switzerland to Philipsville in Africa, into an UNRRA camp, to fulfill an obligation to Switzerland. After various protests from the group, which was increased to a "resistance" by Dr. D. Hermann, the plan was dropped, with the consent of the Swiss government.

Later on, 700 from the group received immigration certificates. In August 1945, they started their trip from Switzerland to Palestine, in a closed group, under the leadership of Dr. Joseph Fischer.

An Aliyah, dreamed of and planned under strange circumstances in Budapest, finally, though a little late, came to fruition. It really can be called an "Aliyah" in the truest sense of the word.

In London, in September 1945, in a detailed eyewitness report, I described to the American Investigation Commission, chaired by Judge Jackson, the techniques and methods of the Jewish destruction organization, as I got to know it. This evidence was read and put into the record during the Nuremberg Trials, on December 12, 1945, by the American lawyer, Dodd.

From statements of Eichmann and Wisliczeny, I learned about the role the Mufti of Jerusalem had played. My testimony in this matter, published by the world press, gave cause for an interpolation in Britain's House of Commons....

pp. 3-6:
For the higher SS leaders, for the leaders of the Judenkommandos in Budapest, especially Eichmann, the Joint was a concept, which formed the psychological basis for their conduct of the negotiations. To them, the Joint was the embodiment of their idea of the "Jewish world power," "the Jewish world conspiracy," and "Jewish wealth." Their belief in the omnipotency of "World Jewry" over capitalists and Communists, over Allies and neutrals, over money and politics, was one of the driving forces in the Nazis' business schemes. World Jewry could, so they believed, exert the same power over the rest of the world, as the Nazi Party in their domain. Eichmann saw in us in Budapest, a sort of secret agent of this world power, the "Zionist shock troops" section, and he believed he was opposed to a malicious, camouflaged unit, as we declared, at the beginning, that we did not belong to the Joint.

The Germans gave us credit for many things. Until the end they did not completely grasp the complete absurdity of their demands for delivery of goods, their hope of political help. Himmler made no secret of his disappointment at the end. They saw in "Jewish delay tactics," sooner cunning and bad will, than an expression of weakness, which was much more real, as we could imagine, and many fearful Jewish leaders abroad, also assumed.

Philip von Freudiger, President of the Budapest Orthodox Congregation, resigned from the leadership of his Congregation in August, 1944 and fled to Rumania. His memoirs, edited in Bucharest, give a description of what happened, which is not incontestable in some parts. With all good intentions, it seems difficult, if not impossible, to retain a consistent objectivity in such a situation, especially if someone is involved, who could and would personally play a role in the happenings.

We mention Freudiger's memoirs mainly because they are the basis of the editing of the chapter in which the Budapest Journalist Ludwig Levai argues about the actions of our Vaadah. Levai's *Gray Book*, a work which contains many valuable dates and documents, but also numerous personal and objective errors, brings the critical remarks of Freudiger into a remarkable impressive viewpoint. Levai admits that the Zionists performed a "International rescue work on a grand scale," but some of the present leaders of Budapest Jewry, and some who play a role in the new Hungary, have been given an importance in the *Gray Book*, which has little to do with reality at that time.

The *Gray Book* also becomes a cautious echo of the various insinuations and rumors which are circulated about the "financial behavior" of our Vaadah. In reality, absolute personal confidence in the members and coworkers of the Vaadah was the basis of our activity. When we were forced to demand money and valuables from wealthy Jews, so that we could assist needy ones at the same time, we knowingly took the risk of subsequent abuse of us.

Our operation with the Germans, financing of Tijul, support of the hidden, had to be kept secret from the Hungarians. Today's critics are hardly identical with those who were willing, yesterday, to share with us the superhuman responsibility. That among these were also those who thank us for saving lives, is not surprising. It belongs to a chapter that could be written, titled "Humans in danger—and afterwards."

With an overzealousness, which could have been more prudent, we not only tried to save lives, but we also undertook the job of trying to get possibly a part of their lost fortunes transferred abroad. The honoring of the so-called Ha Avara Transfer, for which we had the Joint's, as well as the Jewish Agency's authorization, was delayed through bureaucratic procedures, for which, naturally, the Jewish organizations named were not to blame.

The unusual and, for the uninitiated, incomprehensible circumstances of our work, and the disorientation of public opinion, subsequently made it possible for Jewish Know-it-alls to try to discredit the Vaadah, and to make its work seem trivial. Two Budapest newspapers, *Villag* and *Vilagossag*, lent their names to "exposing" the case. *Villag* wrote (May 23, 1946),

"Under the Szotojay government, an extortion company, founded by Dr. Kasztner, occupied itself with the smuggling abroad of rich Jews... Dr. Kasztner had the reputation of having won great influence with the Gestapo. He aided rich Jews, not only to escape to Switzerland but also to Rumania.... He left the country, together with Gestapo officers, and took the obtained money and jewelry with him...." Villagossay limited itself to formulating questions: "Do the members of the Jewish Council know that Rezsö Kasztner, as confidant of the Gestapo, acted as a spy in Hungary and abroad? That before the collapse, he served as an SS First Lieutenant in Pressburg."

The investigation, started by Hungarian Justice officials, ended in dismissal of the case....

p. 6-7:

It shall be stressed at the end, that this report can only approximate a full understanding. Some connections and background, especially concerning international politics, are still not clear up to this date. They will probably stay this way for a long time, and for a reason. For example, one is not in a hurry to publish how an Allied diplomat reacted to the information that 100,000 Jews could be saved from being gassed, "But where will we put them?"

When some of our coworkers are not mentioned, or have not been sufficiently appreciated, it only happened because detailed reports from individual work sectors are very scarce. These reports will have to be written. The time cannot be far away, when one will not only be interested in the numerical balance of the tragedy. Perhaps an authority will be constituted to check the material, and as far as the destruction also involved Jewish responsibilities, deeds and failures, merit and errors, will prove their genuineness and judge accordingly.

Allow us to express our sincerest thanks to Mr. McClelland, the Representative of the War Refugee Board and incomparable mentor of Jewish rescue work.

Finally, we want to point to the fact that the Swiss government, with a grand gesture, granted permission for us to carry out our unusual diplomatic negotiations on Swiss territory. The generous acceptance of the Bergen-Belson group can also not remain unmentioned.

ROSWELL D. MCCLELLAND

Letter to Dr. Kasztner

February 6, 1946

*The Report of the Budapest Jewish Rescue
Committee—1942 – 1945*

*Kasztner appended this document and the next to his Report.
McClelland was the Representative for Switzerland of the
American War Refugee Board, involved in the Swiss border
negotiations arranged by Kasztner, between Jewish organizations there and the SS.—LB*

**The Foreign Service of the United States of America
American Legation**

As former Special Representative in Switzerland of the War Refugee Board,
established on January 22, 1944, by the President of the United States of
America in order "to take all measures within its power to rescue the victims
of enemy oppression who are in imminent danger of death and otherwise to
afford such victims all possible relief and assistance consistent with the successful prosecution of the war," I wish to make the following statement:

In spring 1944 the "SS" showed signs of shifting their interest from the
biological aspects of Jewish extermination to the purely military benefits in
labor, goods and money which could be derived from the Jews in their hands.

Seeing the defection in Nazi ranks, certain illegal Jewish rescue and relief
committees attempted to take advantage of this new situation by approaching representatives of the Nazi authorities, in order to obtain better treatment
for the Jewish population. As a result of these approaches some German officials, frightened by world reaction to the persecution of Jews in Hungary, by
the rapid deterioration of the German military situation, and doubtless in the
hope of gaining a measure of personal protection, displayed a willingness to

accord better treatment to Jewish hostages under their control. This readiness was typified by a series of German proposals which came to the attention of the War Refugee Board commencing in May 1944. Overtures were made by the German authorities through Portugal, Switzerland and Sweden for the discussion of terms for the release of Jews in Nazi hands.

As the result of these initiatives a protracted series of meetings took place during the fall of 1944 and spring of 1945 between Mr. Saly Mayer, representative of the Joint Distribution Committee in Switzerland and German representatives, in the presence of Dr. Kasztner, head of a Jewish rescue committee in Budapest. These meetings were held with the full knowledge of the War Refugee Board and of the Department of State. The British and Russian Governments also were kept advised.

Some tangible results were obtained during the course of these prolonged discussions. Two groups of Jews from Hungary totaling 1,673 persons were brought to Switzerland from the concentration camp at Bergen-Belson as a token of "good faith" on the part of the German negotiators. These two groups consisting of Jews partly saved from the ghettos of Transylvania, especially from Cluj, had left Budapest at the end of June 1944 for the camp of Bergen-Belson and were subsequently brought to Switzerland in August and December of the same year.

I wish to state that, in my capacity as representative in Switzerland of the War Refugee Board, I was fully informed of the various phases of the negotiations which led to the rescuing of these two Jewish groups, as were the War Refugee Board and Department of State in Washington.

I wish to add that, to the best of my knowledge, no charges could be made against those Jews on the spot who organized the release of these two groups nor against those who were included in these transports either because of their activities as organizers or members of these groups.

I can see no basis on which those who organized the departure of these people can reasonably be held responsible for the limited number of Jews who were authorized by the German authorities to leave the territory under their control, nor can the participants of these transports be held responsible for the fact that they and not other Jews were saved.

In view of the desperate circumstances prevailing at that time, and the mentality of the Nazi leaders involved, the very fact of bringing these two groups safely to Switzerland was to be considered as an achievement of great importance.

The attitude of the participants of these transports who have in the meantime returned to Rumania, Hungary and other countries should be considered in the light of the above-mentioned facts.

Bern, February 6, 1946
Roswell D. McClelland
Formerly Representative of the War Refugee Board and Special Assistant
to the American Minister at Bern

ROSWELL D. MCCLELLAND

Letter to Dr. Kasztner
July 18, 1946
The Report of the Budapest Jewish Rescue
Committee—1942 – 1945

> *There is no doubt that the U.S. government did not think*
> *Kasztner collaborated. They took his War Crimes Tribunal tes-*
> *timony re Eichmann & Co. precisely because of this. However*
> *McClelland had no firsthand knowledge of what transpired in*
> *Hungary. Nor is he likely to have known, then or later, what*
> *Kasztner had or would say on behalf of all seven war crimi-*
> *nals.—LB*

American Legation
Bern, July 18, 1946
Dr. I. Kasztner
1, rue Marignac, Geneva

Dear Dr. Kasztner:
In view of your impending departure for Hungary where, I believe, there has
been some misunderstanding concerning the valuable services performed by
you during the war in the rescue of Jews from Hungary and elsewhere, I am
pleased to take this opportunity, as former special representative for
Switzerland of the President's WAR REFUGEE BOARD, to rectify certain
regrettable omissions in the final report of the WAR REFUGEE BOARD
issued in Washington, D.C. on September 15, 1945.

With reference to the prolonged and difficult negotiations which took
place at the Swiss border and in Switzerland during the fall, winter and early
spring of 1944-1945 in an effort to alleviate the situation of and to rescue
persecuted Jews from Hungary, there has never been any question, certainly

262

in my mind, that along with Mr. Saly Mayer, Kurt Becher of the SS, of course, and a few others for both the Hungarian and German sides, you played an indispensable and highly important role. Had it not been for your original initiative in Budapest in establishing the necessary contact and "working agreement" and for your constant mediatory action throughout (in enemy-occupied territory, it might be added) it is difficult to imagine that these negotiations could have taken place at all, or at least that they could have produced anywhere near as successful results as they did. I therefore feel that the omission of your name in the section of the WAR REFUGEE BOARD'S report dealing with this question, when Mr. Mayer's was mentioned, distinctly calls for this amending statement on my part as the one person on the WAR REFUGEE BOARD'S side who was intimately acquainted with this effort.

In closing may I wish you every success in your future endeavors in behalf of your people. I trust that they may be as successful, though not as difficult, as those which you have already accomplished.

Very truly yours,
Roswell D. McClelland
Former Representative of the War Refugee Board

"'I Transported Them to the Butcher,' Eichmann's Own Story: Part I"

Life
November 28, 1960

Adolf Eichmann must have followed Kasztner's trial in 1954 in the international press. He described his relations with him in taped interviews he gave a Dutch Nazi journalist in 1955. Parts of them were published by Life *magazine after his capture, by Israeli agents, in 1960.*

All the interviews were submitted to the court during Eichmann's trial. Only some were admitted into evidence, in the court's concern to uphold this singular defendant's rights, so that nothing would smudge what it knew would be their guilty verdict. Today of course everyone accepts them as indisputably his statement. But the Life *version acquired independent documentary quality as they were what the Israeli and world public read.*

Israelis assumed that Eichmann would be questioned about his relations with Kasztner. But a Jewish witness wanted to defend him. The prosecutor realized there would be an outcry if he praised the Laborite. If Eichmann was questioned and implicated Kasztner, Israelis would reexamine Labor's Holocaust record. So the witness was dropped.—LB

Introduction

How much time fate allows me to live, I do not know. I do know that someone must inform this generation and those to come about the happenings of my era. I am writing this story at a time when I am in full possession of my physical and mental freedom, influenced or pressed by no one. May future historians be objective enough not to stray from the path of the true facts recorded here.

I have slowly tired of living as an anonymous wanderer between two worlds, wanted even by the police of my homeland. At Nürnberg, my most trusted subordinate testified against me. So did others. Perhaps these people referred to me to whitewash themselves. But when such a thing goes on for years and everyone joins in, blaming me for the deeds of all, a legend is created in which exaggeration plays a large part.

In actual fact, I was merely a little cog in the machinery that carried out the directives and orders of the German Reich. I am neither a murderer nor a mass-murderer. I am a man of average character, with good qualities and many faults. I was not "Czar of the Jews," as a Paris newspaper once called me, nor was I responsible for all the good and evil deeds done against them. Where I was implicated in the physical annihilation of the Jews, I admit my participation freely and without pressure. After all, I was the one who transported the Jews to the camps. If I had not transported them, they would not have been delivered to the butcher.

Yet what is there to "admit?" I carried out my orders. It would be as pointless to blame me for the whole Final Solution of the Jewish Problem as to blame the official in charge of the railroads over which the Jewish transports traveled. Where would we have been if everyone had thought things out in those days? You can do that today in the "new" German army. But with us an order was an order. If I had sabotaged the order of the onetime Führer of the German Reich, Adolf Hitler, I would have been not only a scoundrel but a despicable pig, like those who broke their military oath to join the ranks of the anti-Hitler criminals in the conspiracy of July 20, 1944.

The order for annihilation

At the Nürnberg trial the world was given a new interpretation of justice. Not one Russian, no Israeli, no Englishman or North American was punished in even a single instance because he carried out commands given to him while he was in an official position or under military oath. Why should the gallows or the penitentiary be reserved for Germans only?

But I am getting ahead of my story. It is time to outline my rank and duties in the events which I shall discuss, and to introduce myself:

Name: Adolf Otto Eichmann
Nationality: German
Occupation: Lieutenant Colonel SS (retired)

The area of my section's authority was those Jewish matters within the competence of the Gestapo. Originally this centered on the problems of finding out whether a person was a Gentile or a Jew. If he turned out to be a Jew, we were the administrative authority which deprived him of his German citizenship and confiscated his property. Ultimately we declared him an enemy of the state. After the onetime German Führer gave the order for the physical annihilation of the Jews, our duties shifted. We supervised Gestapo seizures of German Jews and the trains that took them to their final destination. And throughout German-occupied Europe my advisers from my office saw to it that the local governments turned their Jewish citizens over to the German Reich. For all this, of course, I will answer. I was not asleep during the war years.

I began my work with the Jewish question in 1935 in Berlin where I had been transferred after service with one of the early SS training companies. My first assignment there had been extremely dull, sorting what ultimately became a huge card index of Jews, Freemasons, members of various secret societies and other subversive elements in the Reich. In time, however, my superiors allowed me to start work on the solution of the Jewish problem.

I must confess that I did not greet this assignment with the apathy of an ox being led to his stall. On the contrary, I was fascinated with it. My chief, General Reinhard Heydrich, encouraged me to study and acquaint myself even with its theological aspects. In the end I learned to speak Hebrew, although badly.

Some of my early work was with the Nürnberg laws, in force since 1935. Under the formula adopted at that time for "Final Solution of the Jewish Question," the laws were intended to drive Jews out of all phases of German life. My experience in this field was often of a confidential and rather embarrassing nature, as when I established that the Führer's diet cook, who was at one time his mistress, was 1/32nd Jewish. My immediate superior, Lieutenant General Heinrich Müller, quickly classified my report as Top Secret.

In 1937 after I had been struggling with Hebrew for two and a half years, I had a chance to take a trip to Palestine. We were most interested in the Palestine emigration and I wanted to find out at what point a Jewish state in Palestine might be set up. Unfortunately Palestine was then in turmoil and the British turned down my application for an extended stay. I did see enough to be very impressed by what the Jewish colonists were building up their land. I admired their desperate will to live, the more so since I was myself an idealist.

In the years that followed I often said to Jews with whom I had dealings that, had I been a Jew, I would have been a fanatical Zionist. I could not imagine being anything else. In fact, I would have been the most ardent Zionist imaginable.

A yellow star on their clothing

In those days before the outbreak of the war, the former government of the Reich hoped to solve the Jewish problem by forced emigration. This was easier said than done, since one had to reckon here the difficulties of emigration as a mass project. The Jewish organizations with the widest experience in this had already been closed down as unacceptable to the government. There was also a tendency among Jews to wait it out on the theory that the Hitler regime would be of short duration. Of the 500,000 avowed Jews who were in Germany in 1933, plus a number who were considered Jews under the Nürnberg Laws, not more than 130,000 managed to leave before 1938.

It may have been the Propaganda Ministry that first thought up the idea of forcing all Jews to wear a yellow star on their clothing. I remember that when Julius Streicher heard about it he whinnied with delight. His newspaper, *Der Stürmer*, devoted an entire issue to this matter, I naturally took part in the administrative details, since as the department head for Jewish affairs in the Gestapo, my countersignature was required. In fact, I recall the day when I received bolts and bolts of yellow cloth to distribute. I issued the cloth to my Jewish functionaries and they trotted off with them.

We did not devise the yellow star to put pressure on the Jews themselves. On the contrary, its purpose was to control the natural tendency of our German people to come to the aid of someone in trouble. The marking was intended to hinder any such assistance to Jews who were being harassed. We wanted Germans to feel embarrassed, to feel afraid of having any contact with Jews. So our administration was quite happy to distribute these bolts of yellow cloth and to regulate the time limit by which the stars would have to be worn.

It was in 1938, at the reunion of Austria with the German Reich, that General Heydrich gave me the order, in my capacity as a specialist in Jewish affairs, to set the Jewish emigration in motion from Vienna.

I found Jewish life in Austria completely disorganized. Most Jewish organizations had already been closed down by the police and their leaders put under arrest. To speed up emigration I called in local Jewish leaders and established a central office for Jewish emigration. It was located in the Rothschild Palace in the Prinz Eugen Strasse.

As with the other, similar central offices, the Vienna office permitted emigrating Jews to take household goods with them. For the custody and administration of Jewish property so-called administrative and accounting centers were later created which worked with tidy accuracy and correctness. Reichsführer Heinrich Himmler, who surprisingly enough often busied himself with the smallest details of the Jewish problem, personally set up the strict administrative standards which were observed in this field. In Vienna alone we were able to prepare as many as 1,000 Jews daily for emigration.

The Jewish SS sergeant

One of the most useful of the Jewish leaders in these days was a Dr. Storfer, a senior civil servant who had been a major in the Austrian army in World War I. I had a weakness for this Dr. Storfer. He never took a penny from his racial comrades and he had a very nice, proper way of negotiating. Unfortunately, years later Storfer made a stupid blunder. He tried to escape. My second in command had never liked him and he had him shot at Auschwitz.

In general we respected Jewish combat veterans of World War I. We even had some Jewish SS men who had taken part in the early struggles of the Nazis—about 50 of them in Germany and Austria. I remember giving my personal attention to a Jewish SS sergeant, a good man, who wanted to leave for Switzerland. I had instructed the border control to let him pass, but when he reached the Swiss border he apparently thought something had gone wrong. He tried to cross illegally through the woods and he was shot. He was a 100 percent Jew, a man of the most honorable outlook.

Through all this period I saw the Jewish problem as a question to be solved politically. So did Himmler and the entire Gestapo. It was not a matter of emotion. My SS comrades and I rejected the crude devices of burning temples, robbing Jewish stores and maltreating Jews on the streets. We wanted no violence. One of my former officers was expelled from the SS for beating up four or five Jews in the cellar of our offices. Barring such exceptions, each of us, as an individual, had no wish to harm the individual Jew personally.

For the sake of the truth I cannot refrain from mentioning a small incident in which I myself violated this code of correctness. On day I called in Dr. Löwenherz, whom I appointed director of the Jewish community in Vienna. He answered my questions with evasions and, I believe, untruth. Owing to a temporary lack of self-control, I hit him in the face. I mentioned this affair to Dr. Löwenherz later in the presence of some of my subordinates and expressed my regrets to him over the matter.

As late as 1940, after we beat the French, we were devising plans for further mass emigration of the Jews to Madagascar. I had my legal experts draft a complete law covering the resettlement of the Jews there on territory which was to be declared Jewish. They would live there without restraint except, of course, they would be under the protectorate of the German Reich. Unfortunately, by the time the obstacles created by bureaucracy for this plan had been overcome, the scales of victory were balanced in such a way that Madagascar was out of our grasp.

The final solution: liquidation

The continuance of the war finally changed out attitude on emigration entirely. In 1941 the Führer himself ordered the physical annihilation of the Jewish enemy. What made him take this step I do not know. But for one thing the war in Russia was not going along in the Blitz fashion the High Command had planned. The ruinous struggle on two fronts had begun. And already Dr. Chaim Weizmann, the world Zionist leader, had declared war on Germany in the name of Jewry. It was inevitable that the answer of the Führer would not be long in coming.

Soon after the order General Heydrich called me to his office in the Prinz Albrecht Strasse. He told me about Reichsführer Himmler's order that all emigration of Jews was to be prohibited—with no more exceptions. He assured me that neither I nor my men would have anything to do with the physical liquidation. We would act only as policemen; that is, we would round up the Jews for the others.

By this time the formula "Final Solution for the Jewish Question" had taken on a new meaning: liquidation. In this new sense we discussed it at a special conference on Jan. 10, 1942 in the Wannsee section of Berlin. It was I who had to bustle over to Heydrich with the portfolio of invitations on which he scribbled his "Heydrich," stroke for stroke. So we sent out the whole thing. A few people declined to participate, on grounds principally of other duties.

After the conference, as I recall, Heydrich, Müller and your humble servant sat cozily around the fireplace. I noticed for the first time that Heydrich was smoking. Not only that, but he had a cognac. Normally he touched nothing alcoholic. The only other time I had seen him drinking was at an office party years before. We all had drinks then. We sang songs. After a while we got up on the chairs and drank a toast, then on the table and then round and round—on the chairs and on the table again. Heydrich taught it to us. It was an old North German custom.

But we sat around peacefully after our Wannsee Conference, not just talking shop but giving ourselves a rest after so many taxing hours.

It is not true that Reichsführer Himmler set down in writing anything ordering the annihilation of the Jews. Do you think he sat down to write, "My dear Eichmann, the Führer has ordered the physical annihilation of the Jews?" The truth is that Himmler never put a line in writing on this subject. I know that he always gave his instructions orally to Lieut. General Oswald Pohl, in charge of the economic administration which ran the concentration camps. I never received any order of this sort.

I would like to stress again, however, that my department never gave a single annihilation order. We were responsible only for deportations. In every European country under our jurisdiction it was the job of the Jewish Adviser (the representative of my office) to work through local officials until he had attained our goal: a roundup of the Jews and their delivery to the transports.

I had Captain Richter sitting in Bucharest, Captain Wisliceny in Pressburg [Bratislava], Dannecker in Paris, etc. All these Jewish Advisers enjoyed the greatest respect, for each of them was really the long arm of Himmler himself. Although I myself had a relatively low rank, I was the only department head in the Gestapo with my own representatives in foreign countries. If one of my specialists got in trouble with a local commander, I would then have my bureau chief, General Müller, give the necessary orders. Müller was more feared than Reichsführer Himmler.

I carefully set up my timetables for the transports with the Ministry of Transportation, and the trains were soon rolling. But through the years we met many difficulties. In France the French police helped only hesitantly. After its initial enthusiasm for the project, the Laval government itself became more and more cautious. Italy and Belgium were by and large failures. And in Holland the battle for the Jews was especially hard and bitter. The Dutch, for one thing, did not make the distinction between Dutchmen and Jews with Dutch citizenship. A person was either Dutch, they said, or he wasn't. Denmark posed the greatest difficulties of all. The King intervened for the Jews there, and most of them escaped.

Yet we managed after a struggle to get the deportations going. Trainloads of Jews were soon leaving from France and Holland. It was not for nothing that I made so many trips to Paris and The Hague. My interest here was only in the number of transport trains I had to provide. Whether they were bank directors or mental cases, the people who were loaded on these trains meant nothing to me. It was really none of my business.

In general, I found that there were fewer problems with local authorities the farther east you went—with the exception of the assimilated Jews in Hungary. The Romanian operations went off without friction. Captain Richter in Bucharest was a good man. Eager to strike against these parasites, the Romanians astonishingly enough liquidated thousands and thousands of their own Jews. Slovakian officials offered their Jews to us like someone throwing away sour beer. Tiso, the Catholic priest who ran the government there, was an anti-Semite.

Tiso's attitude contrasted with mine. I am no anti-Semite. I was just politically opposed to Jews because they were stealing the breath of life from us.

The chambers at Maidenek

It was in the latter part of 1941 that I saw the first preparations for annihilating the Jews. General Heydrich ordered me to visit Maidanek, a Polish village near Lublin. A German police captain showed me how they had managed to build airtight chambers disguised as ordinary Polish farmers' huts, seal them hermetically, then inject the exhaust gas from a Russian U-boat motor. I remember it all very exactly because I never thought that anything like that would be possible, technically speaking.

Not long afterward Heydrich had me carry an order to Major General Odilo Globocnik, SS commander of the Lublin district. I cannot remember whether Heydrich gave me the actual message or whether I had to draw it up. It ordered Globocnik to start liquidating a quarter million Polish Jews.

Later that year I watched my first execution. It was at Minsk, which had recently come under German occupation. I was sent by my immediate superior, General Müller. Müller never stirred from behind his desk at Gestapo headquarters but he knew everything that went on in Europe. He liked to send me around on his behalf. I was in effect a traveling salesman for the Gestapo, just as I had once been a traveling salesman for an oil company in Austria.

Müller had heard that Jews were being shot near Minsk, and he wanted a report. I went there and showed my orders to the local SS commander. "That's a fine coincidence," he said. "Tomorrow 5,000 of them are getting theirs."

When I rode out the next morning, they had already started, so I could see only the finish. Although I was wearing a leather coat which reached almost to my ankles, it was very cold. I watched the last group of Jews undress, down to their shirts. They walked the last 100 or 200 yards—they were not driven—then they jumped into the pit. It was impressive to see them all jumping into the pit without offering any resistance whatsoever. Then the men of the squad banged away into the pit with their rifles and machine pistols.

Why did the scene linger so long in my memory? Perhaps because I had children myself. And there were children in the pit. I saw a women hold a child of a year or two into the air, pleading. At that moment all I wanted to say was, "Don't shoot, hand over the child...." Then the child was hit.

I was so close that later I found bits of brains splattered on my long leather coat. My driver helped me remove them. Then we returned to Berlin. The Gestapo chauffeurs did not like to drive me, principally because I rarely spoke more than 20 words during a 12-hour trip, as for instance the long haul from Berlin to Paris. On this trip back from Minsk I spoke hardly a word. I was thinking. Not that I had become contemptuous of National Socialism after watching this previously unimaginable event. I was reflecting on the meaning of life in general.

Having seen what I had in Minsk, I said this when I reported back to Müller: "The solution, Gruppenführer, was supposed to have been a political one. But now that the Führer has ordered a physical solution, obviously a physical solution it must be. But we cannot go on conducting executions as they were done in Minsk and, I believe, other places. Of necessity our men will be educated to become sadists. We cannot solve the Jewish problem by putting a bullet through the brain of a defenseless woman who is holding her child up to us."

Müller did not answer. He just looked at me in a fatherly, benevolent fashion. I never could figure him out.

Later in that same winter Müller sent me to watch Jews being gassed in the Litzmannstadt [Lodz] area of central Poland. I must stress that the gassing was not done on his orders, but Müller did want to know about it. He was a very thorough government official.

Arriving at Litzmannstadt, I drove out to the designated place where a thousand Jews were about to board buses. The buses were normal, high-windowed affairs with all their windows closed. During the trip, I was told, the carbon monoxide from the exhaust pipe was conducted into the interior of the buses. It was intended to kill the passengers immediately.

A doctor who was there suggested that I look at the people inside one bus through a peephole in the driver's seat. I refused. I couldn't look. This was the first time that I had seen and heard such a thing and my knees were buckling under me. I had been told that the whole process took only three minutes, but the buses rode along for about a quarter of an hour.

We reached our destination and hell opened up for me for the first time. The bus in which I was riding turned and backed up before a pit about two meters deep. The doors opened. Some Poles who stood there jumped into the buses and threw the corpses into the pit. I was badly shaken by what I then saw. Another Pole with a pair of pliers in his hand jumped into the pit. He went through the corpses, opening their mouths. Whenever he saw a gold tooth, he pulled it out and dumped it into a small bag he was carrying.

When I reported back to Müller in Berlin, he chided me for not having timed the procedure with a stopwatch. I said to him, "This sort of thing can't go on. Things shouldn't be done this way." I admitted I had not been able to look through the peephole. This time, too, Müller behaved like a sphinx. He forgave me, so to speak, for not having looked. Perhaps "forgive" sounds like an odd expression here.

The executions at Litzmannstadt and Minsk were a deep shock to me. Certainly I too had been aiming at a solution of the Jewish problem, but not like this. Of course, at that time I had not yet seen burned Germans, Germans shrunken like mummies in death. I had yet to see the heavy, imploring eyes of the old couple in a Berlin air raid shelter who lay crushed beneath a beam, begging me to shoot them. I couldn't bear to shoot them, but I told my sergeant to do so, if he could. If I had known then the horrors that would later happen to Germans, it would have been easier for me to watch the Jewish executions. At heart I am a very sensitive man. I simply can't look at any suffering without trembling myself.

The gas chambers at Auschwitz

I never had anything directly to do with the gas chambers, which evolved from early measures like those at Litzmannstadt. But I did visit Auschwitz repeatedly. It had an unpleasant smell. Even today I do not know how the gassing was carried out. I never watched the entire process. Even a man like Hoess, the commandant at Auschwitz, described the matter to me in a rather rose-colored way.

I knew Hoess well. He did his duty at Auschwitz, as any other man would have done it. It was Hoess who once told me that Reichsführer Himmler, taking a personal look at the entire liquidating action, had declared that this was a bloody fight which our coming generations would need to fight no more. I valued Hoess as an excellent comrade and a very proper fellow. He was a good family man, and he held the Iron Cross from the first World War.

Since the war I have read that two and a half million Jews were physically liquidated under Hoess's command. I find this figure incredible. The capacity of the camp argues against it. Many of the Jews confined there were put on work details and survived. After the war the Auschwitzers sprouted like mushrooms out of the forest floor after a rain. Hundreds of thousands of them are today in the best of health.

Along with the liquidation camps we continued to maintain the ghetto system. I would not say I originated the ghetto system. That would be to claim too great a distinction. The father of the ghetto system was the orthodox Jew, who wanted to remain by himself. In 1939, when we marched into Poland, we found a system of ghettos already in existence, begun and maintained by the Jews. We merely regulated these, sealed them off with walls and barbed wire and included even more Jews than were dwelling in them.

The assimilated Jew was of course very unhappy about being moved to a ghetto. But the Orthodox were pleased with the arrangement, as were the Zionists. The latter found ghettos a wonderful device for accustoming Jews to community living. Dr. Epstein from Berlin once said to me that Jewry was grateful for the chance I gave it to learn community life at the ghetto I founded at Theresienstadt, 40 miles from Prague. He said it made an excellent school for the future in Israel. The assimilated Jews found ghetto life degrading and non-Jews may have seen an unpleasant element of force in it. But basically most Jews feel well and happy in their ghetto life, which cultivates their peculiar sense of unity.

Revolt of Warsaw Jews
The uprising of the Warsaw Ghetto in 1943, however, taught us a bitter lesson about putting excessive numbers of people into these enclosures. Not long after this uprising I received in my office a photo album with an accompanying memo from Reichsführer Himmler, the album showed the phases of that battle, whose severity surprised even the German units fighting in it. I still recall today how we in the SS and the Wehrmacht suffered disproportionately high casualties putting down this revolt. I could not believe, seeing the pictures, that men in a ghetto could fight like that.

During this great bloodletting in Warsaw the order went out to the German occupation authorities to comb the country relentlessly. This was done so thoroughly that after a while there was no more Jewish question in Poland at all.

Elsewhere, even inside the Reich itself, the Warsaw Ghetto uprising had its effect in stringent measures against those Jews still engaged in forced factory labor. It was not in vain that Himmler put his entire weight behind this severity. Previously the directors of the big German factories, even Göring himself, the administrator of the Four Year Plan, had intervened on behalf of sparing Jews for the labor force. Now we in the Gestapo said simply, "Very well, you take the responsibility that things do not come to an uprising like the Warsaw Ghetto." When we said that, the urge to intervene left them.

The Warsaw Ghetto uprising had an equally strong effect with authorities in the other occupied countries. Every national leadership was anxious to remove factors of unrest. My advisers now had a perfect entree in the countries where they were assigned. We could and did use the Warsaw example like a traveling salesman who sells an article all the more easily by showing a special advertising attraction.

With Hungary we were particularly concerned. The Hungarian Jews had lived through the war relatively untouched by severe restrictions. Now Himmler made it clear that he wanted Hungary combed with a tremendous thoroughness before the Jews could really wake up to our plans and organize partisan resistance. For this reason, he chose me to lead the march into Hungary in person.

Before dawn on March 19, 1944, I was leading an SS convoy from the Mauthausen concentration camp toward Budapest, on these orders from Reichsführer Himmler to clear the Jews out of Hungary. My men were equipped with combat gear in case the Hungarians resisted. We had several air raid warnings along the way. Suddenly my advance guard halted. The column came to a stop. Tipped off probably by one of my assistants, the unit commanders gathered around my personal truck and drank a toast to me with the rum they were issued for the march. It was my 38th birthday, my seventh as an SS officer.

On a Sunday morning in brilliant sunshine we crossed the border into Hungary. Instead of rifle fire or rebellious shouts we were greeted with cheers by the villagers and treated to white bread and wine. We put away our small arms then, because it was obvious there would be no resistance. That afternoon we rolled into Budapest and I immediately set up a small office in a corner of my bedroom in one of the great hotels.

I worked almost all that night putting out decrees calling the Jewish political officials to the first conferences the following day. I had already given orders to collect these Jewish officials in advance. Because I planned to work with them, I wanted to insure that they would not be harmed by any right-wing hysteria.

In Hungary my basic orders were to ship all Jews out of the country in as short a time as possible. Now, after years of working behind a desk, I had come out into the raw reality of the field. As Müller put it, they had sent me, the "master" himself, to make sure the Jews did not revolt as they had in the Warsaw Ghetto. I use the word "master" in quotation marks because people used it to describe me. I did not use it first.

Since they had sent the "master," however, I wanted to act like a master. I resolved to show how well a job could be done when the commander stands 100 percent behind it. By shipping the Jews off in a lightening operation, I wanted to set an example for future campaigns elsewhere.

The shipments to Auschwitz

All told, we succeeded in processing about half a million Jews in Hungary. I once knew the exact number that we shipped to Auschwitz, but today I can only estimate that it was around 350,000 in a period of about four months. But, contrary to legend, the majority of the deportees were not gassed at all but put to work in munitions plants. That is why there are thousands of Jews happily alive today who are included in the statistical totals of the "liquidated." Besides those we sent to Auschwitz, there were thousands and thousands who fled, some secretly, some with our connivance. It was child's play for a Jew to reach relative safety in Rumania if he could muster the few pengö to pay for a railroad ticket or an auto ride to the border. There were also 200,000 Jews left in a huge ghetto when the Russians arrived, and thousands more waiting to emigrate illegally to Palestine or simply hiding out from the Hungarian Gendarmerie.

It is clear from statistics, then, that our operation was not a battle fought with knives, pistols, carbines or poison gas. We used spiritual methods to reach our goal. Let us keep this distinction clear, because physical liquidation is a vulgar, coarse action.

Soon after we arrived in Budapest I met a Dr. László Endre, then a Budapest country official, who was eager to free Hungary of the Jewish "plague," as he put it. One evening he arranged a little supper for me and my assistant, Captain Dieter Wisliceny. Two or three other Hungarian officials were present and an orderly in livery who stood at Dr. Endre's side. On this evening the fate of the Jews in Hungary was sealed.

As I got to know Dr. Endre, I noticed his energy and his ardent desire to serve his Hungarian fatherland. He made it clear that in his present position he was unable to do positive work toward solving the Jewish question. So, I suggested to Major General Winkelmann, the ranking SS officer in Hungary, that Dr. Endre be transferred to the Ministry of the Interior. The transfer took several weeks, which I spent conferring with various Jewish officials and learning about Jewish life in Hungary. Then one day Dr. Endre became second secretary in the Ministry of the Interior, and a certain László Baky became first secretary.

Over the years I had learned through practice which hooks to use to catch which fish, and I was now able to make the operation easy for myself. It was clear to me that I, as a German, could not demand the Jews from the Hungarians. We had had too much trouble with that in Denmark. So I left the entire matter to the Hungarian authorities. Dr. Endre, who became one of the best friends I have had in my life, put out the necessary regulations, and Bakay and his Hungarian Gendarmerie carried them out. Once these two secretaries gave their orders, the Minister of the Interior had to sign them. And so it was no miracle that the first transport trains were soon rolling toward Auschwitz.

The Hungarian police caught the Jews, brought them together and loaded them on the trains under the direct command of Lieut. Colonel László Ferenczy of the Gendarmerie, who came from an old, landed family. If I may digress for a moment, I remember that he invited me once to his country estate, where we had a little Hungarian snack of slices of bacon and onion stuck on sticks and roasted over a fire. We ate them with wine from the lieutenant colonel's vineyards. I since have read that he was hanged after 1945.

I never watched the Jews being loaded onto the trains. It was a minor matter for which I had no time. Since the job was the responsibility of the Gendarmerie, it would have constituted an interference with the internal affairs of Hungary if I had even observed the loadings. After all, the Hungarian government was still a sovereign power, although it had reached certain agreements with the Reich.

Himmler's instructions were for me to comb the Jews out of eastern Hungary first. The two secretaries gave the appropriate orders to the Hungarian police. I was also instructed to send almost all transports to the railroad station at Auschwitz, and I ordered Captain Novak to draw up a timetable and arrange for the necessary trains from the Reich's transportation ministry. To each train I assigned a squad of Orpos—uniformed German police—from the several hundred assigned to me.

My men had as one of their basic orders that all necessary harshness was to be avoided. This fundamental principle was also accepted by the Hungarian officials. In practice they may not have adhered to it 100 percent. But that did not and could not interest me, because it was not my responsibility.

Inhumanity among the Hungarians

There were, however, individual cases where my men were shocked by the inhumanity of the Hungarian police. Wisliceny reported to me that the Gendarmes were driving the Jews into the cars like cattle to a slaughterhouse, not everywhere but in some districts. Several times I reminded the Hungarian government in writing—nothing was done orally in my office—that we did not want to punish individual Jews. We wanted to work toward a political solution.

Nevertheless, even as our own units were guilty of roughness here and there. I once saw a soldier beat a frail old Jew over the head with a rubber club. I spoke to the soldier, reported him to his commander and demanded he be punished and demoted. Himmler would not stand for that kind of thing. That is sadism.

I would like to add here that when millions of Germans were deported by the Allies after the war from Eastern Europe to Germany, the operation was not carried out the way we did it with Prussian exactness about provisions and transportation. Although we had the greatest difficulty in obtaining trains, the Jews were always shipped in covered, not open cars, and always by the quickest possible routes.

In Hungary it sometimes happened that there were too few slop buckets on the trains, too little drinking water or no drinking water at all, or that the provisions were bad or stolen during the loading. The Gendarmes sometimes overloaded the cars to empty the debarkation camp as quickly as possible. You can imagine how it was when the Hungarians peremptorily ordered "Everybody in, in, in. The border comes in 240 kilometers, and then Germany. Let the Germans finish things up."

Matters were different on Reich territory where we had full powers. The lieutenant of the guard, for example, could hold the train up until fresh water was provided and the slop buckets emptied and cleaned out, if only to avoid epidemics. After all, we were supposed to bring the material to the concentration camp ready to start work, not sickly and exhausted.

In spite of all our efforts Commandant Hoess at Auschwitz often complained about the condition of the Jews who arrived from Hungary. This proves that Auschwitz was not primarily a death camp. If Hoess simply sent the Jews into the oven, it would not have made any difference to him. He would not have complained to General Pohl, his chief, when a few corpses were lying around in the cars because people had given them too little to eat or drink. And Pohl would certainly not have asked to see me, making the complaints known to me in rather blunt terms. I replied of course that I was not really responsible because the Hungarian government had arranged the details of the loading.

As the transport trains rolled into Auschwitz, sometimes bringing as many as 10,000 units a day, the camp staff had to work day and night. I was on close, comradely terms with Hoess and he told me he could not understand why I showed absolutely no consideration for him and his staff. But how could I? I was just as limited a specialist in my own sector as he was in his. Yet I liked to visit him. He lived with his wife and children in a five-room house on the campgrounds. It was a homey place, clean and simple and furnished in SS-style natural wood.

The charred mountain of corpses

I remember clearly the first time he guided me around the camp. He showed me everything, and at the end he took me to a grave where the corpses of the gassed Jews lay piled on a strong iron grill. Hoess's men poured some inflammable liquid over them and set them on fire. The flesh stewed like stew meat. The sight made such an impression on me that today, after a dozen years, I can still see that mountain of corpses in front of me.

Hoess may have seen disgust in my face, but I spoke to him sternly: "When I see your corpses, I think of those charred German bodies in the air raid shelters in Berlin."

Once the deportations to Auschwitz were running smoothly, I turned to concentrate on negotiations with the Jewish political community officials in Budapest. In this I was carrying out the second basic objective of Reichsführer Himmler: to arrange if possible for a million Jews to go free in exchange for 10,000 winterized trucks, with trailers, for use against the Russians on the Eastern Front.

" 'To Sum It All Up, I Regret Nothing,' Eichmann's Own Story: Part II"
Life
December 5, 1960

Only Heinrich Himmler could turn off the liquidation machine. It was in 1944, the year of the assassination attempt on Hitler, when Reichsführer Himmler took over as commander of the Reserve Army, that he authorized me to propose an exchange: one million Jews for 10,000 winterized trucks with trailers. The world Jewish organization could decide for itself what Jews it wanted to choose. We asked only that they get us 10,000 trucks. Thanks to Himmler's directive, I could assure them, on my word of honor, that these trucks would be used only on the Eastern front. As I said at the time, "When the 10,000 winterized trucks with trailers are here, then the liquidation machine in Auschwitz will be stopped."

In obedience to Himmler's directive I now concentrated on negotiations with the Jewish political officials in Budapest. One man stood out among them, Dr. Rudolf Kastner, authorized representative of the Zionist movement. This Dr. Kastner was a young man about my age, an ice-cold lawyer and a fanatical Zionist. He agreed to help keep the Jews from resisting deportation and even keep order in the collection camps if I would close my eyes and let a few hundred or a few thousand young Jews emigrate illegally to Palestine. It was a good bargain. For keeping order in the camps, the price of 15,000 to 20,000 Jews—in the end there may have been more—was not too high for me.

Except perhaps for the first few sessions, Kastner never came to me fearful of the Gestapo strong man. We negotiated entirely as equals. People forget that. We were political opponents trying to arrive at a settlement, and we trusted each other perfectly. When he was with me, Kastner smoked cigarettes as though he were in a coffeehouse. While we talked he would smoke

one aromatic cigarette after another, taking them from a silver case and lighting them with a little silver lighter. With his great polish and reserve he
would have made an ideal Gestapo officer himself.

Dr. Kastner's main concern was to make it possible for a select group of
Hungarian Jews to emigrate to Israel. But the Arrow Cross, the Hungarian
fascist party, had grown strong and stubborn. Its inspectors permitted no
exceptions to the mass deportations. So the Jewish officials turned to the
German occupation authorities. They realized that we were specialists who
had learned about Jewish affairs through years of practice.

Immensely idealistic Zionists
As a matter of fact, there was a very strong similarity between our attitudes in
the SS and the viewpoint of these immensely idealistic Zionist leaders who
were fighting what might be their last battle. As I told Kastner: "We, too, are
idealists and we, too, had to sacrifice our own blood before we came to power."

I believe that Kastner would have sacrificed a thousand or a hundred
thousand of his blood to achieve his political goal. He was not interested in
old Jews or those who had become assimilated into Hungarian society. But
he was incredibly persistent in trying to save biologically valuable Jewish
blood, that is, human material that was capable of reproduction and hard
work. "You can have the others," he would say, "but let me have this group
here." And because Kastner rendered us a great service by helping keep the
deportation camps peaceful, I would let his groups escape. After all, I was not
concerned with small groups of a thousand or so Jews.

At the same time Kastner was bargaining with another SS official, a
Colonel Kurt Becker. Becher was bartering Jews for foreign exchange and
goods on direct orders from Himmler. A crafty operator, Becher had come to
Hungary originally to salvage a stud farm which the SS wanted. He soon
wormed his way into dealings with the Jews. In a way, Reichsführer Himmler
was Becher's captive. Becher showed me once a gold necklace he was taking
to our chief, a gift for a little lady by whom Himmler had a child. There were
other agencies, German and Hungarian, which tapped Kastner for foreign
exchange in return for Jews, but I held aloof from money affairs and left the
material transactions to Becher.

Men under Becher's command guarded a special group of 700 Jews
whom Kastner had requested from a list. They were mostly young people,
although the group also included Kastner's entire family. I did not care if
Kastner took his relatives along. He could take them wherever he wanted to.

The gentleman's agreement

This is how most of the illegal emigrations were arranged: a group of special Jews was taken into custody and brought together in a place designated by Kastner and his men, where they were put under SS guard to keep them from harm. After the Jewish political organizations arranged transportation out of the country, I instructed the border police to let these transports pass unhindered. They traveled generally by night. That was the "gentleman's agreement" I had with Kastner.

After leaving Hungary, the Jews could then travel through neutral foreign countries or stay hidden, usually in Romania, until the necessary steamships arrived to take them on board. When they reached Israel, the ships waited offshore until a few courageous Jews helped the passengers land against the orders of the British mandate authorities. Since the refugees had no valid papers, the Jewish organization must have spent enormous sums of money to bribe Romanian officials, who did not do these favors for nothing. All this went on with Himmler's permission. I would never have dared to dance to my own waltz. If I demanded rigid obedience from my own subordinates, I had to be just as rigid in carrying out my own superior's orders. Otherwise I would have been a bad SS commander, and I think I was a good SS commander.

By the same token, my relationship with Dr. Kastner was strictly correct. He never saw me or my subordinates ever drink a single glass of wine or Schnaps, and there were certainly never any drunken orgies with Jews. If anything like that had happened, I would have heard of it and I would have punished the offenders the way I punished my chauffeur, who once unscrewed a toilet lid from my office because he needed a new toilet seat for his rented room. He was expelled from the SS. Once, when the same man fell asleep while driving my car, I made him march on foot all the way from Dresden to Berlin. That is how I would have treated any of my men who got drunk or even had a drink with a Jew.

All my own agreements with the Jewish officials were more or less side-transactions to the exchange of the million Jews for 10,000 winterized trucks with trailers. Becher and I were twice ordered to Himmler in Berlin to discuss it. Whether Himmler settled the actual terms of the exchange or whether he left it to me, I do not remember. When I think back though, it seems to me that Himmler may have authorized the offer for an "appropriate number," and I set the figure at 10,000 to one million because I was an idealist and wanted to accomplish as much as possible for the Reich.

It was clear to me that for lack of numbers I could never have squeezed a million Jews out of Hungary. But it was obvious that Jews were piled on Jews in Auschwitz and the various concentration camps. So I assumed that we could easily produce a million Jews. Jews from Hungary supplemented with Jews from Germany, from Austria, from wherever they wanted to take them. It would be a tragedy if the international Jewish community was not able or willing to accept them.

Motorize the divisions

I do remember Himmler specifically saying to me, "Eichmann, motorize the 8th and 22nd Cavalry Divisions." This indicated the personal concern of Himmler, who was soon to take over the Reserve Army, in receiving those trucks. They were far more important than the lives of individual Jews. What did he care about a million Jews? His concern was his divisions. He apparently did not want to motorize these two divisions, but rather to equip them for use as a sort of fast-moving task force. It was for this that he gave instructions to Lieut. General Oswald Pohl, who was in charge of the concentration camp system, to kill no more Jews, to save them up, more or less.

After I received Himmler's authorization I told my assistant Krumey to bring me Joel Brand, a Hungarian Jew whom we had chosen to send to Palestine to take a proposal to the Jewish leaders. Brand left on his trip some time before the grain was high, as an old country boy I remember the time well. Krumey brought him to Vienna, had him furnished with the proper papers and shipped him by plane to Istanbul, because Turkey was still neutral. When he got as far as Syria, he was arrested by the British, interrogated, and imprisoned in Cairo. The Jewish leaders never accepted our proposal.

I knew at the time that Brand was being held by the British because Kastner was giving me constant reports. But when I let Brand leave the country, I had made sure his family stayed in Budapest so that I could have a guarantee of his return. Then as the weeks went by I said to Kastner, "Kastner, you know what we agreed. Brand's family stays here because he must return. Why doesn't he come back?" And so for the first time I did use family pressure, but I never turned pressure into practice because Dr. Kastner's reports still held out some hope. I never took any steps to keep Brand's family from emigrating illegally. If they had, I would never have known it.

Meanwhile the deportations had to continue in spite of our pending deal. But the Jews were to a certain extent "put on ice," held in a camp ready to be moved at any time. Suppose Brand had come back and told me, "Obersturmbannführer, the matter is settled. Five or ten thousand trucks are on their way. Give me a half million or a million Jews. You promised me that if I brought you a positive report, you'd send 100,000 Jews to a neutral country as a deposit." Then it would have been easy for us to ship the Jews off.

If the deal had succeeded, I believe I could have arranged to ship the first 20,000 Jews in two days via Romania to Palestine or even via France to Spain. If there had been any delay it would have come from the side of the receivers. The plain fact was that there was no place on earth that would have been ready to accept the Jews, not even this one million.

We had a hearty, comradely relationship with the Hungarian secret police until they learned that we were letting Jews emigrate behind their backs. The gentlemen reacted strongly. They refused to visit or consult with us, and it became my job to smooth things over. Fortunately I had formed a warm friendship with Dr. Lászlo Endre, the second secretary in the Ministry of the Interior. I had even given him my own machine pistol as a gift (naturally with the approval of my superiors). The two of us managed to restore good relations, and I even spent a few weeks on Dr. Endre's country estate. At the time I was virtually out of work for lack of further numbers to deport.

Meanwhile, as the Russians advanced and the first symptoms of the coming chaos were noticeable, the transports were halted. A series of Allied air raids had torn up the Budapest-Vienna railroad track so that for a time no trains could get through. This made Dr. Endre impatient. He wanted to get on with the solution of the Jewish problem. "So I resolved to teach our opponents a lesson, to say, "Look, it does you no good when you bomb out our railroads, because your allies, the Jews, have to endure the consequences." I proposed a forced march of the Jews to the Reich's border. General Ernst Kaltenbrunner, the new chief of the Security Police and the Security Service, gave me orders to that effect.

To preserve appearances
As it turned out, the march cost more trouble than if I had sent 100, no, 500 trains to Auschwitz. Hungary was the window that showed the Reich to the neutral foreign countries, and we Germans had accordingly to preserve appearances. "You smashed our transportation routes but we will carry on in the most elegant manner." That was what the trek was for. The actual number of marchers was so unimportant that I have forgotten it. In any case it was less than 20,000.

The plan was for the Jews to march to the border at Burgenland, about 180 kilometers away. Every day a unit of 2,000 Jews began the march, and then in ten or twelve days the first of the marchers must have reached the border. Everything possible was done to make the trip hygienic and safe. I drove the route once myself, and on the whole distance I saw only two corpses. They were old people. It is clear, as they say, that where planing goes on, chips will fall. The overall natural decrease on the trek, however, was only one percent. When the groups arrived on the border, they were put to work helping German women, children and old people digging tank traps to defend the Reich.

With the march over, Dr. Endre congratulated me on the splendid fulfillment of the mission, and I must admit, we had a drink to celebrate, a kind of Schnaps called "mare's milk" which I had never drunk before. It was excellent.

With the Russian advance moving closer, conditions in Hungary became more and more chaotic. In Budapest the situation was tense. My old friend and comrade, Major General August Zehender, commander of the 22nd SS Cavalry Division, which we had hoped to motorize, was defending Budapest as the Russians drew near it. Then his artillery ran out of shells. Zehender's position was near a streetcar station on the east side of the city, but his ammunition depot was several kilometers beyond the last streetcar stop to the west. He told me in despair that the Russians were about to attack his division and he had no ammunition for his hundred guns.

A living chain for shells

I proposed a living chain of Jews to carry shells from the depot and load them on streetcars at the west end station. The streetcars could carry them through the center of Budapest to the eastern end of the line where his own units could move them to the front line. My idea worked. We made a living chain of them, six or eight kilometers long, to carry the shells from the depot to the station. Then dozens of streetcars, one after the other, sped across Budapest to meet Zehender's men in the east. The guns blazed away.

As Christmas approached, I has nothing more to do in Hungary but no orders to withdraw. I was having a drink with Zehender one day when he told me that many of his officers had been killed and a whole company had gone over to the Russians.

"Give me a squadron," I told my friend, "and I'll stay here through New Years' Day." Then, in the presence of my aide, Zehender telephoned Kaltenbrunner, who had replaced Heydrich as Himmler's deputy. I put my head close to his ear to hear what my chief said, but Zehender broke the news: "Kaltenbrunner tells me it's impossible. You are too valuable. Himmler would have his head." And so my last attempt to see some action was reduced to absurdity.

One or two days before Christmas Eve, 1944, all the German police units were ordered to withdraw, except for one Gestapo group which stayed behind as a gesture to the Hungarians. They were all killed. So was my comrade Zehender, shot as he fought off the enemy with his machine pistol. I left Budapest at 3 PM on Christmas Eve, the last member of the German police to leave the city. As my Mercedes raced westward, the road was already under Russian artillery fire. A great flood of refugees streaming toward Vienna had choked the highway for days, but now it was suddenly empty. It was as though the road had died.

I made my last report to Himmler less than a month before the final surrender of Germany. The Reichsführer had been for some time negotiating with Count Bernadotte about the Jews. He wanted to make sure that at least 100 of the most prominent Jews we could lay our hands on would be held in a safe place. Thus he hoped to strengthen our hand, for almost to the end Himmler was optimistic about making separate peace terms. "We'll get a treaty," he said to me, slapping his thigh. "We'll lose a few feathers, but it will be a good one." It was then mid-April 1945.

Himmler went on to say that he had made some mistakes. "I'll tell you one thing, Eichmann," he said, "if I have to do it over again, I will set up the concentration camps the way the British do. I made a big mistake there." I didn't know exactly what he meant by that, but he said it in such a pleasant, soft way that I understood him to mean the concentration camps should have been more elegant, more artful, more polite.

During those last days I called my men into my Berlin office in the Kurfürsten Strasse and formally took leave of them. "If it has to be," I told them, "I will gladly jump into my grave in the knowledge that five million enemies of the Reich have already died like animals." ("Enemies of the Reich," I said, not "Jews.") I spoke these words harshly and with emphasis. In fact, it gave me an extraordinary sense of elation to think I was exiting from the stage in this way.

My immediate superior, General Müller, had just said to me: "If we had had 50 Eichmanns, then we would have won the war." This made me proud even though, ironically, he spoke on the same day that I learned all was finally lost. By that time my department was one of the few offices which was not burned out from the bombing. I had set my subordinates like bloodhounds on the trail of every incendiary bomb. I helped them myself. So the office was in good condition. Later the whole Gestapo head office moved in and squeezed me out.

Each one of the Gestapo officials was now out to select a civilian firm for which he could say he had worked during the last few years. He could receive employment certificates, "instructions" or correspondence from the company, in a word, anything that would permit him to hide his real job from postwar investigators. There were hundreds of civilian letterheads on file in that office, and if a particular one was not available, we could always have it printed.

You could see how closely they crowded around the official in charge, who made detailed notes on how each man wanted his faked papers to read. The press was so thick that Müller and I had a large space in the back of the room where I used to play music with my subordinates. (I had played second violin: my sergeant played first violin—he was a far better musician than I.) "Well, Eichmann," Müller said, "what's the matter with you?" Since my return from Hungary I had carried a Steyr army pistol. I said to Müller, indicating the gun: " Gruppenführer, I don't need these papers. Look here, this is my certificate. When I see no other way out, it is my last medicine. I have no need for anything else."

This is the truth: of all the Gestapo department heads in Berlin, I was the only one who spat on these false certificates. Müller must have known I was a regular guy.

Resistance in the Alps

My last journey was to Prague, where I visited Karl Hermann Frank, the SS commander there. He told me I could not go back to Berlin. "Nothing is left in Berlin," he said, "the Russians have broken through somewhere."

I was finally able to get through to Kaltenbrunner. He ordered me to proceed to the resort town of Altaussee in the Austrian Alps. I arrived there, accordingly, at about the beginning of May and went directly to the slopes of the Loser, the mountain above the village. In one of the tidy summer villas in the Loser's slope, the chief of the Security Service was quartered.

I was received by his aide, an old and trusted friend of mine, Major Scheidler. I walked into the next room to report and found Kaltenbrunner himself sitting behind a table, clothed in the uniform blouse of an SS general and some wedge-shaped ski pants tucked into some wonderful ski boots. It was an odd costume for the "Last Days of Pompeii" feeling that then oppressed us all, at least it did me. It was after lunch and he was playing solitaire, with a small cognac on the table. I asked him how things had come out. "It's bad," he said, "the solitaire, I mean."

He had Scheidler bring me a cognac, the usual orderly was not around. The white snow of the Loser slope gleamed through the window. It had snowed heavily in the region, which would not be clear of snow until the end of May. The room was comfortably warm. The cognac tasted awfully good despite my gloomy mood.

"What are you going to do now?" Kaltenbrunner said. You must realize this was not like those occasions when I had been ordered to report in the line of duty. Now the die had been cast and all these matters had become of secondary importance. One's brain was in a sense only half present. It was hard to concentrate on what was happening at the moment. This was the beginning of that nervous shock which a few days later hit me like a hammer. For it was now a fact that the Reich, for which we had feared and cared so much, was smashed in pieces.

Answering Kaltenbrunner's question, I told him that I was going into the mountains. "That's good," he said. "Good for Reichsführer Himmler, too. Now he can talk to Eisenhower differently in his negotiations, for he will know that if Eichmann is in the mountains he will never surrender, because he can't."

So we concluded our official business and I went off to become a partisan chief in Austria. I took my leave formally without any personal overtones, as did Kaltenbrunner. He remained sitting at his solitaire, only his expression revealing a certain friendliness to me. "It's all a lot of crap. The game is up." These were the last words I ever heard from my good friend Kaltenbrunner.

I had quartered my people at one of the large resort hotels in Altaussee. The hotel proprietor years afterward kept railing against "that dog Eichmann" who requisitioned his hotel and let his gang run it, inflicting all sorts of fancied damages. The complaint was merely something rooted in his wretched shopkeeper's mind. By no means did we wreck everything in his hotel. On the contrary, I finally yielded to the pressure of the doctor in charge of the neighboring field hospital, who had tearfully begged me to take my combat troops out of Altaussee so that he might declare it an open city. So we evacuated. Before my troops left, I personally saw the Red Cross nurses scrubbing and cleaning up, room by room, since the overcrowded hospital had to expand into this pig's hotel. It was set up as a hospital annex. The beneficiary of all this clean-up operation was thus enabled to feather his own nest.

Since Kaltenbrunner had given his orders, I collected all the heavy equipment we had there and set out to organize a resistance movement in the Totes Gebirge, above the town. The whole thing had now been dumped in my lap. Besides, the regularly assigned people in my department, I had some groups of Waffen SS soldiers and a wild bunch from Schellenberg's Intelligence Section of the SS. Schellenberg's crowd had been burned out of the

Kremsmünster monastery. I think they set it on fire themselves, but they managed to get a few truckloads out with them. In the trucks were scattered piles of uniforms, all kinds of uniforms except winter equipment and ski gear. Instead they had down sleeping bags and emergency rations—chocolate, hard sausage, etc., of the sort we hadn't seen for a long time. They also bought a small chest full of dollars, pounds and gold coins.

Snow on the mountains

I decided to head for the Blaa-Alm, a stretch of mountain pastureland about an hour's march from Altausee. Suddenly it began to snow heavily. I had the Bürgermeister order out 150 of the Hitler Youth—they were all we had—to shovel the snow out of our path. It was already one or two meters deep in spots. At least we could get through with the vehicles.

There was only one inn on the Blaa-Alm, and I requisitioned a room from the innkeeper to store the weapons and the uniforms. An old party man in the town had warned me about the innkeeper. He said I would do well to have the traitorous anti-Nazi clerical done in, and I decided to do so. (It was the time when everybody was doing everybody else in.) But when I saw him, a little sausage of a man, I said to myself: "No, you don't need to do away with him." And so we didn't.

The SS boys had brought a barrel of wine with them from the Kremsmünster storehouse. I set it upon the street so that all the soldiers coming up to the mountain could stop for a few glasses before going on. I allowed each man only a five-minute stop. The barrel was soon empty.

At sunup on the first day after we reached the mountain, one of the officers from the Intelligence Section came up to get some emergency rations "by order of Obergruppenführer Kaltenbrunner." He was a fresh, arrogant fellow, and my Captain Burger said to me, "Shall I rub him out." I told the man he could have half a case and no more. "Otherwise," I said, "I'll have you done in." So he took off somewhere with a half suitcase full of chocolate and hard sausage, perhaps to Switzerland.

Another SS man came four or five times with a note saying that we should deliver a quantity of gold to him. The signature always Ernst Kaltenbrunner's. I knew the writing and it seemed genuine to me, although I had no reason to test its authenticity. In any case gold or money meant nothing to us in the mountains, while bread and emergency rations were everything. Although I was harsh to this fellow at first, I finally had Hunsche, who was acting as our paymaster, pay out the gold that he requested, thus translating Kaltenbrunner's wish into the fact.

The next morning I heard loud noises and confusions outside my window. There was Burger boxing a civilian's ears. Through an orderly I ordered Burger to report to me in my room. He told me the man was a teacher from one of the villages in the valley who was trying to make off with the supply of lard in one of the trucks. Burger was giving him a tangible answer for his conduct. I told Burger that an officer never hits anybody. If the man was looting, he should be hauled before a court martial and shot but never beaten up.

Fighting a war on the Blaa-Alm

What a bunch of good-for-nothings you have here, I said to myself. There were guys from the Waffen SS, who probably were just out of hospital and at the disposal of almost any unit, rounded up and turned over to me by the Security Police; this absolutely insubordinate gang from the Intelligence Section, a few women, my own men. And add to this 150 Hitler Youth. Then there were some Romanians on my neck, too. With this I was supposed to fight a war.

I had plenty of the most modern weapons, however, I had never before seen assault rifles, and now I had piles of them. I had never seen as much ammunition as I had up here—bazookas lying in heaps. Nevertheless I gave the order to evacuate the Blaa-Alm and go farther away to the Rettenbachalm, which lies even higher.

Burger, who was my best skier, I sent on patrol ahead of us to investigate snow conditions and the chances for finding lodging. Meanwhile I had all the weapons we were not using thrown in a stream. I had decided to release the majority of the men. Discipline had suffered irreparably. I had 5,000 Reichsmark paid out to each one against his signature. I was hard and brusque with them. Each man, on hearing he was no longer needed, gladly took off down the mountain without further formalities. I was even hard on a little SS girl, an office worker, who had begged and implored me to take her along. Scorning all her feminine wiles, I said, "Pay out 5,000 marks. Dismissed."

While we were moving, an orderly arrived from Kaltenbrunner with a directive from Reichsführer Himmler ordering us not to shoot at Americans or Englishmen. I countersigned it and the boy rushed off back to the valley. I later conveyed this order to the men. It looked like the end. The Americans were now sitting in Bad Ischl, not very far away, and we heard that our girls were already dancing with the Americans in the marketplace. Even the huntsmen were hostile to us. Gangs of them—home guardists they called themselves—were crawling around us in the hills, all of them punks. They were probably people who had shouted themselves hoarse yelling Heil Hitler in

1938. Now they prowled about us, with weapons of course. Whether or not my men shot at them I did not know, nor do I know now if they ever did. There was shooting everywhere at that confused time.

My driver Polanski asked me if I would give him a car and a truck or two so that he might go off and set up a peacetime trucking concern on his own. It occurred to me that I no longer needed any cars, so I decided to fulfill his wish. After all, he had served me loyally for many years. "Take a truck for yourself," I told him, "or whatever you need from the Blaa-Alm, and make off with my Fiat Topolino."

I later heard that he abandoned the Fiat in a ditch, but he did succeed in taking off with one truck. I wish him success in his trucking business.

Ultimately, even my trusty Burger sought me out for a private conversation. "Obersturmbannführer," he said, "you are being sought as a war criminal. The rest of us are not. We have thoroughly discussed the matter. We feel that you would be doing your comrades a great service if you would leave us and appoint another commander."

I had already decided the answer myself. "Men," I said, "I will leave you alone on the Rettenbachalm. The war is over. You are not allowed to shoot at the enemy any longer. So take care of yourselves."

Lieutenant Jaenisch, my aide for many years, asked if he might accompany me. We drank a last Schnaps together.

There was only one thing I regretted. If I had not been in a state of shock at this time, I would have done more for my wife and children. Unfortunately I did not make provision for them ahead of time, unlike the gentlemen from the Intelligence Section of Schellenberg's, the so-called kid-glove boys of the SS. I, too, could have had my family securely wrapped in a very comfortable cocoon of foreign exchange and gold. In fact, I could easily have sent them on to the farthest, the most neutral of foreign countries. Long before the end, any of the Jews I dealt with would have set up foreign exchange for me in any country I had named, if I had promised any special privileges for them.

As it was, I was able to give my wife only a briefcase full of grapes and a sack of flour before going into the mountains from Altaussee. I had also given them poison capsules, one for my wife and one for each child, to be swallowed if they fell into the hands of the Russians.

A corporal named Barth

I gave myself up to the Americans under an assumed name. I knew the Allied investigators were searching for Eichmann, but luckily I was always just a shade more clever than the CIC officer who interrogated me. I started off in one small American prison camp, posing as a Luftwaffe corporal named Barth.

After studying the psychology of the American CIC, however, I changed my rank from corporal to second lieutenant in the SS. Lieutenant Eckmann, Otto Eckmann, became my name. I moved my birth date back one year to March 19, 1905, and the place to Breslau. I did this so I could remember the figures more easily, avoiding the fiasco of a momentary lapse of memory when I was filling out their forms.

Ultimately I was transferred to the large POW collection center at Weiden. By coincidence, my former aide, Lieutenant Jaenisch, had been sent to the same place. I volunteered to head a work detail and in this capacity I was moved to Oberdachstetten in Franconia. It was then August, 1945. I remained there until the beginning of January, 1946.

In these months we were being interrogated by the CIC office in Ansbach. I knew that if the interrogations continued I might come under suspicion. So I decided to escape. Due to the fear of reprisals, there existed an unwritten code of honor that no officer could escape from a camp without his fellow officers' approval. Since there were about ten officers in the camp, I asked the camp leader, a major, to call an officers' meeting.

I had revealed to the major my real name, rank and official position. "My dear comrade Eckmann," he said, "I have know that for a long time. Your Lieutenant Jaenisch told me about it in confidence. As long as you said nothing to me, I kept the information locked in my heart."

At the officers' meeting I explained merely that I was probably wanted by the Americans because I had been politically active. Nobody asked many questions in those days, and the major, as camp leader, gave his approval. It was simply a matter of form. After all, I could hardly imagine that any group of SS officers would have withheld their approval, knowing that one of their leaders found it necessary to get away.

After leaving the prison camp, I managed to procure papers which gave my name as Otto Henninger. I lived on one of the wooded heaths in the Celle area, and it was there that I was shown a pile of newspapers with articles about me. They were under headlines like "Mass-murderer Eichmann" or "Where is 'Lieutenant Eckmann' hiding out?" The articles noted that I had escaped from the camp.

I started to think about who could have given the name Eckmann to the CIC. There seemed to be only two possible sources for the information. One was my Lieutenant Jaenisch. The other possibility, which seemed highly unlikely, was that the CIC had interrogated the major, who probably reasoned that I was far enough away by then to be safe. I rather think it was Jaenisch who told them. He had a type of pigheadedness peculiar to Lower Saxons.

Though the intervening years since then people searched for me in vain. I would like to find peace with my former opponents. And I would be the first to surrender myself to the German authorities if I did not always feel that the political interest in my case would be too great to lead to a clear, objective way out.

If there had been a trial in 1945, I would have had all my subordinates with me. Today I am not so sure. Some of them may be serving with the new police. Others may have had a hard life through these years, each damning the stupidity that led him to become a Nazi in the first place. And prosperity and democratic reeducation have borne fruit in Germany, so I would not know today what witnesses an attorney for the defense might properly call. I believe, in fact, that if I brought on Jews as witnesses for the defense, I would come out almost better with them than with my own men as witnesses, sad though it may sound. Dr. Kastner, Dr. Epstein, Dr. Rottenberg, Dr. Baeck, the entire Council of Elders in Theresenstadt ghetto—all of them I would have to summon. After all, there were also relatively harmless actions which took place under the general heading "Final Solution of the Jewish Problem."

But to sum it all up, I must say that I regret nothing. Adolf Hitler may have been wrong all down the line, but one thing is beyond dispute: the man was able to work his way up from lance corporal in the German army to Führer of a people of almost 80 million. I never met him personally, but his success alone proves to me that I should subordinate myself to this man. He was somehow so supremely capable that the people recognized him. And so with that justification I recognized him joyfully, and I still defend him.

I will not humble myself or repent in any way. I could do it too cheaply in today's climate of opinion. It would be too easy to pretend that I had turned suddenly from a Saul to a Paul. No, I must say truthfully that if we had killed all the 10 million Jews that Himmler's statisticians originally listed in 1933, I would say, "Good, we have destroyed an enemy." But here I do not mean wiping them out entirely. That would not be proper—and we carried on a proper war.

Now, however, when through the malice of fate a large part of these Jews whom we fought against are alive, I must concede that fate must have wanted it so. I always claimed that we were fighting against a foe who through thousands of years of learning and development had become superior to us.

I no longer remember exactly when, but it was even before Rome itself had been founded that the Jews could already write. It is very depressing for me to think of that people writing laws over 6,000 years of written history. But it tells me that they must be a people of the first magnitude, for law-givers have always been great.

MAURICE CARR
"The Belated Awakening: Dr. Goldmann Accuses World Jewry of Moral Bankruptcy in Nazi Era"
Jerusalem Post
May 5, 1964

Nahum Goldmann was Zionism's star diplomat in the age of the dictators. After the Holocaust, he was elected President of the WZO for 12 years, and was in office when he gave the speech below.—LB

It is all very strange. What are the more than 3,000 Jews—to say nothing of the three black-robed, white-wimpled nuns—doing here tonight, packing every seat and even filling the aisles of the Mutualité? No such large assembly of Jews has been seen in this city since that awesome July in 1942 when 30,000 men, women and children, wearing the Shield of David emblem, were rounded up in a sports stadium, to be dispatched to the extermination camps of Eastern Europe.

It is always very strange when the Mutualité is thronged. For the Mutualité is more than the largest hall in the French capital. It is a sort of floodgate for collective passions. Not so long ago for example, Poujade and his little fascist shopkeepers were pouring out their venom here and threatening to flood the country with it. Then came the deluge of bitterness from the Algerie Francaise zealots, bent on sweeping away the Gaullist regime. More latterly, cleansing waters splashed over never-to-be erased bloodstains as the young Russian poet Yevtushenko declared from this platform his lament for Babi Yar.

It is exceedingly strange that this evening so many Jews should be gathered to commemorate the Warsaw Ghetto Rising, considering that at anniversary meetings in previous years they came, not by the thousand, but by the score. True, there is a star attraction—the main speaker is Dr. Nahum

Goldmann. But there is also another explanation, which Dr. Goldmann himself offers in these words. "The world conscience is belatedly awakening to the unspeakably monstrous crimes of the Auschwitz era."

Dr. Goldmann tells his vast audience that he has just flown in from Frankfurt, where earlier in the day he attended the current trial of 21 Auschwitz guards. What he heard there had made him weep. Even the judges had had tears in their eyes. More impressive even than the Eichmann proceedings was this Frankfurt trial "where Germans today dispense justice with the same total thoroughness that they used yesterday for the perpetration of mass murder."

West Germany will stage more such trials "over the next six to 10 years. Dr. Goldmann discloses, adding: "I told the Germans that these trials, more so than reparations, will show the world to what extent Germany means to break with her past and attain, insofar as it is possible, a certain moral rehabilitation and psychological purification."

One cannot help wondering how "new" is this Germany where convicted SS killers are generally let off with such light sentences that they more often than not serve less than a day's prison for each Jew they murdered.

Jewish Behavior
On the principle, however, that morality like charity begins at home, Dr. Goldmann is primarily concerned tonight—and rightly so—with the conduct of the Jews during the Holocaust. He denounced the "indecency, the arrogance, the effrontery" of those Jews who, themselves belonging to communities that happily remained beyond the Nazis' clutches, speak slightingly of the alleged failure of East European Jewry to resist extermination.

There were Jewish revolts, he points out, in Vilna, Bialystok and many other places besides Warsaw. It should be remembered that not only were the Germans "diabolically skillful" in reducing human beings to uttermost degradation through all manner of bestial torments, but that when the Jews did resist they were performing near-miraculous feats such as no other people were called upon to do. For unlike the Gentiles in Hitler's Festungeuropa, the Jews were herded into isolated ghettos "where they lived and perished as if on a different, an infernal planet."

But what of the Jews, and more particularly their leaders, in the free countries? Had they understood the peril in the early thirties when Hitler first came to power, and had they done anything like their duty afterwards when disaster befell, they could "certainly have saved the lives of many hundreds of thousands, if not millions of Jews."

"They are moral bankrupts," declares Dr. Goldmann, "and I have no qualms in saying 'they,' for this 'they' includes myself." He goes on to indict, first and foremost, the American Jews who 30 years ago refused to campaign against the Nazis for fear of "spoiling relations between the United States and Germany."

Passive Elite

"I was never so ashamed in my life," Dr. Goldmann recalls, "as when I had to admit to Benes how passive the Western Jewish elite were. This was the day after promulgation of the Nuremberg laws. Benes, who was not yet President of Czechoslovakia, called me to his hotel in Geneva. He shouted: 'Don't you Jews see that this is not only the end of German Jewry, but a threat to all of you and to all humanity? You Jews are powerful in finance, in the press, in other walks of life. Why don't you act? Why don't you summon a world conference?' I had to explain to him that it would do more harm than good to call such a conference since the most influential Jews would stay away, causing a fiasco."

Dr. Goldmann remembers, aloud, how at the height of the calamity he and the late Dr. S. Wise received from the Jewish Resistance Movement in Poland a telegram exhorting "twelve top American Jews to go and sit day and night on the steps outside the White House until the Allies are moved to bomb Auschwitz and Treblinka."

Instead, the Jewish leaders made discreet if pressing representations to Roosevelt and Churchill, who had other things to do than to knock out the gas chambers and the crematoria where Jews were being destroyed wholesale.

Dr. Goldmann does not dwell, though, on the responsibilities of other people. He insists that the Jews must, if only to find their future bearings, make a spiritual self-reckoning, a heshbon hanefesh. To this end, he himself has written a book of memoirs, exposing what he terms our "moral bankruptcy" (which one hopes will be published the sooner, the better).

The next speaker, Joseph Weinberg, is a survivor of Auschwitz and other Nazi camps, where he spent three and a half years. Kiddush Hashem, that is, the sanctification of the Name, or martyrdom, by which concept Jewry preserved its identity through nearly 2,000 years of exile, has given way in Israel to kiddush haam, that is, the sanctification of the People or national revival, and the bridge between the two, between kiddush hashem and kiddush haam, he proclaims, was thrown by the heroes of the Warsaw Ghetto.

After the singing of "Hatikva," the multitude streams out into the street, where strong police forces are on hand as they always are on hand as they always are when the Mutualité is full. Some Zionist youths unfurl their blue-and-white banner with the Shield of David. A plainclothes police officer—belonging no doubt to the special Jewish Affairs section—dashes up and orders the boys to put the flag away. They bite their lips and comply.

PART V
The Stern Gang and the Nazis

Fundamental Features of the Proposal of the National Military Organization in Palestine [Irgun Zvai Leumi] Concerning the Solution of the Jewish Question in Europe and the Participation of the NMO in the War on the Side of Germany

David Yisraeli, *The Palestine Problem in German Politics 1889-1945*
Bar Ilan University, Israel, 1974
(German) pp. 315-17

This proposal to Hitler was written in late 1940, when Avraham Stern (Yair), (1907-1942), still called his movement the "real" Irgun, from which they had split earlier that year. Later they took the name Lohamei Herut Yisrael (Lehi for short), Fighters for the Freedom of Israel. They were, however, universally known by the name the British in Palestine gave them: the Stern Gang.

The document was presented to two German diplomats in 1941, in Lebanon, then run by Germany's Vichy French ally. They deposited the proposal in the German embassy in Turkey, where it was found after the war.—LB

It is often stated in the speeches and utterances of the leading statesmen of National Socialist Germany that a prerequisite of the New Order in Europe requires the radical solution of the Jewish question through evacuation ("Jew-free Europe").

The evacuation of the Jewish masses from Europe is a precondition for solving the Jewish question; but this can only be made possible and complete through the settlement of these masses in the home of the Jewish people, Palestine, and through the establishment of a Jewish state in its historic boundaries.

The solving in this manner of the Jewish problem, thus bringing with it once and for all the liberation of the Jewish people, is the objective of the political activity and the years-long struggle of the Israeli freedom movement, the National Military Organization (Irgun Zvai Leumi) in Palestine.

The NMO, which is well-acquainted with the goodwill of the German Reich government and its authorities towards Zionist activity inside Germany and towards Zionist emigration plans, is of the opinion that:

1. Common interests could exist between the establishment of a new order in Europe in conformity with the German concept, and the true national aspirations of the Jewish people as they are embodied by the NMO.
2. Cooperation between the new Germany and a renewed folkish-national Hebraium would be possible and,
3. The establishment of the historic Jewish state on a national and totalitarian basis, bound by a treaty with the German Reich, would be in the interest of a maintained and strengthened future German position of power in the Near East.

Proceeding from these considerations, the NMO in Palestine, under the condition the above-mentioned national aspirations of the Israeli freedom movement are recognized on the side of the German Reich, offers to actively take part in the war on Germany's side.

This offer by the NMO, covering activity in the military, political and information fields, in Palestine and, according to our determined preparations, outside Palestine, would be connected to the military training and organizing of Jewish manpower in Europe, under the leadership and command of the NMO. These military units would take part in the fight to conquer Palestine, should such a front be decided upon.

The indirect participation of the Israeli freedom movement in the New Order in Europe, already in the preparatory stage, would be linked with a positive-radical solution of the European Jewish problem in conformity with the above-mentioned national aspirations of the Jewish people. This would extraordinarily strengthen the moral basis of the New Order in the eyes of all humanity.

The cooperation of the Israeli freedom movement would also be along the lines of one of the last speeches of the German Reich Chancellor, in which Herr Hitler emphasized that he would utilize every combination and coalition in order to isolate and defeat England.

A brief general view of the formation, essence, and activity of the NMO in Palestine:

The NMO developed partly out of the Jewish self-defense in Palestine and the Revisionist movement (New Zionist Organization), with which the NMO was loosely connected through the person of Mr. V. Jabotinsky until his death.

The pro-English attitude of the Revisionist Organization in Palestine, which prevented the renewal of the personal union, led in the autumn of this year to a complete break between it and the NMO as well as to a thereupon following split in the Revisionist movement.

The goal of the NMO is the establishment of the Jewish state within its historic borders.

The NMO, in contrast to all Zionist trends, rejects colonizatory infiltration as the only means of making accessible and gradually taking possession of the fatherland and practices its slogan, the struggle and the sacrifice, as the only true means for the conquest and liberation of Palestine.

On account of its militant character and its anti-English disposition the NMO is forced, under constant persecutions by the English administration, to exercise its political activity and the military training of its members in Palestine in secret.

The NMO, whose terrorist activities began as early as the autumn of the year 1936, became, after the publication of the British White Papers, especially prominent in the summer of 1939 through successful intensification of its terroristic activity and sabotage of English property. At that time these activities, as well as daily secret radio broadcasts, were noticed and discussed by virtually the entire world press.

The NMO maintained independent political offices in Warsaw, Paris, London and New York until the beginning of the war.

The office in Warsaw was mainly concerned with the military organization and training of the national Zionist youth and was closely connected with the Jewish masses who, especially in Poland, sustained and enthusiastically supported, in every manner, the fight of the NMO in Palestine. Two newspapers were published in Warsaw (*The Deed* and *Liberated Jerusalem*): these were organs of the NMO.

The office in Warsaw maintained close relations with the former Polish government and those military circles, who brought greatest sympathy and understanding towards the aims of the NMO. Thus, in the year 1939 selected groups of NMO members were sent from Palestine to Poland, where their military training was completed in barracks by Polish officers.

The negotiations, for the purpose of activating and concretizing their aid, took place between the NMO and the Polish government in Warsaw—the evidence of which can easily be found in the archives of the former Polish government—were terminated because of the beginning of the war.

The NMO is closely related to the totalitarian movements of Europe in its ideology and structure.

The fighting capacity of the NMO could never be paralyzed or seriously weakened, neither through strong defensive measures by the English administration and the Arabs, nor by those of the Jewish socialists.

WERNER OTTO VON HENTIG

My Life in the Diplomatic Service

pp. 338–339

Werner Otto von Hentig, head of the Foreign Office's Oriental Department, was touring the Middle East. He had dealt with Zionists under the Kaiser and Weimar, and had been a passionate supporter of Ha Avara. But that was history.

Germany wanted Arab support against Britain. But it was allied to Vichy France, which dominated Lebanon, Syria, and a vast empire in Arab West Africa, and Mussolini, horrific ruler of Libya. Open support for Arab nationalism against France was out. However the wily diplomat, encountering equally guileful Beirutis, made it clear that things could change for the better.

But not even a virtuoso talker could have given any hope to the strangest intriguer ever to step foot in a city where archeologists have dug up Phoenician plots and schemes by the thousands.—LB

In Beirut, I didn't take a room in the first class Hotel St. George, with a very beautiful ocean view, but in an older Austrian Hotel Monopol, located in the narrow streets of the old city.

With uncanny, un-understandable speed, with which word spreads in the Orient, my arrival was immediately known to politically interested circles. Not only Arabs, but also Chaldeans, Kurds, Armenians and, not least, the different religious communities, at whose head was naturally Cardinal Tarpuni of the Maronites, in Lebanon extraordinarily numerous and French oriented. Here again I benefited by the already mentioned purposeful oriental custom to greet the new arrival, but in such a shady manner that I wasn't sure who didn't put any value in relations, or didn't want to compromise themselves in the eyes of the French.

In the first line appeared, naturally, the Arabs, lead by Lebanese Minister-President Riad el Solh. The representative of Palestinian Arabs, Musa Alami, also came, asking sympathy for their concerns. Also the President of the Kurdish throne, Emir Kamuran Bedir Chan, the Elders of the Armenian community, then came the representative of the Uniate oriental churches, with more than a half million members, the so called Thomist Christians of Southern India; the Syrian Catholic Church was there, among the sects, mostly unknown to us, who live and are politically active. The strangest delegation came from Palestine itself. The leader, a very good-looking officer type, offered to work together with the National Socialists against his own people, above all, the orthodox Zionists, if Hitler would genuinely agree to give the Jews their own state in Palestine. So many people, so many problems, so many requests to the Reich. However I'm only there to observe.

There are two tasks. First, our Arab friends should be warned of the crude plans of the powers-that-be, and also, if possible, to free them from jails and camps. Secondly not to leave them in doubt as to our inner opinions. Riad el Solh encountered me at a tea reception, where he asked me candidly in front of others, about German politics and their aims. I mentioned that a government, out of specific political needs, must from time to time restrain its declarations. The "policy of the German people," however, supports the independence of the Arab countries. Riad el Sohl understood immediately.

To the Jewish delegation, however, I could only respond that their condition could never be accepted out of consideration of the Arabs and in regard to our general principles. However, I personally, always was for an Israeli national state, in a climactically favorable area where one could settle. I had even given Hitler the suggestion in writing that it would be more advantageous to German policies to deal with a responsible government and a sovereign state, rather than an unaccountable and therefore more dangerous worldwide power.

NATHAN YELLIN-MOR
Israel, Israel
1978
(From Yellin – Mor's original English
manuscript, pp 83 – 86)

The Sternists were too fanatically fascist to give up. In December 1941, after the British had taken Lebanon from Vichy, Stern sent Nathan Yellin-Mor to try to contact the Nazis again, in neutral Turkey.

After the British killed Stern in 1942, Yellin-Mor was one of the triumvirate that led the Sternists. Later yet, after the establishment of Israel, he moved left, and became a "peace Zionist," sympathetic to the Palestinian cause.

Stern's underground name, Yair, was after Eleazer ben Yair, commander at Masada in 73 AD, the finale of the Jewish revolt. When the Romans stormed the fortress, his Zealots committed suicide rather than surrender.—LB

Yair didn't go along with the "no choice" theory. Did anyone test it? There were some objective reasons for attempts to form ties with Britain's enemies. First, there was their desire to weaken the Empire by setting off a conflagration within its boundaries. Then again, one of Germany's stated aims was to make Europe, and perhaps other continents as well, Judenrein. This could be done only by having world Jewry concentrated in its own land. The Germans, it was reported, were moving all of Poland's Jews into the Lublin area. This was obviously a temporary measure. Now they were talking about settling all the Jews, after the war, in Madagascar, a plan which Yair considered far more dangerous than the Lublin move, involving as it did a land which was not ours and toward which we bore no affinity. But the idea of centralization, as such, seemed desirable. What remained to be done was to convince the

Germans that the centralization should be in Palestine, rather than Madagascar, and that this move should be made not after they take Madagascar but now, by us, in Palestine.

The more enmeshed in the war that it would become, the more likely would Germany be ready for talks. Britain was also being battered, but it would probably emerge strengthened. Its present state should therefore be exploited for an assault on the British in Palestine, not only in repayment of what had been done to us but also to further our objectives.

Why should we be fighting the British and trying to gain the support of their enemies? Had not Germany declared war on the Jewish "race?" The reason, said Yair, was that there is a basic distinction between their roles vis-à-vis our people. We have to differentiate between the foe and the arch enemy. The foe may be any foreign power which is in control of our homeland and denies the Hebrew people statehood and freedom. The arch enemy hates Jews wherever they may be found. The arch enemy may be of the stripe and dimensions of Haman, seeking to kill, destroy and annihilate all the Jews within reach. But the presence of an arch enemy must not put off the struggle against the foe, the despoiler of our land, even for a single day. The incidence of the arch enemy is an extension of the people's subjugation in its homeland. Were it not so, the land could take in all Jews threatened by the designs of the arch enemy.

If we are duty bound to fight the foe, we may utilize the aid of the arch enemy, given because he is the foe of our foe. This may even resolve in persuading the arch enemy to cease persecuting the Jews, seeing that his aim would be realized as soon as our objective of national independence is attained.

There is no assurance that we may carry our point. But the effort must be made. Yair was willing to assume full responsibility for this dangerous course. There were enough precedents, in the wars of liberation of other peoples—the Italians, Poles, Irish.

In the early stages of our conversations on this topic, I didn't know that one of Yair's men had already been dispatched from Palestine to study the feasibility of the attempt. Only later, after Naftali Lubentchik's arrest, did Yair tell me about his mission. Naftali used his former connections as an employee of "Lloyd Triestino" to cross the Lebanese border, without the required permit. After France fell, Lebanon and Syria came under Vichy authority. The top-level supervision was in the hands of a Vichy-Italian armistice commission, to which German representatives were later added. Naftali

Lubentchik met with members of this commission and asked them to pass on a proposal to Berlin and Rome for a pact with the Hebrew liberation movement, represented by the underground. In outline, the proposed pact stipulated that the IZL in Israel would continue to war on Britain, and in return the other side would recognize the right of the Hebrew people to establish a state in Palestine and would help transfer Jews from Europe to Palestine while the fighting was still in progress.

The German representative, Otto von Hentig, did not hide from Lubentchik the fact that, in Germany, there was some sentiment in favor of establishing a Jewish State in Palestine, as a workable solution of the Jewish problem. He felt, however, that the number of people sharing this sentiment was too ineffectual and that the hour was too late. The ruling circles in Germany had already decided that the campaign against the British in the Middle East should be via the millions of Arabs, rather than through the minute Hebrew element. However, he did promise to submit the proposal to Berlin.

Lubentchik did not take along any written memorandum for the German representative. Had there been need for one, he would have formulated it on the spot, since he was familiar with the episode of the Italian "intermediary" and with the numerous drafts connected with it. Apparently one of von Hentig's secretaries noted down the essence of the proposal in his own words.

Lubentchik didn't get any reply. When Syria and Lebanon were taken by the British in June, 1941, their intelligence men found him working as a librarian in a French air force base. They checked his citizenship. His reasons for being in the locality didn't satisfy them. He was arrested and sent to Mazra'a.

Yair received a detailed report of Lubentchik's experience in Beirut, but he still thought that an effort should be made to ascertain Italy's stand—and Germany's, even more. Today, when the outcome of the war is known, and after the annihilation of 6 million Jews, people are ready to agree that Yair was a Hebrew patriot but a naive politician, rendered irrational by his hatred for the British.

This hindsight wisdom is no more justified today than it was then. In the life of nations there are moments of total crisis, when oblivion and survival hang in the balance. At such junctures, the principles of conventional morality lose all meaning. All the spiritual and lofty values may be observed—only to fall into the fathomless abyss. In order to survive in the jungle, certain means must at times be used which would ordinarily seem to be immoral. This is particularly justifiable when he that preaches morality is also wielding a heavy club with which he wishes to crack your skull. Of course, not every end justifies the means. However, the purpose of the struggle for survival, growing out of the desire to remain alive, justifies means which cannot be countenanced in normal times.

The state of the Hebrew nation, during the Second World War, was without parallel, either in the East or the West. Its temporary abodes were in flames. It tried to escape from the fire, but no rescuing hand was extended to it. The refugees from the flames were pushed back into the burning abode, and anyone fortunate enough to save himself from this hell and reach the water's edge to safety was thrust, brutally, violently, into the deep. Great Britain was ostensibly fighting for liberty, for democracy. Freedom—for whom? Democracy—where? Britain was concerned primarily with its own threatened freedom. The British were attached to a democratic way of life; even in their darkest days they did not waive their right to free expression. This is a laudable standpoint. But we are not the British. We are not citizens of Great Britain, scrupulously zealous about maintaining the trappings of perfect parliamentary procedure. We are but one of its colonies, in the great British Empire. A colony under domination, its people worse off than other peoples. Poland was an ally, and others went in to fight for it. Czechoslovakia is an ally, as well as France, overrun with only a small segment in the struggle against the conqueror. All have assurances, guarantees, pacts. What do we have? Nothing but Britain's formal declaration that it would never allow us to attain statehood and sovereignty in our homeland. Only a fraction of the nation is in Palestine. Many millions are in the diaspora, and those in conquered Europe are in a most precarious situation. They must get to their homeland. They are striving to reach its shores. What has been their fate?

"Israeli Stamp Honors Stern Gang Founder"

San Francisco Chronicle
August 15, 1977

In 1944, the Stern Gang assassinated Lord Moyne, Churchill's High Commissioner for the Middle East. In 1948, they assassinated Swedish Count Folke Bernadotte, formerly of the Red Cross, then the UN Special Mediator for Palestine, and the new Labor-led Israeli government outlawed the group. Altho individuals were later allowed to integrate into the military/police complex, the Laborites saw these assassins as Zionism's lunatic fringe. But, post-48, most of them rejoined the Revisionist Herut Party, and Menachem Begin's government brought them retroactively into the Pantheon of official Zionist heros. Today, an envelope with a Stern stamp will get to Beit Yair, the Stern Gang museum on Stern Street in Tel Aviv.—LB

Tel Aviv—Israel will issue a postage stamp honoring Avraham Stern, founder of the notorious Stern Gang linked to the killing of British and Swedish diplomats before Israeli independence.

A government spokesman said yesterday the stamp would be one of a series honoring underground fighters for Jewish freedom thirty years ago.

Stern, code-named "Yair," was the most extreme of the rightist guerrillas, led by current Prime Minister Menachem Begin, who battled against British rule in Palestine before establishment of the Jewish state. Stern was captured and killed by British authorities in 1942.

The Stern Gang allegedly killed Lord Moyne, British minister of the Middle East, in Cairo in 1944, and gunned down Swedish UN Mediator

Count Folke Bernadotte at a roadblock outside Jerusalem in 1948.

The Labor party, which ruled Israel until last May, considered Stern a terrorist and never gave him any official honor.

CHRISTOPHER WALKER

"Holocaust Relived: Shamir Defends Terrorism"

The Times (London)
October 21, 1983

*Yitzhak Shamir, born Yitzhak Yzernitsky, in Byelorussia, in
1915, was one of the three Lehi leaders after Stern. He definitely organized the Moyne assassination, and many Israeli historians see him as organizing the Bernadotte slaying.*

*In 1955, Labor recruited the assassin-master into the
secret police. He retired in 1965. He joined Herut and became
the successive Likud Party's choice to replace Menachem Begin
after the Prime Minister went mad, blaming himself for his
wife's death.—LB*

Mr. Yitzhak Shamir, the Israeli Prime Minister, has given an interview covering the most controversial aspects of his past as leader of the Jewish terrorist
group known as the Stern Gang and one of the top undercover agents in the
Mossad, Israel's secret service.

Mr. Shamir defended the murder of Lord Moyne, the British Cabinet
minister assassinated on his order in 1944, and denied that he had any part
in the efforts by Mr. Abraham Stern, the original commander of Lehi
(Fighters for the Freedom of Israel) to establish contact with the Nazis and
Italian Fascists.

"There was a plan to turn to Italy for help and to make contact with
Germany on the assumption that these could bring about a massive Jewish
immigration to Palestine. I opposed this," he told the Tel Aviv newspaper
Yediot Ahranot, "but I did join Lehi after the idea of contacts with the Axis
countries was dropped."

Referring to the shooting of Lord Moyne in Cairo, Mr. Shamir stated:

"We always regretted the loss of life. But look at what the British author and investigator, Nicholas Bethell (Lord Bethell) has written about Lord Moyne: he was Colonel Secretary when the unfortunate immigrant ship, the Struma reached Istanbul, and he was the one who pressured the Turks into pushing it back out into the Black Sea.

"He accused Zionism of seeking large immigration into a crowded country over the 'displaced residents.' He came out against large-scale immigration into the country. He was the one who asked, when there was a chance of saving one million Jews from the Nazi holocaust 'What will I do with them?' One must not forget the era in which these various events were taking place in the region. Today, at a distance of more than 40 years it is difficult for a person who is unaware of the circumstances of that time to understand things properly."

Mr. Shamir described how after escaping from a British prison camp in Eritrea, he made one leg of the journey to Djibouti in French Somaliland in a crammed cell built into the hull of an oil tanker.

Dr. Shmuel Ariel, who was the representative in France of the Irgun (the other Jewish terrorist group) disclosed how the French political system was manipulated to ensure that Mr. Shamir and another escaped detainee were not extradited to the British.

"Among those involved was the French Prime Minister, M. Robert Schumann who signed a personal letter ordering the transport of the two to France to be assured," Dr. Ariel claimed. "French Navy ships brought Shamir and Ben-Eliezer from Djibouti to France in 1948 with the status of political refugees."

LENNI BRENNER
"Mr. Shamir and Lehi"
(Letters)
The Times (London)
November 4, 1983

I had come to London from Jerusalem to lecture on Zionism in the Age of the Dictators, when Shamir's denial of involvement in the Stern Gang's approach to the Nazis appeared in the Times. I brought in the letter below, and their Proposal. When an editor saw that the incredible document was real, they had no hesitation running the letter, certain that my claim of his membership, and my admitted speculation as to Shamir's psychology in denying membership in the organization when they wrote the Proposal, were equally true.—LB

Sir, Your October 21 issue contains a denial, by Yitzhak Shamir, Israel's new Prime Minister, of any part in the efforts of the "Stern Gang" to ally themselves to Adolf Hitler in 1940-41. He admitted that "There was a plan to turn to Italy for help and to make contact with Germany on the assumption that these could bring about a massive Jewish immigration (to Palestine); I opposed this, but I did join Lehi (Fighters for the Freedom of Israel) after the idea of contacts with the Axis countries was dropped."

As an American, away from my files, I cannot be certain exactly when in 1940 Shamir joined the group. But in any case, isn't he confessing that he knowingly joined an organization of traitors which had offered to ally itself to the archenemy of the Jews? Nor can there be any doubt that he joined up with Stern before December 1941, when the Sternists tried to send Nathan Yallin-Mor to Turkey to contact the German ambassador there with the same proposal: that they be allowed to ally themselves to the Third Reich.

After Stern's death in February, 1942, Shamir served as operations commander in the triumvirate that took over the organization. At his side were Israel Scheib-Eldad, now with the rightist Tehiya Party, and, after his escape, Nathan Yallin-Mor. May I suggest that Shamir is primarily deceiving himself, that he cannot face the reality that he was then a leader of a group of pro-Nazi Jews?

Respectfully,
Lenni Brenner

GEROLD FRANK
The Deed
1963, pp. 90–93

Gerold Frank reported the Cairo trial of the youths who killed Moyne in 1944. As Yzernitsky/Shamir organized the assassination, he is a major personage in the book. Frank, pro-Zionist and sympathetic to the assassins on the human level, had no reason, in 1963, to make up what was a secondary event in the book, occuring in 1940, well before Lubentchik's expedition, that only took on historic significance when Shamir denied his membership in Stern's Irgun splinter until "after the idea of contacts with the Axis countries was dropped." On the other hand, Shamir had the best reasons in the world to deny the facts.

Eliahu Bet Zouri and Eliahu Hakim were hung for the crime. The source for the account in The Deed *is obviously Bet Zouri's comrade, David Danon, who witnessed the memorable event described.—LB*

Meanwhile, the outbreak of war posed a problem, too, to the dissidents—the Irgun High Command.

Their strategy was to have a direct effect on Eliahu Bet Zouri. Meeting behind barbed wire at Sarafend Detention Camp, they decided that since the British were fighting the Germans, they would call a truce against the mandatory administration in Palestine, and resume their revolt only at the end of the war.

On this rock—cooperation with the British—the organization split wide-open into two factions, one led by David Raziel, the other by Abraham Stern.

Stern flatly opposed the truce. He would not cooperate with the British Administration when, he declared, the British, by refusing to save Jewish refugees, were in fact collaborating with Hitler in their destruction. The argument boiled over two months later, in January 1940, when Raziel was unexpectedly released from internment and Stern and his followers were not. Stern charged that Raziel had made a secret deal with the British.

Five months later, in June, Stern and the others were released. Raziel confronted them in a dramatic meeting, denied he had made any deal, denounced Stern for "flinging mud" at him and resigned as commander of the Irgun: Stern took over. An appeal to settle the dispute was made to Jabotinsky, who as head of the Revisionist party was spiritual leader of the Irgun. Jabotinsky, then in the U.S. on a lecture tour, had always distrusted Stern's fanatic Anglophobia. In August he cabled Raziel to resume command and Stern to step down and cooperate.

Stern refused; the situation remained tense for another eight days. Then news came that Jabotinsky had suddenly died of a heart attack in a Betar camp in upstate New York.

At this major blow the movement all but disintegrated. In September Stern walked out of the Irgun and set up his own group. He serviced notice he would fight not only the British in Palestine but British imperialism everywhere. He severed all ties with the Revisionist party; he rejected all authority but himself, his group would go forward on its own.

The split demoralized Bet Zouri and his friends. As Irgunists they were already members of a tiny minority, ostracized by the Jewish community. They had been able to endure this only because they believed in the rightness of their cause. That their commanders could quarrel over aims and methods, even attack each other, dismayed them. Even more shattering was the manner in which they were pulled by their various leaders, first this way, then that.

One memorable Saturday night Eliahu and David Danon, who had left the Haganah and joined the Irgun because he had become convinced that self-restraint was not an effective policy, were summoned to a remote schoolhouse. Irgun guards silently directed them to a classroom where to their astonishment they found nearly 50 other youths aged 15 to 20—obviously, like themselves, members of the Irgun. This was unheard of, to meet in so large a group, to allow so many to recognize each other. The faces about them were solemn; this disregard of all rules of conspiracy could only mean disaster. They soon learned why they had been called together: they were to be addressed by a representative of each faction.

First, their twenty-two-year-old group commander spoke. He was obviously labor under great emotion. Undoubtedly most of them, he began, had heard of the "difficulties" within the organization following the "disagreement at headquarters." He, personally, did not feel he could advise them—he dared not take the responsibility—where their duty lay; to remain with Raziel or leave with Stern. "Let each of you make your own decision in such a matter of conscience–" He wanted to say more but his voice began to betray him, his eyes grew moist, and he turned and ran from the room.

He was followed by the Irgun commander in Tel Aviv. Far more controlled, he made a brief speech. "If you are ready to follow our great leader, Jabotinsky, then accept his judgment and be loyal to the man he named." He read Jabotinsky's cable to Raziel: "I reappoint you to functions heretofore held with full power to appoint and remove any colleagues," and the one sent to Stern: "Reappointing R and formally ordering you to comply with these directives." He concluded: "Long live Jabotinsky!"

David leaned toward Eliahu and whispered, "I cannot understand such blind devotion to any man." No matter how wise, how could another decide a question of one's own conscience?

Eliahu nodded but said nothing.

Now the entire group of fifty were ordered to proceed in utter silence to another classroom. Here a short, square-shouldered, square-faced, muscular man awaited them, Itzhak Yizernitsky, who had once taken Eliahu with him to burn down the tax booths in Tel Aviv.

He stood, solid as an oak, as if he had grown where he stood, waiting for them to file in and stand at attention. Then he spoke tersely, summing up the reason, behind Stern's decision to walk out of the Irgun. "I tell you no fairy tales," he said. "If you join us, you must bring money to buy arms and ammunition—we have no organization behind us, no political party, no one to help us, no one to back us but ourselves. We will demand painful sacrifices from you."

He paused, and looked at them from under his heavy black brows.

"Men!" His deep voice rumbled. "If you want to smell fire and powder, come with us!"

He turned on his heel and left the room.

Silently the two boys walked home from the meeting. David spoke first. "Fire and powder! Is that an aim in life?"

He remembered later Eliahu's slow reply, "If only we could do without it...."

In the course of their walk, they agreed they could not go with either group.

The three had discussed for some time the problems faced by their little cell. The MacMichael plan, which seemed so brilliant at the beginning, grew increasingly complex. Suppose they succeeded: what then? Was it logical to kill MacMichael if such an act was not part of a long-range program? They had no such program: even if they could formulate one, they certainly could not carry it out by themselves. What was needed was an apparatus—an organization? Either they must create a new one or join one already existing. Both David and Amihai had already made overtures to reenter the Irgun. Now Eliahu was asking them, instead, to join the reorganized Stern group—the FFI.

Both David and Amihai had reservations. "I'd have to know these people better," Amihai said. "Especially your Yizernitsky-Shamir. These people are the only bridge between you and the idea for which you must be ready to die. In other words, you're wagering your life on their political judgment." He shook his head. "I have no way of knowing if they are right or wrong, but it doesn't follow that just because they are first-rate fighters their political judgment is also first-rate."

David, for his part, could not forget Yizernitsky's "fire and powder" remark in the days immediately following the Raziel-Stern split. "I hate the smell of both fire and powder," he said, with some heat. "I'll live with them if that's the only way to drive the British out—but is it the only way?"

YITZHAK SHAMIR

"Freedom Fighters"

Summing Up
1994
pp. 32–35

After his debacle in the Times, *and other exposés, Shamir must have realized that denying involvement in what the Sternists had done was impossible. So he fell back to the next line of defense: It was well intended.*

But if it was sane in 1940-41, why did he deny he had anything to do with the plan, in 1983, and only claim it was virtue incarnate, in 1994?—LB

"We are all recruited for all of our lives; only death can discharge from the ranks," wrote Yair in his best-known poem. He called it *Anonymous Soldiers*, set it to music and it became the Lehi anthem. It put into short words the way we felt about that fight for freedom which history, as we saw it, made synonymous with a fight to the death against the Palestine government. Parting from former comrades, leaving the Irgun, setting out on a precarious and lonely campaign—unaided, at times even hated, by much of the Yishuv—against forces committed to crushing us was not easy. That Lehi existed, that we had never lost heart and that, until the Jewish state came into being, the organization endured despite these odds was due almost entirely to our continuing belief in Yair's credo. And when he was killed, 2 years after Lehi's formation, we were able to go on without him on the strength of what we had learnt from him.

Born in Poland (the part which was then Russia) in 1907, Yair settled in Palestine in 1925 and attended the Hebrew University. Like so many of us he was drawn to, and became active in, the Irgun Zvai Leumi and, in the late 1930s, was sent to Europe to contact the Polish authorities in the hope of obtaining their active cooperation in the Irgun's battle for Jewish independence in Palestine. He succeeded on two counts: the Poles agreed to help establish advanced Irgun training courses in Poland and provided us with arms. One course graduated but another, in which I was to take part, never came into existence because then the war broke out. As for the arms, the Poles had intended to give us enough to equip a division—they thought they were helping to lay the foundations for a Jewish army—but only managed to supply a small number of machine guns, rifles, pistols and some ammunition. Part of this was smuggled into Palestine, the rest was to be stored by the Irgun in Poland until it could be transported there. But that was lost. Why the "generosity?" To some extent it was due to Yair's magnetism, but also to the idea that assisting the Irgun would eventually serve to take more Jews out of Poland, thus reducing the dimensions of that country's "Jewish problem."

Yair made an ideal spokesman; he was exceedingly intelligent, erudite (he translated Homer into Hebrew), unusually good-looking, polite and very controlled. He spoke to people respectfully, seriously and calmly, and looked at them when he talked to them. He was also somewhat of a dandy, very well-dressed, always in a suit with a tie—even in Palestine, where the tone was set in those days by men in shorts, open-necked shirts and sandals. He sounded and behaved like a young university professor at some acknowledged European center of higher learning, a man marked for distinction as a political scientist or philosopher—and, in fact, to some extent, he was both of these. But the subject matter of his discussions, reflections and reading, the conclusions he reached and lived by, and his overwhelming preoccupations could hardly have been further from the academic.

Above all, he was a true revolutionary, unable and unwilling to suffer any distraction from the main effort; wildly impatient for the Jews to be free. He believed, with that depth of conviction that is, I think, the outstanding attribute of all visionaries, that only the here and now counted; that the future wouldn't be determined in Jerusalem, not in Whitehall or Washington. He didn't want a better or more enlightened Mandate; he wanted none at all. He wanted the Jews to be sovereign in their country and, in 1941, he wrote a manifesto which he called "The Principles of Rebirth." In it, he declared, that the borders of Israel "are explicitly stated" in Genesis 15:18; that the right of the Jews to the Land is one of ownership and cannot be rescinded; and that the fate of the Jews of Palestine lay in their own hands. He had no time or use for politics; he wasn't in the least interested in party platforms, or sectarian maneuvering, or bickering about the advantages and disadvantages of

Socialism and so forth. These issues didn't belong in the category of things that concerned or intrigued him. Nor did the spit and polish of the Irgun.

Creating Lehi, Yair did away at once with military trappings. We had no hierarchy, no GHQ, just a central committee; there were no officers, and we didn't stand to attention or salute anyone or follow-the-leader, although discipline was extremely strict. Yair believed that people should think for themselves. "Study, train and think," he told us. He schooled us in the rudiments of covert life, including the art of camouflage: be inconspicuous, quiet, walk in the shade, be a little stooped, a little shabby, never preen or show off. Although he was a master of practical conspiracy, his craving for secrecy came out in unexpected ways sometimes. For instance, he wrote by hand, in capital letters, extremely quickly so that his handwriting would reveal as little as possible about him, be as anonymous, as impersonal as possible.

What Yair hoped for was that the Nazis, so eager to rid themselves of Jews, would help to bring the majority of Jews from Europe, through the British blockade, to Palestine, thus making havoc of British illusions regarding post-war control of the Middle East, facilitating Allied defeat and, possibly, if Britain knew what was afoot, even producing the withdrawal of the White Paper. Whatever the result, he reasoned, Jews would be brought to Palestine. He didn't make this plan public, but Lehi openly termed the world war a conflict between the forces of evil, between Gog and Magog, and made unmistakable its position—again it must be remembered that all this was in 1940 and 1941—when it was reasonable to feel that there was little for Jews to choose from between the Germans and the British. All that counted for Yair was that this idea might, after all, be a way to save Jews about whom no one else, least of all the British seemed to care. Nothing came of it, of course. By that time, though no one yet knew it, the Nazis were already at work on a very different solution to the Jewish problem. In the meantime, however, Lehi was not only feared and disapproved of by the Yishuv, but also suspected of Fifth Column activities by a public that went on believing—incredibly, in the face of accumulating evidence to the contrary—that the British would open the gates of Palestine to the anguished Jews and which refused to be weaned of emotional and political dependence on Britain.

It is not easy for me to write about Yair without sounding a melodramatic note because his personality and life were so dramatic. But it is a fact that he raised a banner only unfurled in Israel before by men like the hero whose name he took for his nom de guerre: Eleazar Ben-Yair, the first-century leader of the Zealots who, for three years, held out on Masada, the last outpost of the Jews in 70 AD, after the destruction of Jerusalem by Roman troops. The night before the final and victorious Roman assault on the rock fortress, Eleazar Ben-Yair spoke to the Jews: "Never be servants to the Romans," he said, "or to any other than God Himself." Next day, when the Romans came, they found only two women and five children alive; all the others had decided to kill themselves. However, his choice of name notwithstanding, I am sure that Yair himself would not have regarded the saga of Masada as a model for the future of the Jewish people. On the contrary, when he spoke of the future it was always logically—and optimistically. That, I imagine, is what the founder of Lehi would have said and done had he been on Masada that night.

CONCLUSION
A Final Word on the
Final Solution

Zionism was little more than an off-stage noise in the America of the '30s. In contrast, the Communist Party was ten times more active among Jews, organizing hundreds of thousands of workers, Jewish and gentile, into unions.

All of this changed with the Holocaust. A nationalist wave consumed the Jewish community, terrorized out of their wits by the enormity of Hitler's crime. Ninety percent supported the creation of Israel, which they saw as sort of the silver lining on the clouds, after the Nazi storm.

That was then. Today, circa 50 percent plus say they reject the Jewish religion. Over half of young Jews intermarry. Now, less than 22 percent of all Jews say they are Zionists. But that sea change is primarily based on rejection of Judaism, not anything either the Zionists or the Palestinians have done. They are now the most educated population stratum in the world, and bronze-age Orthodoxy, and prettied up Reform and Conservative versions, have been abandoned for physics.

But, for all their education, the new generation only knows what it knows. And the secular realities of today's Jews isn't on their current agenda. Sociologists and pollsters say that Jews are circa 2.3 percent of Americans. But a March-April,1998 poll by the *Los Angeles Times* and the Israeli daily, *Yedioth Ahronoth*, asked American Jews, 18 and older, "Just your best guess: What percentage of the population in the U.S. do you think is Jewish?"

7% of American Jews think Jews are 1% of Americans.
Margin of error: minus 43%

12% of American Jews think Jews are 2%.

13% of American Jews think Jews are 3%.

5% of American Jews think Jews are 4%.
Margin of error: +174%

10% of American Jews think Jews are 5%.
Margin of error: +217%

18% of American Jews think Jews are 6-10%.
Margin of error: +260%/435%

6% of American Jews think Jews are 11-15%.
Margin of error: +478%/652%

18% of American Jews think Jews are over 15%.
Margin of error: +652% plus

11% of American Jews say they don't know.

As 5 percent is over 100 percent above the demographers' estimate, 52 percent of all American Jews overestimate their numbers by 100 percent or more.

The *American Jewish Yearbook* would have given them a real picture of themselves. But most of them don't even know it exists. Left to their own devises, they will never learn enough about themselves, much less about Zionism, to make them serious observers of the ongoing crisis in the Middle East.

Their fantastic notion of their own numbers has to be put in context. The Gallup Poll Monthly for March 1990, reported that "the average American thinks that America is...18 percent Jewish." And the wild Jewish estimates of their numbers is not any different than the situation with Blacks. The census says that Blacks are 12.8 percent of Americans, but the Gallup Poll says the average Black thinks they are 42 percent of the U.S.

In plain words, average American Jews, for all their book learning, are like unto the people of Ninevah of old, who God decided to spare, for all their sins, because they couldn't "discern between their right hand and their left hand," when it came to politics.

In 1948, Jews knew what Hitler did to the Jews. Most knew nothing about what Zionists did or didn't do for them and, if possible, most

Americans knew even less. Nor did most Jews or Americans know what, if anything, the U.S. had done to help European Jewry in the '30s or the Holocaust era.

But we know, or should know, what they didn't. America, under Democrat Roosevelt, did nothing to open the immigration gates for German Jews in the '30s, and helping the Jews was never a priority during the Holocaust.

Roosevelt was immensely popular among Jews, getting ca. 90 percent of their votes, in spite of his indifference to their brethern's plight. But today most historians have nothing but contempt for him. He put 140,000 of his own citizens, Japanese-Americans, into concentration camps. To be sure, he didn't kill them. But there can be no mincing words: putting those innocents into camps for their race was a war crime. And fighting Hitler with Blacks herded into segregated units was also criminal.

Today, if Churchill is still incorrectly popularly esteemed, his British empire is gone, to no one's regret. And another anti-Nazi, Stalin, is reviled and his Soviet Union has vanished into the history books.

In this context, exposing the Zionist role in the Hitler era is part of the scrutiny of the past, required of historians, and is no different in principle than denouncing Roosevelt or Stalin for their crimes, committed while they were fighting Hitler.

The question is whether it will do some good, today, whether it will help Americans, Jew and gentile, understand Zionism and thereby help save lives, Palestinian and Israeli, by subjecting today's Israel to the scrutiny called for by its crimes, past and present.

I can't answer that. Time will tell. But it doesn't matter, at least for me. As a historian I can do no other than to dig up the facts and proclaim them. The proverb still is true: although the people may not heed, yet must the truth be told.

GLOSSARY
Abbreviations, Foreign Words, and Organizations

Abyssinia—Ethiopia.

Agudas Yisrael—Union of Israel—Pre-Holocaust anti-Zionist Orthodox movement.

AJC—American Jewish Committee—Right-wing assimilationist grouping.

AJC—American Jewish Congress—Zionist organization identified with rabbi Stephen Wise.

Aliyah—Immigration to Palestine.

Altneuland—Old-new homeland—Palestine.

Alliance Israelite Universelle—French Jewish philanthropy.

American Jewish Joint Distribution Committee—Major conservative overseas charity.

Anglo-Palestine Bank—Zionist bank in Palestine.

Angriff—The Attack—Propaganda Minister Goebbels' organ.

Anti-Comintern pact—Treaty between Germany, Italy and Japan, against the Communist International, the Stalinist world organization, the political basis of the war time "Axis."

Anti-Dreyfusard—Opponent of Alfred Dreyfus, French Jew wrongly accused of being a spy for the German Kaiser.

Arrow Cross—Hungarian pro-Nazis.

Ashkenazim—Jews who settled in northern and eastern Europe. Distinguished from Sephardim, the minority of other Jews.

Atem taylu—tiyul—to walk—excursion—Zionist term for rescue, escape.

Autonomism—Movement believing that Jews should have some form of autonomous self government within Russian and Austro-Hungarian empires.

Av—Month in Orthodox, 13 month lunar calendar.

Baal—Canaanite god.

Bank of Temple Society—The Templers were a German Protestant sect in Palestine.

Bar mitzvah—Ceremony at 13, when boys become men.

Besciùv Adonái—Betar hymn.

Betar—Brit Trumpeldor—Sons of Trumpeldor—Revisionist youth organization. *See* Revisionists.

B'nai B'rith—Sons of the Covenant—Pre-Holocaust conservative assimilationist fraternal order, now pro-Zionist.

Bolsheviki—Majorityites—Name of Russian socialist faction which became the Communist Party.

BUF—British Union of Fascists—Mosleyites.

Brit Habiryonim—Union of Terrorists—Revisionist fascist organization.

Brith Hachayal—Union of Soldiers—Revisionist group.

Brith Hashomrim—Union of Watchmen—Revisionist organization in Nazi Germany.

Bukra, insha' allah—Arabic—Tomorrow, God willing.

Bund—General Jewish Workers League—Yiddish socialist movement in Russia and Poland; anti-Zionist.

Cabala—Medieval Jewish mysticism. Now English for magic, secrecy, etc.

Center Party—German Catholic party.

Central Bureau for the Settlement of German Jews—Headed by Chaim Weizmann, it organized German immigration to Palestine.

CV—Centralverein—Central Union of German Citizens of the Jewish Faith—Defense organization of assimilationist bourgeoisie.

Chaldeans—Middle Eastern Christian sect.

Chazan/mohel/shamash—Cantor/circumcizer/sexton.

Dat Ha-Avoda—Religion of Labor—Labor Zionist glorification of manual labor.

Deutschen Staatsangehoerigen juedischen Volkstums—German subjects of Jewish nationality.

Diaspora—Dispersion—Galut.

Dibbuk—A spirit that takes possession of a body.

Dreidel—A top for games on Chanukah, a minor holiday beefed up to be the equivalent of Christmas for modern Jewish kids.

Dror Habonim—Labor Zionist organization.

Deuxième Bureau—French secret police.

Einiklech—Grandsons of famous hasidic rabbis, who often inherit their leadership over their predecessor's synagogue, unlike more traditional synagogues.

Emergency Committee for Zionist Affairs—Official voice of World Zionist Organization in the United States during the Second World War.

Eretz Yisrael—Land of Israel. Literally the land, not the state.

Fasces—Latin—Bunch of rods with an axle in the middle. Party symbol.

Fronterlebnis—Experience at the front.

Galut (aka Golah)—Diaspora—Dispersion.

General Zionists—Bourgeois Zionists divided into rival factions.

Gesellschaft—German—Society.

Ghedud—Betar unit.

Giovinezza—Youth—Fascist Party's anthem.

G(ioventù) U(niversitaria) F(ascista)—University Fascist Youth.

Gobi—Manchukuo currency.

Gog and Magog—The Old Testament final war against Judaism.

Ha'avara Ltd.—The Transfer. Trading company set up by World Zionist Organization to trade with Nazi Germany.

Ha Dagel—The Banner.

Hadassah—Zionist women's organization.

Hadàr Betari—Majesty of Betar.

Ha Doar—The Post—Jerusalem newspaper.

Haganah—Defense—Underground militia in Palestine, dominated by Labor Zionists.

Haman—Enemy of Daniel and Hebrews in Book of Esther.

Ha Note'a Ltd.—Citrus corporation in Palestine which entered into trade agreement with Nazi Germany.

Hapoel—The Worker—Labor Zionist sports movement.

Hashomer Hatzair—Young Watchmen—Left Zionist youth movement.

Hasidism—Ultra-Orthodox mystic current widespread among Eastern European Jews.

Hechalutz—Pioneers—Labor Zionist youth movement.

Herut—*See* Tnuat Haherut.

Histadrut—General Federation of Jewish Labor in Palestine.

HOG—Hitachdut Olei Germania—German Immigrants' Association in Palestine.

INTRIA—International Trade and Investment Agency—Zionist company selling German goods in Britain, affiliate of Ha'avara Ltd.

In Zwei Welten—German—In 2 Worlds.

Irgun Zvei Leumi—National Military Organization—Revisionist underground.

Izvestia—Official Soviet gazette.

Jewish Agency for Palestine—Central office of World Zionist Organization in Palestine; originally it nominally included non-Zionist sympathizers.

Jewish Colonial Trust—Zionist bank.

JLC—Jewish Labor Committee—Union organization in America, dominated by Bundist sympathizers, anti-Zionist in 1930s.

Jewish Legion—Zionist military organization in British Army during conquest of Palestine in WW I.

JNF—Jewish National Fund—Zionist agricultural fund.

Jewish Telegraphic Agency—Zionist news service.

JWV—Jewish War Veterans—right-wing American ex-servicemen's grouping.

Joint—See American Jewish Joint Distribution Committee.

Joint Boycott Council of the American Jewish Congress and the Jewish Labor Committee—Anti-Nazi boycott organization.

Joshua ben Nun—Joshua the son of Nun—The biblical Joshua.

Juden Kommandos—The Nazi Jewish-deportation commandos, Eichmann & Co.

Judenrat—Jewish Council—Nazi puppet council in the ghettos.

Judenrein—Jew-free.

Judenstaat—Jewish State—Title of Theodor Herzl's book.

Judenstaat Partei—Jewish State Party—Revisionist splinter group, post-1934, loyal to World Zionist Organization.

Juedische Rundschau—Jewish Review.

Jüdische Volkspartei—Jewish People's Party—Right-wing party in German Jewish communal politics, dominated by Zionists.

Jüdischen Rettungskomitees aus Budapest—*See* Vaadah.

Jüdischer Verlag—Jewish Publishers—German Zionist publishing house.

Keren Hayesod—Palestine Foundation Fund.

Keren Ka Yemeth—Zionist fund.

Kiova-Kay—Obscure Russian term for Japanese regime in Manchukuo; Name of sect of pro-Zionists.

KPD—Kommunistische Partei Deutschlands—Communist Party of Germany.

Labor Zionists—*See* Poale Zion.

Left Poale Zion—Labor Zionist splinter grouping with strong Yiddishist orientation.

Lohamei Herut Yisrael—Fighters for the Freedom of Israel—Stern Gang—Revisionist splinter group.

Luftmenchen/luftparnosses—Men who live on air, speculators, wishful-thinkers.

Maccabi—Zionist sports organization.

Maki—Israeli Communist Party.

Mapai—The Labor Party.

Mapam—A "left" labor party, including Hashomer Hatzair.

Maronites—Lebanese sect. They recognize the Pope, but they are allowed their own rituals.

Menorah—Seven armed candelabra; symbol of Orthodox Judaism.

Mezuzah—Scroll in small tube on doorpost.

Mizrachi—Religious Zionist party.

Mossad—Bureau in charge of illegal immigration for World Zionist Organization.

Narodnaya Volya—People's Will—Nineteenth century Russian non-Marxist peasant socialists, frequently assassins. Forerunner of the Social-Revolutionary Party.

Nationale Jugend Herzlia—Revisionist youth movement in Nazi Germany.

NSDAP—Nationalsozialistische Deutsche Arbeiterpartei—National Socialist German Workers' Party.

NEMICO—Near and Middle East Commercial Corporation—Affiliated to Ha'avara Ltd.—Zionist company selling German goods in the Middle East.

Neologes—Hungarian equivalent to American Reform Jewry.

NZO—New Zionist Organization—Revisionist international organization set up in 1935.

Noar Hazion—Zionist organization.

Ostjuden—Eastern or Yiddish Jews.

Palestine Labor Party—Labor Zionist party in Palestine; *See* Poale Zion.

Palestine Offices—Fourteen worldwide offices for immigration to Palestine.

Palestine Telegraphic Agency—Zionist news bureau.

Paltreu—Palestine Economic Organization of German Jews.

Pengö—Hungarian currency.

Pilpul—Talmudic nitpicking.

Poale Zion—Workers of Zion—Labor Zionists.

Pressburg/Bratislava—German and Slovak for city in Slovakia.

Rak b'dam—Hebrew—Only with blood.

Reichshauptbank—German Central Bank.

Reichsverband jüdischer Kulturebunde—German Union of Jewish Culture Leagues—Segregationist organization established by Nazis.

Reichsvertretung der deutschen Juden—Reich Representation of Jews in Germany—United organization of Jewish bourgeoisie under the Nazis.

Revisionists—Political party established by Vladimir Jabotinsky in 1925.

Rosh Betar—High Betar—Head of Betar.

Schnorrers—Yiddish—beggars.

Seder—Passover meal and ceremony.

Sejm—Polish parliament—pronounced Shem.

Shiksa—Hebrew—blemish—From Yiddish into English, now universally meaning gentile woman.

Shoah—Holocaust.

Sicarii—Assassins during Judean revolt against Rome.

SD—Sicherheitsdienst—Security Service of the SS.

Shtadlanuth—Backstairs diplomacy done by rich Jews.

Siebenburgen—Seven fortified "Saxon" towns in southern Transylvania, in Rumania prior to WW II, annexed to Hungary during Holocaust.

SPD—Sozialdemokratische Partei Deutschlands—Social Democratic Party of Germany.

Sprachenkampf—German—Language war in Palestine over establishing Hebrew as the dominant language in Palestinian Zionism.

Spartacus-Weishaupt—Meaning obscure. Spartacus was the leader of a Roman slave revolt. Spartacus League was the name of the early KPD. Adam Weishaupt was the head of the Illuminati, a rationalist society, 1776-85.

Sperrmarks—German blocked account marks.

SS—Schutzstaffel—Protection Corps.

Staatszionistische Organisation—State Zionist Organization—Revisionist movement in Nazi Germany, technically unaffiliated to world Revisionist movement.

Stern Gang—Lohamei Herut Yisrael—Fighters for the Freedom of Israel.

Sukkah—A booth for meals and ceremonies during the Feast of Tabernacles.

Talmud—Centuries of comment and debate over Old Testament.

Theresienstadt—Nazi propaganda's model concentration camp, for Czech and prominent foreign Jews.

Tnuat Haherut—Freedom Movement—Revisionist party in Israel, founded by Menachem Begin.

UNRRA—Post-War United Nations Refugee Relief Agency.

Vaad Hazalah—Jewish Agency's Rescue Committee during the Holocaust.

Vaadah—Vaadat Ezra Vö-Hazalah Bö-Budapest – Budapest Jewish Help and Rescue Committee.

Vaad Leumi—National Council—Semi-government of Zionist settlement under the British.

Van-Dao—Japanese imperialist ideological term in Manchukuo.

Verboten—German—Forbidden.

Viva L'Italia! Viva IL Re! Viva IL Duce!—Long live Italy! Long live the King! Long live the Leader!—Mussolini's title.

Working Group—Jewish rescue group in Slovakia.

WJC—World Jewish Congress—Pro-Zionist Jewish defense organization established in 1936.

WZO—World Zionist Organization—Central body of Zionist movement.

Yamato—Name for ancient Japan. Term for imperial ideology.

Yishuv—Zionist settlement in Palestine.

Zibor—Community.

Zimri—Murdered in Numbers 25: 1-15, by Phinehas, Aaron's grandson, for having a Midianite girlfriend.

ZVfD—Zionistische Vereinigung für Deutschland—German Zionist Federation.

INDEX

Index

Index